BEYOND INFORMALITY

GLOBALIZATION IN EVERYDAY LIFE

SERIES EDITORS
Rhacel Salazar Parreñas
Hung Cam Thai

EDITORIAL BOARD
Héctor Carrillo
Jennifer Cole
Kimberly Kay Hoang
Sanyu A. Mojola
Saskia Sassen

Beyond Informality

*How Chinese Migrants Transformed
a Border Economy*

DOUGLAS DE TOLEDO PIZA

STANFORD UNIVERSITY PRESS
Stanford, California

Stanford University Press
Stanford, California

© 2025 by Douglas de Toledo Piza. All rights reserved.

No part of this book may be reproduced or transmitted in any form or by any means, electronic or mechanical, including photocopying and recording, or in any information storage or retrieval system, without the prior written permission of Stanford University Press.

Printed in the United States of America on acid-free, archival-quality paper

Library of Congress Cataloging-in-Publication Data
Names: De Toledo Piza, Douglas, author.
Title: Beyond informality : how Chinese migrants transformed a border economy / Douglas de Toledo Piza.
Other titles: Globalization in everyday life.
Description: Stanford, California : Stanford University Press, [2025] | Series: Globalization in everyday life | Includes bibliographical references and index.
Identifiers: LCCN 2024049092 (print) | LCCN 2024049093 (ebook) | ISBN 9781503641914 (cloth) | ISBN 9781503643314 (paperback) | ISBN 9781503643321 (ebook)
Subjects: LCSH: Chinese—Brazil—São Paulo—Economic conditions. | Chinese—Paraguay—Ciudad del Este—Economic conditions. | Street vendors—Brazil—São Paulo. | Street vendors—Paraguay—Ciudad del Este. | Informal sector (Economics)—Brazil—São Paulo. | Informal sector (Economics)—Paraguay—Ciudad del Este. | Markets—Brazil—São Paulo. | Markets—Paraguay—Ciudad del Este.
Classification: LCC F2651.S29 C534 2025 (print) | LCC F2651.S29 (ebook) | DDC 381.18098161—dc23/eng/20250305
LC record available at https://lccn.loc.gov/2024049092
LC ebook record available at https://lccn.loc.gov/2024049093

Cover design: Lindy Kasler

The authorized representative in the EU for product safety and compliance is: Mare Nostrum Group B.V. | Mauritskade 21D | 1091 GC Amsterdam | The Netherlands | Email address: gpsr@mare-nostrum.co.uk | KVK chamber of commerce number: 96249943

To Vera and Stélio, with infinite gratitude.

Contents

	Foreword	ix
	Preface: Beyond Borders	xv
	Acknowledgments	xxi
	INTRODUCTION **INFORMALITY, ACCUMULATION, CAPTURE**	1
1	**THE MAKING OF A COMMERCIAL BORDERLAND** *Overseas Chinese Importers in a Trade Outpost*	34
2	**CAPTURING WEALTH** *Chinese Vendors, Shifting Legality, and Shopping Tourism in São Paulo*	65
3	**ENTREPRENEURIALISM FROM AFAR** *Engaging Migrants' Associations and Implementing China's Trade Policies*	96
4	**SPACES OF ILLEGALITY, TACTICS OF LEGIBILITY** *Cross-Border Mobility and Translocal Emplacement*	125
	CONCLUSION **SUBVERTING EXPLOITATION**	156
	Translation Glossary	163
	Notes	169
	References	171
	Index	193

Foreword

This book is a tale of many tales. Critically tackling the issue of the informal economy, it makes key contributions to the analysis of contemporary capitalism. Following the history and geographies of Chinese migration to South American countries, it carefully analyzes the roles of borders in shaping and containing this migration. Focusing on the metropolitan space of São Paulo, it takes "popular markets" as a lens to shed new light on the urban development of one of the most vibrant, turbulent, and unequal Latin American cities. Investigating the transnational spaces carved out by movements of migration between China, Taiwan, Paraguay, and Brazil, it provides an original and effective viewpoint on the rise of China in today's world. Taking the perspective of Chinese migrants as an epistemic and political razor, it stages productive dialogues with some of the most interesting theoretical trends in migration studies.

It would be easy to go on. But I leave to readers to discover other issues and research fields at stake in *Beyond Informality*. My tentative list should be enough to give an idea of the unique character of Douglas de Toledo Piza's book, which works the boundaries of several academic disciplines to provide a full-fledged analysis of a specific migratory movement that has contributed to transform the urban spaces of Ciudad del Este and São Paulo. In the beginning, one could quip, there was a border zone. In what came to be known as *triple frontera* (the triple border between Paraguay, Argentina, and Brazil), a free trade zone was established in 1957 on the Paraguayan side, shortly after the coup that inaugurated the dictatorship of Alfredo Stroessner. The border was seen as a trade opportunity, and the founders of the new city of Ciudad del Este were keen to turn uneven development, a key issue in dependency theory in Latin America at the time, into a dynamic stimulus to promote commercial exchanges across borders. Monetary and wealth differentials were of course crucial to this project.

As it is the case in most free (or special) economic zones across the world, the growth of Ciudad del Este in the following decades was predicated upon migration. Trade colonies have emerged since the establishment of the city, with complex hierarchies and relations of subordination within different national groups. Taiwanese are today the second largest migrant group in Ciudad del Este, with migration peaking in the late 1970s and early 1980s and many migrants' associations popping up in the following years. The wave of liberalization of trade in the 1990s created the conditions for a different kind of Chinese migration, from the mainland. Taking the opportunity to seek economic prosperity as importers, these new Chinese migrants added complexity and new power dynamics to the Chinese community in Ciudad del Este. They laid the foundation for a different kind of relation with Chinese migrants based in other Latin American cities, including São Paulo.

Beyond Informality reconstructs the presence of Chinese migrants in Brazil—a history that begins in colonial times—and focuses on two moments in which Chinese migration (again, both from the PRC and from Taiwan) took a new dynamic, respectively in the 1960s and 1970s and the mid-1990s. In this latter moment, in the wake of Deng Xiaoping's economic reforms, a multitude of working-class migrants, often with precarious immigration status, settled in Brazilian cities, most notably in São Paulo. Low-skilled and lacking financial resources, those migrants found (and continue to find) in "popular markets" their main opportunity to make a living. Working as vendors, they entered complex relations with Chinese importers that were starting to establish new "commodity circuits" with Ciudad del Este. What resulted from these encounters and from this transnational web of exchanges was a booming of popular markets as well as a powerful dynamic that reshaped entire portions of the metropolitan space of São Paulo. Conflicts, negotiations, and clashes abounded both within the Chinese transnational economy and in the relation with the city at large, duly accounted for in *Beyond Informality*.

As I noted at the beginning of this foreword, this book is important for the understanding of key dimensions of contemporary capitalism. One thinks for instance about the roles of Chinese diasporic communities ("overseas Chinese") in economic development in Brazil, and the complex interplay of geoeconomics and geopolitics they imply, including the relations between migrants from the mainland and from Taiwan as well as their associations and respective governments. Even more important in *Beyond Informality* is the critical approach to the notion of informality, or "informal sector," which is already signaled by his use of the phrase "popular markets." Used by street vendors, activists, and scholars across Latin America, this phrase encapsulates the struggle against the stigma of irregularity and suggests the vibrancy and economic relevance of what Piza defines as "non-hegemonic modes of production, distribution, and consumption." Far from being marginal, these modes of economic activity generate an "immense wealth" and must be understood in their crucial function in contemporary capitalist accumulation.

The notion of informal sector has been criticized and contested since British anthropologist Keith Hart introduced it in 1973. What makes Piza's intervention original is, on the one hand, the acknowledgment of the general crisis of the wage labor relation, long considered to be a standard and the basic hallmark of the formal sector. The persistence and extension of economic activities once dubbed "informal" is rather a key feature of capitalism today, even beyond the divide between Global South and Global North. On the other hand, Piza joins a lively debate in Latin America and beyond on popular markets and economies, emphasizing a wide fabric of conflicts and antagonisms that traverse them. Speaking of non-hegemonic modes, he masterfully registers the powerful push of popular forces that strive to make a living within these economic spaces. But he is far from providing an idyllic picture of popular markets. He rather points out that the immense accumulation of wealth facilitated by those markets is predicated on multiple forms of exploitation, dispossession, and private appropriation.

Chinese vendors are the subjects whose experience allows him to shed light on this persistent predicament.

From a theoretical point of view, one of the most creative aspects of *Beyond Informality* is the combination of a compelling critique of "orthodox Marxism" and an original use of Marx, along with Foucault, to come to grips with the working of popular markets. As I already wrote, and contrary to orthodox Marxist views, there is no contradiction between the planetary expansion of capitalism and the persistence of the informal economy in many parts of the world. The opposite is the case. What remains to be accounted for is the role of the state and the legal system, which on the one hand seem to acknowledge and even promote popular markets, while on the other—as this book amply demonstrates—criminalize certain economic activities. Working through the Foucauldian notion of "illegalisms" against the background of Marx's analysis of "primitive accumulation," Piza forges a theory of postcolonial capitalism centered upon the concept of "capture by illegality." What he means by this is that a flexible application of the law and the differential management of legality enable an elite to explore loopholes in the law, changes in regulation, and uneven enforcement, reproducing dispossession and exploitation and facilitating accumulation.

The notion of "capture by illegality" is key to the analysis pursued in this book. It has important theoretical implications, since it sheds light on the deep imbrication of David Harvey's famous distinction between "accumulation by exploitation" and "accumulation by dispossession." It also guides Piza's examination of what he calls—using another Foucauldian term—the governmentality of popular markets. While he includes in his analysis migrants' associations and other diasporic actors, he insists on the relevance and pitfalls of the acknowledgment of "popular entrepreneurialism" by the Workers' Party mayor of São Paulo, Fernando Haddad (2013–2016). Along with law enforcement, popular entrepreneurialism is a pole that defines the field of tensions within which governmental attitudes and policies towards popular markets take shape. Both in Ciudad del Este and São Paulo, the two sites of Piza's investigation, such governmental attitudes must accommodate the needs of a booming tourism that takes popular markets as an occasion both for sightseeing and for shopping.

Conceived as an investigation of a transnational circuit, Piza's work focuses on what he considers strategic nodes. Qualitative research techniques (from interviews to observation to firsthand experiences) give *Beyond Informality* a characteristic width of analysis without in any way sacrificing its depth. Multilayered and theoretically sophisticated in his analysis, Piza never loses sight of Chinese migrants, who steer the narrative and shape the politics of the book. Strategically altering the title of a famous book by James Scott, he urges "seeing like a migrant." This is indeed the perspective he takes even when analyzing the state and the legal system. More generally, his investigation of practices of migration and mobility (as well as emplacement) remains always attentive to the strivings, to the imaginaries, to the desires of Chinese migrants—and in particular of those street vendors that are the soul and the body of popular markets. Piza knows that mobility can be a promise of autonomy as well as a risk of deception. He does not romanticize migration, but he compellingly reveals the fabric of struggles and the moments of autonomy that interweave migratory practices and movements. And these struggles and moments of autonomy crisscross every chapter of this book, adding a political twist to a remarkable ethnographic investigation.

Sandro Mezzadra,
Professor of Political Theory at University of Bologna
September 2024

Preface:
Beyond Borders

The first time I crossed the International Friendship Bridge between Brazil and Paraguay, I was eight years old. I was mesmerized to see so many shoppers making their way back to Foz do Iguaçu, on the Brazilian side of the Paraná River. On the other side, Ciudad del Este's vibrant, colorful, and polyphonic streets were exciting to say the least. My eyes were pleasantly confused, and I kept looking back to the lined-up toys displayed on vending tables, one after another. My mother held my hands tightly to make sure her little child was not left behind, carelessly staring at the irresistible bunch of teddy bears and racing cars with all their lights and sounds. At every step, a vendor surprised me with a personal offer amidst the indistinctive mass of people: "Batman, boy? Take one for each child, madam, or five for the price of four." I nodded to vendors and looked to my parents as if they would understand I wanted all the toys. I was just not capable of choosing one. It was September 1996, and the holiday season with its gift exchange seemed disappointingly distant in the future.

My family did not share similar feelings about Ciudad del Este. My father was tense and disgusted about wandering in the city's alleys. The eight-year-old boy did not understand the reasons for his repugnance for a day trip that was a paradise for me. For hours, he remained restlessly attentive to what he feared could be scammers and robbers. He was not anxious on our way to Ciudad del Este; he had fun with jokes the tour guide made about the city's infamous casinos. Not even the long time we spent in the traffic jam over the half-mile bridge bored him. His discomfort began after crossing the checkpoint, where no immigration officer bothered asking for papers. Like most cars ahead of us, our van was stopped several times by army officials, guns drawn. "No worries, people, we're alright! This is normal procedure in Ciudad del Este," said the tour guide, whom my father no longer regarded as a fun person. Unlike my father, my brother was excited to see so many soldiers in full tactical gear. Perhaps seeing them influenced his insistence in asking for a Rambo action figure at the end of that day. My mother, despite being disappointed by the quality of the imports, was in her comfort zone: she feels at home in street markets.

Ciudad del Este felt strangely familiar to me. Somehow it reminded me of the much quieter street where I grew up in a small Brazilian city far from Paraguay. During my childhood, I counted down the days, anxiously waiting for the Friday flea market, when Auntie Sonia displayed the latest merchandise she bought in Paraguay. Though she was not truly a relative of ours, the kids in the block and I affectionately called her "auntie." She was a lovely lady in her sixties, who still managed to embark twice a week on bus trips to Ciudad del Este, a round trip of more than two thousand miles. On our family trip, I learned that she was like those thousands of shoppers crossing the bridge from Paraguay with their bags full of imports. Neighbors patronized her because they knew she would have something unique when they needed to buy a gift for any occasion or, on demand, the latest electronic appliances for the house: TVs, camcorders, video games, and much more. The first gift I ever bought with my savings was a ballerina music box Auntie Sonia promised me my mother would love for her birthday gift. It cost more money than I had, but Auntie Sonia knew how to close a sale, and upon counting every coin in my piggy bank, she gave me a discount. For me, Ciudad del Este was a place where everyone was like Auntie Sonia.

Our trip to Ciudad del Este was my family's first and only international travel, even though we spent less than ten hours abroad. Planning for what was a rather expensive trip for us required an economy of expectations: the destination had to accommodate everyone's desires for an ideal vacation. Embodying his self-image as the bread winner of the family, my father wanted to give his family the opportunity of having the experience of flying for the first time. That in itself was an attraction for him. He later regretted it, as the domestic flight to Foz do Iguaçu lasted just one hour. "It was too short," he remarked, and added: "Poor Auntie Sonia! Her bus trips take literally fifteen times more." My mother wanted to visit the Iguazu Falls on the border between Brazil and Argentina, just a couple miles south. Though my brother and I were not consulted about our dream vacation destination because no other international trip would fit in the family's budget, my parents promised that we could choose a Christmas gift in Ciudad del Este, one of those electronics we kept asking for but they could never afford.

During my childhood, my family enjoyed upward social mobility to the middle class. The urbanization of our hometown and our family's access to consumer goods coincided. I remember the day our street was paved, the same street my parents lived on for the entirety of their lifetimes. Not until later did some neighbors enjoy the small pleasures of mostly inexpensive but dispensable imports. I was the first, if not the only one, among my friends in the block to have a pair of rollerblades to skate up and down the shining, newly tar-paved street. Auntie Sonia bought the rollerblades in Paraguay. She carried them in a bag over her shoulders, she told me. They were not my size, but I did not care, and neither did my playmates with whom I shared my rollerblades on Sunday afternoons for months until the wheels wore out completely and needed replacement—which was not available in my hometown.

Around the same time, my mother commissioned Auntie Sonia to buy a vacuum cleaner in Paraguay. I did not understand until I was a few years older how significant a boring appliance like a vacuum cleaner could be for my mother; it reduced the labor she spent doing house chores and freed her time for income-generating activities. It symbolized her sense of pride that came with the opportunity to be compensated monetarily for her labor. That opportunity was not to be found in the formal economy, but it did represent a step outside the realm of unpaid domestic, emotional, and child-rearing work she had exclusively performed at home for a decade. My mother resumed working multiple informal part-time jobs to complement the family's finances and to receive her own income again. She worked her many jobs at home, including all the domestic work that still fell primarily on her. As a talented home baker and craftswoman, she made different goods each season, from chocolate Easter eggs to decorated candles, cheap jewelry, or customized uniforms for companies. Like Auntie Sonia, she depended on traveling to procure supplies to buy and resell.

In my teenage years, I helped my mother on bus trips to downtown São Paulo, where one could buy almost anything. My mother used to procure her supplies from local shopkeepers that she patronized, and occasionally from street vendors who had a better price. The São Paulo I knew, after all, was not much different than Ciudad del Este, and its unrivaled buzzing streets oddly reminded me of the Friday flea market in my hometown.

Auntie Sonia suffered from arthritis and eventually stopped taking long trips to Paraguay. She became a fellow bus traveler on our trips to São Paulo. On our way back, she always showed us the items she purchased, hoping she was right about the cartoons kids were watching those days. Though it was easier for her to embark on a three-hour trip to São Paulo than it was to go to Paraguay on overnight bus excursions, it was also less profitable. It was a sad paradox that the more she needed money to afford her medicines, the less feasible it was for an old lady to travel to Ciudad del Este twice a week. The times when she spent more days on the road than at home were gone, but so was her income. Her inability to travel long distances was not the main reason she changed her shopping destination. At the turn of the millennium, her patrons could find the same goods for a cheaper price in São Paulo. To Auntie Sonia's despair, her clients no longer depended on her to buy imported items. That was how our neighborhood experienced Brazil's trade liberalization in the late 1990s. That was how Auntie Sonia felt in her daily life when Brazil lifted protectionist tariffs on the imports found in Paraguay she specialized in selling.

Like in Ciudad del Este, Auntie Sonia shopped in São Paulo from Chinese stallholders. Little did I know that, years later, I would research the experiences of the Chinese, Taiwanese, and Hong Kongese vendors. In the trips to São Paulo with my mother, I became increasingly curious about these vendors. The bus dropped us off in front of a shopping mall where, trip after trip, I noticed the growing number of Chinese stallholders and street vendors. I was fascinated by them and intrigued about what drove them there. São Paulo has a long history spanning across a century and a half of working-class migration from around the world. But still it was not the most obvious destination for Chinese migrants, especially due to the vendors' shared hardship and struggle working in the streets.

My interest in the lives of those Chinese migrants grew when I moved to São Paulo. As an undergraduate student studying Mandarin Chinese, I hung out with them to practice the language and learn more about their culture. The more I learned about their lives, the more involved I became with migrants' rights activism. And the more I did work in advocacy and community outreach, the more I felt like I needed to share the stories I heard. But their stories are not simply local, and I soon realized I had to go beyond borders with them.

Sixteen years after my family's day trip to Ciudad del Este, I returned to Paraguay for the first time to conduct fieldwork. I crossed the International Friendship Bridge again just like the shoppers who inhabit my memories of September 1996. Over these last two and a half decades, however, more has changed in the lives of overseas Chinese vendors in Ciudad del Este and São Paulo than perhaps anyone anticipated. The story I tell in this book is an account of such transformations.

Acknowledgments

A book is never the product of one person alone. This book is the result of years of support, encouragement, and solidarity of many people who have contributed to it in direct and indirect ways.

First, I wanted to thank the migrants, vendors, and other interlocutors who made my research project possible by generously sharing their time, knowledge, experiences, and emotions with me. I recognize our distinct positionalities and the different purposes of our interactions (as a researcher, it is impossible to eliminate my scholarly goals), but I would like to think that this book is theirs as much as it is mine. I am mindful that my perspective might not be exactly like theirs and that their viewpoints are presented here as I understand them. Nonetheless, I truly value this diversity of points of view which informed my understanding and am forever grateful for their shaping of this project. I hope to do justice to the perspectives they shared with me and to serve their struggles with my work whenever possible. Many became friends in this journey, and I thank their companionship and camaraderie.

This book is the product of research spanning over a decade, and I am thankful for the unwavering intellectual support I received along the way. Carlos Forment, Benoît Challand, Anne McNevin, Sandro Mezzadra, Vera Telles, and Nadya Guimarães have shown an incredible amount of trust in my work, and I am grateful for having learned a great deal from them. Many mentors and fellow researchers have supported me since I started researching Chinese migrants in South America as a graduate student at the University of São Paulo, and to them, I owe enormous gratitude: Rosana Pinheiro Machado, Zhou Zhiwei, Ho Ye Chia, Cheng Jing, Shu Changsheng, Fernando Rabossi, and Carlos Freire da Silva. I cannot express my gratitude enough to the scholars I met at The New School, including Miriam Ticktin, Alexandra Délano, Alex Aleinikoff, Lei Ping, Jonathan Bach, Victoria Hattam, Laura Liu, and Fabio Parasecoli. Beyond the academic and intellectual support, which has been abundant, I have had the joy of being friends with the most admirable people I could have ever met there, Zeyno Ustun, Sonia Prelat, Sidra Kamran, and Fabiola de Lachica Huerta, and I am also grateful for the friendship I made through them with Tyler Navoichick, Sam Dinger, and Eli Lichtenstein. There could not have been a better place to finish writing this book than Lafayette College. Since I joined the faculty, I have made new colleagues who have shared their support, inspiration, and friendship. A heartfelt thanks to Angelika von Wahl, Hannah Stewart-Gambino, and Caleb Gallemore.

Over the last decade and across three institutions, my students have raised the toughest questions that helped me rethink my research and never let me take for granted my research, teaching, and outreach to the community. They have helped me become a better educator and scholar, and I am grateful for that.

I am humbled and honored for the distinguished fellowships I received and thank the several institutions that supported the research for this book, including the American Council of Learned Societies, the Coordination for the Improvement of Higher Education Personnel–Brazil, the São Paulo Research Foundation, the Andrew W. Mellon Foundation, Lafayette College, The New School for Social Research, and The New School Department of Sociology. Beyond resources, I am thankful for the communities that provided me with support to develop my scholarship, especially the Zolberg Institute on Migration and Mobility, the Janey Program in Latin American Studies, the India China Institute, the Heilbroner Center for Capitalism Studies, the Institute for Critical Social Inquiry, and the Graduate Institute of Design, Ethnography, and Social Thought.

Many thanks to Marcela Maxfield, the anonymous reviewers, and the series editors Rhacel Salazar Parreñas and Hung Cam Thai for their support and feedback that made this book better. Special thanks to Justine Nicole Sargent, Michael Araujo, and everyone at Stanford University Press for their careful assistance.

My deepest gratitude to the unconditional and caring support I have received from Vera Lúcia de Oliveira Piza, Stélio de Toledo Piza, and Éric de Toledo Piza. No words are enough to thank Ivy Mayumi de Moraes for the loving and wisest support. They fill my journey with courage and the greatest sense of purpose, without which this book would have never been possible.

INTRODUCTION
INFORMALITY, ACCUMULATION, CAPTURE

TWO DECADES AGO, migrant Law Kin Chong was arrested in São Paulo. Law was considered the biggest smuggler in the country and was being investigated by the Brazilian Congress's Special Committee on Counterfeits and Tax Evasion. He was accused of smuggling goods, money laundering, conspiracy, and extortion. Law was arrested, however, for another reason: his attempt to bribe the committee chair with over half a million dollars in exchange for a report that stated his innocence. Hollywood-like images, captured by a hidden camera, showed the precise moment when the police descended on the committee chair's office to intercept the illegal transaction. Law's envoy was arrested on the spot while he handed over a bag full of dollars. Dressed in full tactical gear, the police immediately surrounded Law's house, drawing weapons and pounding on the door, taking him into custody.

Law Kin Chong gained notoriety in São Paulo's most famous low-income shopping district. During his hearing, the committee cited numerous times his family's business in Paraguay. They said his connections with the border town of Ciudad del Este were evidence that Law was a counterfeits smuggler. Born in Hong Kong, Law migrated at a young age with his family to São Paulo in 1963. After a few years in São Paulo, when Law was a teenager, his family moved to Ciudad del Este, where they made a fortune as importers. With a donation he received from his parents of one million dollars—a huge sum by Paraguayan standards at the time—Law left the family in Ciudad del Este in 1994 to open a new business in São Paulo: the largest indoor market in downtown, with over two thousand shops and stalls. Law's personal, familial, and business ties to Paraguay, however, were still deeply associated with his image. Even though evidence suggested that the smuggled counterfeits found in his indoor market were imported through a port near São Paulo, not Paraguay, the committee insisted on inquiring about his connections to Ciudad del Este.

The committee's investigation showed symptoms of the growing discontent in Brazilian society about what many described as the Chinese mafia taking over South America's largest informal economy. The mainstream narrative in media and everyday parlance was that Chinese criminal organizations built an empire of counterfeits smuggled from Paraguay. The investigation focused on the astounding amount of goods and money moved in the transnational informal economy both through legal and illegal avenues. But it did little to understand the complexities of the relationship between Chinese vendors and importers and the very different roles they played in this economy. Nor did it help mitigate the dire conditions vendors continue to face while their work enriches importers, distributors, and sublessors. Law Kin Chong's imprisonment, though representing the Brazilian authorities' attempt to dismantle powerful Chinese groups, did not stop him from running his ever-growing business for two decades.

While other Chinese groups rose to key positions in the distribution of imports in São Paulo and Ciudad del Este, Chinese vendors remain some of the most marginalized workers who provide the labor that sustains that transnational informal economy. Chinese vendors face a double challenge due to their precarious immigration status and their illegal economic activities, making them vulnerable to exploitation and coercion. While they bear the brunt of working on the margins of the law, they do not reap the benefits of their own labor. A transnational elite of Chinese businesspeople, on the other hand, profits and profiteers from the booming informal economy. They leverage their economic, social, and political power to bend the law in their favor and get away with irregularities, violations, and criminal behavior. Moving over ten billion dollars annually, this economy is vital not only to a majority of marginalized Chinese vendors, but also to wealthy Chinese importers who take it as an opportunity to redirect investment for urban redevelopment.

In an informal economy that is constantly on the brink of being shut down, legality is not neutral, but rather instrumentalized to serve special interests that make the powerful thrive and the marginalized suffer. Chinese importers revolutionized the distribution of goods and expanded the informal economy, all while also appropriating the wealth Chinese vendors generate. Yet, it is also from this liminal place of dispossession in the informal economy that migrant vendors engage in collective action and individual practices to resist both criminalization of economic activities and illegalization of immigration status, fundamentally changing deep-seated informal economies in South America.

In this book, I am particularly interested in how different groups use loopholes in the law, changes in regulations, and uneven enforcement in a transnational commodity circuit at the fringes of law. How is legality deployed as a governing tool in the informal economy? I argue that the uses (and misuses) of illegality enable transnational business elites to capture the wealth vendors generate in the informal economy. In the economic circuit between Ciudad del Este and São Paulo, reworking the boundaries of legality serves the double function of restricting the low-income vendors' ability to retain the revenue of their economic activities while preserving and even boosting the informal economy, facilitating the accumulation of wealth by a small group of businesspeople. While Chinese stallholders and street vendors generate value in illegalized markets and remain in a precarious position, Chinese importers, distributors, and sublessors accumulate wealth through the uneven and flexible application of legality.

POPULAR MARKETS AND SHOPPING TOURISM

Across the Global South, the informal economy was seen by policymakers and thinkers of all positions in the ideological spectrum as the epitome of underdevelopment and backwardness. Though the term remains underspecified, the informal economy broadly refers to income opportunities outside recorded wage employment, especially of poor residents of urban centers. At best, the informal economy is recognized as a structural issue of a broken system and is addressed from the perspective of economic inclusion and social rights. At worst, it is condemned as the embodiment of unlawfulness, disorderliness, and unruliness. While practitioners and scholars no longer simply dismiss the informal economy as an incurable economic plague, it is seen either as a means of survival for disenfranchised populations, or as an illegal economy which should not be tolerated. However, as this book will show, neither framing holds true in the case of the Chinese migrants in the transnational economic circuit between Ciudad del Este and São Paulo, where special interests prevail and wealthy merchants have promoted these lucrative markets and capitalized on the work of vendors.

In South America, many vendors refer to marketplaces in the informal economy as "popular markets." The term "popular" in this context refers to the working-class background of workers and consumers and emphasizes class inequalities. By choosing to use "popular markets" over "informal economy," vendors seek to dissociate themselves from the stigma of irregularity, illegality, and criminality. Though it can also be used in a derogatory manner, vendors use the term "popular market" to celebrate the communitarian ties that forge a wider fabric of social cooperation and solidarity. It encapsulates shared histories of economic struggle, vitality, and success. In that sense, popular markets have come to signify the non-hegemonic modes of production, distribution, and consumption that give form to a vibrant system of local and transnational socioeconomic relations (Forment 2015; Gago 2017, 2018; Gordon et al. 2012; Muller and Colloredo-Mansfeld 2019; Ribeiro 2006; Tassi et al. 2015).

This book contributes to filling a gap in the scholarship on the popular markets by analyzing the role of Chinese diasporic communities in the emergence and transformation of the commodity circuits between Paraguay and Brazil. This scholarship focuses on street vending regulation, the struggles of Brazilian long-distance peddlers, and anti-smuggling or anti-counterfeits operations (Aguiar 2012; Cardin 2010; Cardin and Fiorotti 2018; Ferradas 1998; Freire da Silva 2008, 2014a, 2014b; Pinheiro-Machado 2018a; Rabossi 2004; Tucker 2017b, 2020, 2023). In contrast, fewer studies investigate the migrant importers, shopkeepers, and stallholders, particu-

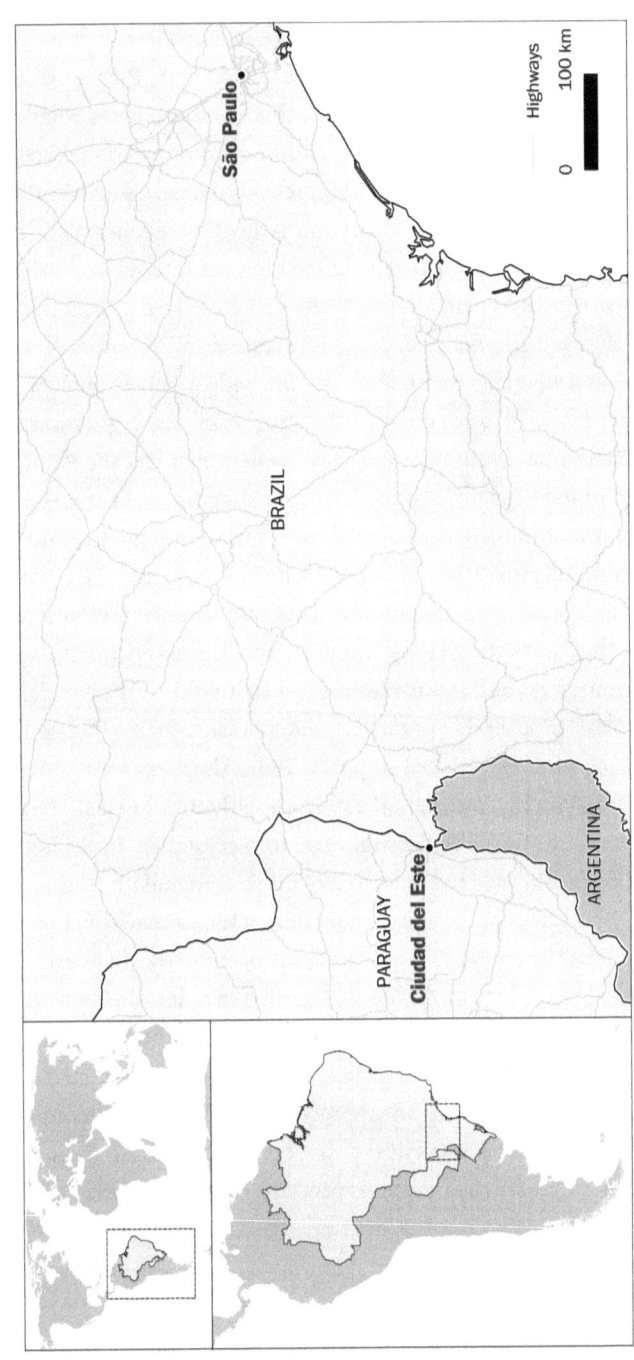

MAP 0.1. Ciudad del Este (Paraguay) and São Paulo (Brazil), 2024. Source: Map by Douglas de Toledo Piza.

larly the Chinese, and the legal architecture that enables such a dynamic transnational circuit to boom (Pinheiro-Machado 2017; Piza 2015; Rabossi 2007). In contributing to filling that gap, this book discusses what migration, borders, and the flow of goods look like in a transnational economic circuit in uneven geographies of development across the Global South.

Being on the borders with Brazil and Argentina, Ciudad del Este is a popular market known for being a destination for international shoppers who want to buy tax-free imports. The city was conceived to be a trade hub, and it has changed dramatically since its creation in the 1950s. A series of legislation lowered tariffs on imports and created loopholes for subsequent exportation, officially and unofficially. This evolving legislation transformed the city into an imports paradise, fomenting what the Paraguayan government branded as *turismo comprista*, or shopping tourism. High-tech electronics, brand name clothing, chic perfumes, fine liquors, cute teddy bears, and shoddy trinkets—Ciudad del Este has them all. The city's economy depends not only on foreign shoppers but also on international migrants like the Taiwanese, Hong Kongese, and Chinese who are some of the largest importers and most traditional distributors in Ciudad del Este.

In the 1990s, thousands of Brazilian shoppers flocked to Ciudad del Este daily in search of tariff-reduced imports. Those shoppers were dubbed *sacoleiros*, a Brazilian neologism that can be roughly translated as "bag holders," in reference to the large bags they use to carry goods. In the heyday of Ciudad del Este, they traveled hundreds of miles as frequently as three times a week, relying on this precarious occupation as the primary or supplemental source of family income. From the legal perspective, they are considered travelers reentering Brazil and are entitled to a duty-free allowance of US$300 on items accompanying them. However, they bring in imports in quantities well beyond the allowed quota, which is widely tolerated on both sides of the border, achieving an unprecedented flow of unrecorded "importation." In Paraguay, these sales are not officially considered exportation because the items never clear customs procedures in Ciudad del Este. Nonetheless, Paraguay's Central Bank developed an original way of accounting for a revenue which at times was higher than a third of the country's GDP (Penner 1998, 2005, 2006; Ruiz Díaz and Ons 2013).

However, starting in the 2000s, São Paulo became the main destination

FIGURE 0.1. The Tri-Border Area of Brazil, Paraguay, and Argentina, 2008. Aerial view showing Ciudad del Este (Paraguay) to the right of Paraná River, the International Friendship Bridge at the center, and Foz do Iguaçu (Brazil) to the left; Puerto Iguazú (Argentina) is in the upper-left corner across the Iguazu River. Source: Secretaria de Estado de Comunicação Social, 2008. Photograph by Julio Cezar Covello Neto. Reprinted with permission.

for the Brazilian shoppers and resellers. Changes in the global economy, particularly international trade liberalization and regional economic integration, repositioned the local popular markets. At the domestic level in Brazil, the gradual increase in the lower classes' purchase power throughout the 2010s unlocked access to consumption goods for larger populations. Locally, municipal authorities in São Paulo did not take long to actively promote what they similarly called *turismo de compra*, or shopping tourism. Shopping centers mushroomed in downtown, catering to low-income shoppers and far-distance resellers who now preferred São Paulo over Ciudad del Este. Downtown São Paulo has a long history of popular markets dating to the late nineteenth century. Like in Ciudad del Este, a significant number of vendors in popular markets in downtown São Paulo are domestic and international migrants, including Chinese, Taiwanese, and Hong Kongese.

In the popular markets of downtown São Paulo, one finds all kinds of goods from a variety of wholesalers, department stores, retailers, stallholders, and street vendors. More than 20,000 establishments offer a wide gamut of domestic and imported goods: garments, shoes, electronics, cheap jewelry, and so on. According to a 2015 study by the São Paulo Department of Labor, Development, and Entrepreneurship, those popular markets represented a yearly sales potential of US$7 billion at the time, with approximately 500,000 daily shoppers, a figure that doubles during peak seasons like the Christmas holidays. That same study shows that more than 250 buses daily filled the parking lot of the Dawn Market. The Dawn Market is the largest indoor market in São Paulo operating from 2 a.m. to 5 p.m. six days a week; about half of its nearly 4,500 stallholders were Chinese during its peak in 2013. The gross product of a nearby popular market alone was ten times higher than the average revenue of a shopping center in Brazil in 2009 (TNS Research International 2009). Vendors proudly say that they are "the biggest open-air shopping center in Latin America," twisting the idea that fancy shopping centers are spaces exclusive to the middle and upper classes in Brazil.

For decades, these popular markets were discredited as an illegal economy that should be eliminated. However, thanks at least in part to Chinese migrants, these popular markets became prime shopping tourism destinations and vibrant spaces of popular entrepreneurialism.

OVERSEAS CHINESE IN THE INFORMAL ECONOMY

On October 4, 2015, I headed to Ciudad del Este to attend the "Double Ten," Taiwan's national day celebration. The event commemorated 104 years of the foundation of the Republic of China as well as 58 years of uninterrupted diplomatic relations between Paraguay and Taiwan. Sandra, a Chinese migrant working in Ciudad del Este for a Taiwanese distributor, drove us across the International Friendship Bridge. Like many fellow Chinese migrants working in Ciudad del Este, she lives in Foz do Iguaçu on the Brazilian side of the border. "You know, Paraguay recognizes Taiwan but it does not recognize China, making it very difficult for us Chinese migrants to live in Ciudad del

FIGURE 0.2. Street vending in 25 de Março Street in downtown São Paulo, 2017. Source: "Consumerism Leads to Economic Improvement," 2017. Photograph by Cris Faga / Shutterstock. Reprinted with permission.

Este." Although it was her first time attending the Double Ten, she was used to going to Taiwanese cultural events in Paraguay. "The Chinese community here is small, it's not like in São Paulo. We don't have many options of Chinese cultural celebrations here. But I think the Taiwanese are like us, they are Chinese, too! It's politics that separates us, not culture. You are going to love the food, I promise you," she said on our way there.

Unlike the majority of Chinese migrants in Brazil who hail from cities in the southern provinces of China, Sandra was born and raised in Beijing. She wanted to escape the expectations her parents had for her life: "I was young, in my early twenties. They had my entire life planned for me, and I didn't want that life for myself. I wanted to live an adventure!" Sandra arrived in Foz do Iguaçu in mid-1996, when commerce in Ciudad del Este was in its most glorious days. The draw for a young adult Chinese woman was not just abundant work opportunities or the prospects of good sales, but especially the financial autonomy she did not think was possible to achieve in China as an unmarried woman. As she said: "It was hard work and long shifts, I didn't speak a word in the local language, but sales were really good. I would never be an independent woman in Beijing and I didn't want to be a housewife."

Like most Chinese migrants in the area, Sandra found a job in no time. She worked as a stallholder for her Taiwanese boss for almost a decade, selling Taiwanese electronics like cameras and laptops and European-brand wristwatches made in Taiwan. At the Double Ten, Sandra introduced me to her boss, Kao. Few people could talk about the history of the Taiwanese community of importers and distributors in Ciudad del Este better than Kao. A short man in his sixties, Kao was softspoken and charming, switching graciously between Spanish and Mandarin. He quickly offered us ice-cold lychee juice. "From my home country. I've been importing this since the 1980s. It's a taste of home, and I hope you like it," he said. As Sandra took a phone call, he waited for the sound of her receding steps to fade away and explained that the taste of home for him was "economic prosperity and freedom." His family left Taichung in the early 1970s fearing annexation by China. Seeing Sandra coming back, he moved on quickly to speak of memories of the nascent Taiwanese community of importers in the 1970s, emphasizing Taipei's enormous governmental support for the community. He spoke of the resilience and success of the Taiwanese community in Ciudad del Este, long before the Paraguayan-born generations left for the United States, Canada, Australia, Hong Kong and, as he proudly said, Taiwan. He checked the time on his wristwatch as if looking for an excuse to segue, and praised Sandra for being his best salesperson ever: "Tell him how many watches you sold a week."

In the late 2000s, as her level of Portuguese and Spanish improved, Sandra moved on to work for the same boss in his import-export company. This career move did not mean a higher salary for Sandra, but it was important to keep her in the area. Even though she made more money as a stallholder, she knew "sales were not as good as they were when I got here, I was not making money like I did before." Meanwhile, however, she had become a mother and was raising her child with limited support from the father, a Chinese migrant who returned to China after they divorced. Accepting a managerial position at her boss's company gave Sandra a more stable source of income that she needed. She had already lived her adventure and no longer seemed so venturesome.

On our way back from the celebration, Sandra told me that her friend Xu Yuhua kept saying that Sandra should move to São Paulo. Xu Yuhua, a Chinese migrant woman from Wen Zhou, is the person Sandra was on the phone with at the Double Ten. Sandra and Xu Yuhua shared a stall working for Kao in Ciudad del Este in the late 1990s, but after three years, Xu Yuhua moved to São Paulo. There, she worked as a stallholder for a Wenzhounese migrant in a market owned by Law Kin Chong. Xu Yuhua was surrounded by Chinese migrants in her work and residence, particularly fellow Wen Zhou natives. The Wenzhou Association of Brazil is one of the largest hometown associations and one of the most active Chinese clubs in Brazil, making connections and facilitating Chinese migration in São Paulo.

As a Beijing native, Sandra did not have access to the same migrant groups. More importantly, for her, moving to São Paulo would mean "starting all over again." She was not ready for the stories she was hearing from Xu Yuhua: unaffordable housing, meager income, and the constant fear of being robbed. Looking pensive, Sandra took a deep breath when we crossed the international bridge and said: "I've made my life here, I don't envy those who moved on."

As the stories of Sandra, Kao, and Xu Yuhua suggest, Chinese diasporic communities are a broad and heterogeneous group. The Chinese diasporic communities are best described by the term *huáqiáo*, which is usually translated as "overseas Chinese." Although the term can strictly refer to migrants who retain their Chinese or Taiwanese citizenship, it is broadly used in ordinary language and even official policy in China, Taiwan, and the diaspora to describe the wider category that includes migrants and their descendants abroad as well as the ethnic Chinese who have been nationals of foreign countries for generations. It is often used together with the term *huárén* (a person born in China or Taiwan who moved overseas and acquired another nationality) to refer broadly to those who identify culturally as Chinese and who reside outside China, Hong Kong, Macau, and Taiwan. The notion of "overseas Chinese" implies the retention of the Chinese identity despite not being physically present in the territory of the nation. It involves a sense of belonging to a presumed homeland to which they are expected to return—in the past, it was translated as "Chinese sojourners," implying that migrants were only temporarily outside of China. It also suggests that descendants naturally inherit the Chinese identity, being considered diasporic Chinese who are expected to make their way "back" to the homeland of their ancestors. However, with China's economic rise and the increase in remittances, foreign direct investment, and trade, the term has come to signify that migrants and their descendants can reconnect with the homeland and contribute from afar (Bourbeau 2001; Ho 2016; Ho and Boyle 2015; Liu 2008; Ma Mung 2009; Roulleau-Berger 2007; Xiang 2007).

The term *huárén* has been steadily used for over a century in diaspora policy by the late Qing dynasty's imperial government (until 1912), the Republic of China (that is, China from 1912 and 1949, and Taiwan since then), and the People's Republic of China (China since 1949). Yet, the overseas Chinese individuals give a more fluid meaning to it. Across the wide range of overseas Chinese communities in Paraguay and Brazil, "Chineseness" represents a category in flux that indexes different forms of ethnic belonging, national identity, and attachment to a symbolic homeland that includes one or more places. As any cultural identity, it is adapted situationally and negotiated over time and across generations. In particular, the issue of self-identification as Chinese or Taiwanese, which remains unresolved in Taiwan's government, political parties, and civil society, is no less contentious among the diasporas. The Taiwanese diaspora in Ciudad del Este and São Paulo includes two camps that have opposite views loosely aligned with the positions of Taiwan's two major parties. Siding with the Kuomintang (Nationalist Party of China), which ruled Taiwan for decades as a one-party state, older generations in the diaspora claim the Republic of China is the rightful successor of the Chinese nation and state, preferring the term Chinese over Taiwanese. In turn, younger cohorts typically take the position of Taiwan's Democratic Progressive Party, a party founded on the principles of anti-authoritarianism and pro-independence in 1986, just a year prior to the end of US-backed martial law in Taiwan. This perspective advocates for Taiwanese nationalism based on a distinct Taiwanese identity. It also defends de-Sinicization and privileges the term "Taiwanese." But there is more at play than age, migration cohort, or alignment with party ideologies.

Numbers matter. Local dynamics between majority and minority groups affect how the overseas Chinese individuals experience and negotiate their Chineseness. In the popular markets of São Paulo, Taiwanese migrants underwent a process of "Chinese-ification," adapting to the Chinese majority. However, this process too is far from straightforward as the relation is not merely one of majority-minority, but also one of hierarchy in work relations and socioeconomic status, with the Chinese migrants consistently occupying subordinate positions.

Geopolitics and the global economy also matter. China's rise has reconfigured the strategic self-identification of diaspora members (Liu 2022). As new trade opened and more business opportunities with China emerged, Taiwanese migrants in Ciudad del Este like Kao flexibly reclaimed their Chineseness. This shift reversed a long-term tendency of Chinese migrants like Sandra going through a process of "Taiwanese-ification" in which they adopted practices of the majority group (Freire da Silva 2014a; Pinheiro-Machado 2010, 2018b).

Not only was Chineseness transformed through business opportunities, the diaspora in Paraguay and Brazil also reactivated ties with this flexible cultural identity to unlock new economic potential. The overseas Chinese individuals of earlier migration have the intercultural abilities, language skills, and bureaucratic knowledge to navigate legal systems as diverse as the Taiwanese, Chinese, Paraguayan, and Brazilian. These individuals are well positioned to enter profitable business sectors like import, export, and shipping. The growing links with globalized China creates transpacific career paths for the South American–born overseas Chinese individuals. Their skills make them valuable bridge builders. China's global economic rise incentivized migrants and descendants to maintain or even create ties with their cultural heritage for business purposes, with Taiwanese migrants not only reconnecting with Taiwan but also bridging gaps with China's soaring business sectors (Stenberg 2012).

The overseas Chinese communities in the popular markets of Ciudad del Este and São Paulo are also stratified socioeconomically. The conditions in their moment of arrival further cement social inequalities and create differential access to economic opportunities, sorting them in groups of importers, distributors, shopkeepers, stallholders, and street vendors. Their occupations correlate with different levels of income and autonomy in work, which in turn vary according to availability of start-up capital, immigration status, education attainment, language skills, and dependency on employers and migration brokers. These overseas Chinese communities also range in terms of language (Mandarin Chinese, Cantonese, Hakka, Hokkien, and several other dialects), national identities (Chinese, Taiwanese, Hong Kongese, Singaporean, and Indonesian), political or ideological views (in favor or against the Chinese Communist Party or Taiwan's independence), and religion (Buddhism, Catholicism, Protestantism, and atheism).

In Ciudad del Este, the largest overseas Chinese community is the Taiwanese, with migration starting in the 1970s and reaching a peak of around 15,000 migrants in the early 1990s. Most Taiwanese migrants came from the city of Taichung, which shows the prevalence of social networks in migration and reflects the role of hometown associations. Because Paraguay maintains diplomatic relations with Taiwan and because China adopted a stricter emigration policy between the mid-1950s and the early 1980s, the Chinese community in Ciudad del Este is smaller but has been present since the 1990s, as have small numbers of Hong Kongese, Macanese, and Singaporeans since the 1970s.

While the official Chinese migration to Brazil dates to the 1810s, Chinese servants, aides, and workers were present throughout colonial Brazil, where they provided labor for the Portuguese Empire and maritime traders. In 1812, a few hundred tea cultivators arrived at the request of the King of Portugal. This experiment in growing tea was intended to both realize the King's desire to get a foothold in the international tea market and to acclimate the Portuguese court, who had just resettled in Rio de Janeiro along with the royal family after escaping Napoleonic forces' impending invasion of Lisbon. It is believed that those Chinese tea cultivators became peddlers after the seat of the Portuguese Empire returned to Lisbon and Brazil became an independent country. In the mid-nineteenth century, when transatlantic slave traffic to Brazil was prohibited, there was a heated debate in the parliament and press known as the "Chinese Question." The debate was about utilizing Chinese laborers to replace enslaved Blacks in the country's transition out of a slave-based economy. At the same time, high-ranking officials of the Qing dynasty became enthusiasts of Chinese migration to Brazil and even proposed large migration projects. Most notably, during a moment of both Westernization and political turmoil in the late Qing dynasty in China, reformer and Guangxu Emperor's influential confidant Kang Youwei penned a plan in 1897 to found a "New China" in Brazil. However, despite the interest of elites in both governments, no large-scale labor-contract migration from China to Brazil was ever concretized. Official entrants throughout the entire nineteenth century did not reach three thousand (Lee 2018; Leite 1999). Occasional chain migration resulted in a small increase of Zhejiangese migrants in the early twentieth century, who were peddlers and small business owners in sectors like restaurants or dyeing in Rio de Janeiro (Gao 2012; Shu 2009; Stenberg 2012).

Significant overseas Chinese migration to São Paulo started only in the mid-twentieth century and can be divided into three moments. The first moment marks the arrival of Chinese migrants who left the country with the rise of the Chinese Communist Party to power in 1949, including wealthy industrialists from Shanghai, traders from Guangdong, and Catholics. These migrants had the economic and social capital to take career paths as liberal professionals in Brazilian society. However, this migration decreased to virtually zero in the mid-1950s with Beijing's rigid migration policies (Baxi Meizhou Huabao 1998; Fausto 2009; Stenberg 2012).

The second moment includes mixed-origin migrations catalyzed by geopolitical shifts in Asia in the 1960s and 1970s. This migration intensified with the United Nations' recognition of Beijing's government in lieu of Taipei's in 1971. Even before that, in the first decade of the People's Republic of China alone, nearly seven thousand Chinese migrants who had left for Taiwan and Southeast Asian countries arrived in Brazil. They joined middle-class Taiwanese from cities like Taichung and Hualien, who feared the looming threat of annexation at the height of China's Cultural Revolution. Additionally, the second moment of migration to São Paulo also included ethnic Chinese migrants who left Southeast Asian countries like Singapore and Indonesia during decolonization as well as Macanese migrants from countries like Portuguese-speaking Mozambique fighting their war for independence from Portugal. Hong Kongese and Macanese holding British or Portuguese citizenship migrated to Brazil in smaller numbers from the 1960s to the last years of European colonial possessions in East Asia. By the mid-1960s, more than 17,000 overseas Chinese migrants arrived in Brazil, a majority becoming small business owners in São Paulo. That figure kept growing, and the total number of entrants is higher because of prevalent return migration and remigration to third countries (Gao and Shu 2023; Macagno 2013; Tang 2013; Veras 2009).

In the third and most recent moment, starting in the mid-1990s and intensifying in the 2000s, the Chinese population in Brazil swelled to over 250,000 while the Taiwanese community reached 40,000. The recent Chinese migration is a product of deep transformations that began with Deng Xiaoping's[1] economic reforms and flexibilization of migration policies in the late 1980s. These migrants are predominantly working-class of rural and urban origin with approximately 100,000 Cantonese, 70,000 Fujianese, and 40,000 Zhejiangese (roughly 30,000 from the city of Qingtian and 10,000 from Wen Zhou) (Freire da Silva 2018). They are also more likely to have a precarious immigration status. Popular markets are often the only opportunity for these migrants who are low skilled and lack the financial resources to more successfully integrate in the local economy and achieve upward social mobility in Brazil. Family chain migration is not negligible (Gao and Shu 2023; Stenberg 2012); however, native-location networks operating transnationally can be credited with increasing new migration. Most migrants I interacted with were driven by economic opportunities in the informal economy and made their way to São Paulo through intermediaries. As a result, they did not exercise much agency over their work recruitment process or job placement, and they worked in precarious conditions as street vendors and stallholders. The lack of agency of these migrants working in the informal economy of Brazil and Paraguay echoes what recent Chinese migrants face in the informal economies in other countries in Latin America, North America, and Europe (Alba Villalever and Rubio 2018; Chan 2018, 2021; Denardi 2016; Gao 2017, 2022; Hearn 2012; Lausent-Herrera 2009; Moraga 2018; Muller 2019).

Although most overseas Chinese individuals of the first two moments of migration were not involved in the popular markets in São Paulo, a small number of them did play a unique role that fundamentally transformed those markets by revolutionizing distribution in two ways. First, as importers, they supplied the popular markets with tariff-reduced imports from Paraguay as early as the 1960s in official and unofficial ways. Second, as developers and real estate owners in Ciudad del Este and São Paulo, they built indoor markets that became highly popular shopping destinations. This small group of well-off overseas Chinese merchants constitutes a transnational business elite that continues to play a double role in imports distribution and real estate development. They expanded from Ciudad del Este to help make São Paulo the epicenter of this commodity circuit, putting newly arrived migrants to work as vendors.

MALLEABLE LEGALITY

Despite the ingrained belief of many, popular markets are not a survival economy of the urban destitute. Or, at least, they are no longer. In fact, the concept of "informal economy" has long been criticized for being poorly defined—and for being defined to talk only about the poor. This classist perspective obfuscates the immense wealth circulating in local and transnational commodity circuits. Still, the concept of the informal economy enjoys enormous popularity in academia and social and economic policymaking.

Key debates on the informal economy span decades of scholarship and government response. Those debates were not simply academic, but they also had tangible ramifications in government policy and international governance. Influential academics holding government offices, and other well-positioned intellectuals moving back and forth from academia to policy, all fiercely defended their competing views. By shaping the government's response to the informal economy in South American countries, they directly affected street vendors and informal economy workers for decades, including the Chinese vendors in Paraguay and Brazil. Those debates did not happen in a vacuum. Quite the contrary, they informed and were informed by larger questions, arguing whether the informal economy was reminiscent of an incomplete transition to a capitalist economy and whether the solution to that issue was national developmentalist policies of industrialization. The debates about the informal economy were deeply subject to three discursive arguments centered around the legacies of colonialism, the fallacies of development, and the perils of neoliberalism.

Globally, the concept of the informal economy emerged during a heated intellectual and political debate about development where postcolonial quests for autonomy clashed with powerful capitalist nations' attempt to hold international sway. British Africanist anthropologist Keith Hart is credited with coining the term "informal sector" in the early 1970s. The informal sector refers to unregulated activities that are the only income opportunities available for the poor urban residents of Africa's largest cities and the Global South more broadly (Hart 1973). This perspective disputed American economist Walt Whitman Rostow's modernization theory predominant at the time in academic and policy circles influenced by Western liberalism (Rostow 1960). According to this theory, economic growth comes in stages—from unindustrialized economy to mass production—as society transitions to capitalism and the modern segment of the economy inevitably absorbs the traditional sectors. At the height of the Cold War, Rostow pushed for the implementation of his theory in policy, when he became an influential adviser to U.S. Presidents John F. Kennedy and Lyndon Johnson. A critical view contends, instead, that the informal sectors of the economy are not the product of an incomplete transition to a capitalist economy. Rather, they are a consequence of colonization, economic imperialism, and the international division of labor that perpetuates the unequal relations between rich countries and countries in the periphery of global capitalism.

However, a report by the International Labor Organization applied the concept descriptively in 1972 to "measure the size of the informal sector." This approach presupposes that the informal economy is a quantifiable, discrete sphere that can be estimated by a set of indicators. By doing so, this approach denies the inextricability of regulated and unregulated economic activities. It rapidly became the prevalent approach worldwide. Its far-reaching dissemination was successful, in large part, because it is applicable to economic and social policymaking. International development organizations and scholars in wealthier countries quickly used metrics of informality to propose policy packages that would presumably help developing countries transition to full capitalism and thus, as the approach insisted, overcome unemployment and economic informality. The informal economy has since been associated with underdevelopment in mainstream policy and international governance. Such an application of the concept subscribes to the ideology of developmentalism, that is, a belief that national development is exportable, being a panacea available to all countries that implement the right policies (Escobar 1995).

The notion of "informal sector" had been the object of contention in academic and political debates in Latin America even before the concept was coined. The debate, in the context of the Latin American structuralist critique of modernization and underdevelopment—the precursor of world-system theories—was framed under the concepts of relative surplus population and marginality. That critique challenged the argument that the typical trajectory of progress in capitalist societies (from early urbanization to industrialization, wage employment, and mass consumption) is inevitable. On the contrary, it maintained that the informal sector would not disappear by simply adopting the policy package disseminated from the more economically developed countries. After all, the Euro-American experience of Fordism and full employment is an unrealistic goal for periphery nations, and it had only been possible in countries that benefited from colonial looting, exploitative extraction, or unfair international trade. Reformist intellectuals in office and academia proposed policy to combat the terms of trade that negatively affected the economy of periphery countries. Those reformists contended that unfavorable terms of trade prevented those countries from fully industrializing and absorbing the labor force in the formal sector of the economy (Cardoso 1971; Furtado 1968; Nun 1969).

Thus, this debate anticipated the informality debate in analyzing whether and how the productive sectors of the economy can absorb the excess labor force in contexts where wage employment is the exception, not the norm.

Brazilian Left academics drawing from a Marxist dialectical perspective argued against the assumption of a dual economy consisting of distinctive pockets of industrialization on the one hand and noncapitalist relations of production on the other hand. In the same year the ILO report was published, Francisco de Oliveira argued in his 1972 publication "The Brazilian Economy: Critique of the Dualist Reason" that the coexistence of formal and informal labor in countries like Brazil is not an anomaly. Rather, in his view, indistinguishable processes of formal and informal labor are interlinked in the Brazilian economy given the position it occupies on the periphery of globalized capitalism. This perspective settled the academic dispute on informality in Brazil, and similar views coincided across Latin America. While progressives and conservatives alike doubled down on national developmentalist solutions in the years ahead, the underlying economic structures locally and globally did not change for at least two decades (Oliveira 2003; Wallerstein 1992). However, in government, that perspective too was engulfed by the ILO's policy-driven approach and its insistence on data that measure the size of the informal sector and policy that supposedly leads to assimilating nonrecorded, nonwage employment into the productive sectors of the economy.

Recently, worldwide renewed interest in the topic of informality is again a passionate and fiery debate in scholarship and policy. This time it is not about imperialism or developmentalism but the promises and pitfalls of neoliberalism. As deregulation became the neoliberal mantra for economic growth, neoliberal ideologues embraced the informal economy to advocate for popular entrepreneurship against what they described as an excessive state. Informality, they argue, is the source of individual freedom and the most effective way for developing countries to achieve economic growth (De Soto 1989). Opponents maintain instead that this argument is misguided because unleashing market forces will lead to more dispossession of workers and the poor, not inclusion. Neoliberalism intensifies the capture of the social and economic value generated in informal markets. Through its promotion of credit, it facilitates the penetration of financial capital into the informal economy, only to enable the appropriation of the wealth through personal indebtedness (Elyachar 2005; Gago 2017; Schuster 2015). Additionally, neoliberalism intensifies intellectual property rights protection mechanisms, resulting in increased globalized technologies of control of economic behavior in the informal economies (Pinheiro-Machado 2017). Furthermore, the informal economy is no longer confined to Global South countries, if it ever was. In the Global North and elsewhere, neoliberalism has informalized labor relations in virtually all forms of employment, bringing about economic and human insecurity (Amar 2013; Antunes 2007; Barbosa 2011; Cacciamali 2000; Machado 2002; Neilson and Rossiter 2008; Standing 2011).

The informal economy has persisted as a phenomenon and a debate. But, in contexts as different as South America, Sub-Saharan Africa, Asia, and the Mediterranean, it has also fundamentally changed from an underground economy to the center of wealth circulation. By recentering Latin American popular markets from the economic margins to the core of transnational commodity circuits, this book shifts attention to how local policymakers and transnational Chinese businesspeople use legality to reframe informality as an opportunity for popular entrepreneurialism. It shows that informality is not synonymous with the lack of state regulation or noncompliance, but rather, with mutating parameters of legality and novel directions in enforcement serving a capitalist-entrepreneurial transnational class (Azaïs et al. 2012; Kalir et al. 2012; Peraldi 2007; Portes 1994, 2010; Roitman 2004; Sassen 1994; Tarrius 2002; Van Schendel and Abraham 2005). A question that remains is how this capitalist-entrepreneurial class captures the wealth generated in informal markets.

CAPTURE BY ILLEGALITY

The popular markets in Ciudad del Este and São Paulo feature a paradox: the promotion of shopping tourism expands the informal economy while it simultaneously cracks down on certain irregular activities. Exploitation and accumulation thrive precisely in this intersection between the expansion of the informal economy and the hindering of specific economic activities. Accumulation happens in the popular markets through what I call "capture by illegality." Capture by illegality is the flexible application of the law that enables an economic elite to explore loopholes in the law, changes in regulations, and uneven enforcement to expand the informal economy and appropriate the wealth workers generate in partially illegal ways.

Marxist thought offers a well-established critique of capitalist accumulation. However, orthodox Marxist approaches are doubly inept to think about the role of legality for accumulation in popular markets. They dismiss popular markets as a residue of noncapitalist relations. Further, these approaches have a limited understanding of the role of law in capitalist accumulation. They are restricted to the argument that, under capitalist relations of production, the law plays a fundamental role in protecting private property and securing the conditions for the appropriation of workers' surplus value in the wage labor economy. It ignores the economic role law plays outside wage labor relations of production. Influenced by the Althusserian reading of Karl Marx's *Capital* (1978), orthodox Marxist approaches see the state as siding with the capitalists in a society characterized by class struggle. However, these perspectives do not explain how legality is used for social control and bent for the private interest of market magnates. Yet, this is crucial in markets that are at the brink of being shut down because targeted enforcement is used for control in a space of widespread evasion to the law and constant contestation of legality.

Marxist scholarship still wrestles with the apparent contradiction between the planetary spread of capitalism and the persistence of the informal economy in the Global South. When applied to the informal economy, British Marxist geographer David Harvey's (2003) framework of accumulation by dispossession is helpful to theorize how informality generates value and enters the circuits of accumulation. A key difference between Harvey's theorization of accumulation by dispossession and the orthodox understanding of Marx's primitive accumulation is that, while the latter is understood as a shift in class relations by separating producers from their means of production and forcing workers to enter wage labor, the former focuses on the erosion of common property rights. From this perspective, primitive accumulation is not only a historical process leading to the transition to wage labor, but also a contemporary manifestation of capitalist accumulation, from land grabbing to extractivism, from gentrification to financialization (Gago and Mezzadra 2017; Levien 2011; Mezzadra and Neilson

2019; Sassen 2014). Capitalist accumulation is not restricted to squeezing workers' surplus value in the relations of production based on wage labor, but rather it encloses the commons and dispossesses people from resources they depend on for living. Thus, Melanie Samson argues, "Dispossession is delinked from proletarianization, as capital values the resources to be enclosed, but not the people who must be dispossessed of them. Rather than being a central mechanism for bringing people into capitalist labor relations, accumulation by dispossession plays the opposite role of rendering increasing numbers of people permanently surplus to the needs of capital" (Samson 2015, 815).

Under global neoliberal capitalism, the state enables magnates of the informal economy to capture new spheres of accumulation created by informal economy workers. Far from being negligent, the state actively reproduces informality, enabling new forms of accumulation and dispossession in the popular markets. Instead of simply taking away the means of production from workers, the state keeps workers in informality so that the wealth they generate can be captured through processes like the privatization of management and the enclosure of public resources. In her analysis of Ciudad del Este's urban and economic informality, Jennifer Tucker (2017a) shows that the state uses ambiguity to regulate by implementing contradictory regulations, exercising discretionary enforcement powers of street vending regulation, leaving land use classifications open, and contingently authorizing development based on the power of political alliances rather than adherence to the law or a master plan. The state invests in producing urban and economic informality to serve the private interests of merchants and political allies of the ruling government officials. This causes "dispossession by informality" and "accumulation by transgression," undermining the informal workers' ability to use public spaces for economic activities and stripping them of common resources that are their means of livelihood (Tucker 2017a). This dispossession is economic, but also political. In places like Brazil, the "misrule of law"—the application of the law with the purpose of dispossessing the poor not only from property and shared resources but also from civic engagement and the idea of rights—is aimed at preventing the achievement of social citizenship (Holston 1991, 2008).

Drawing from the renewed attention to Marx's notion of primitive accumulation, but also informed by French philosopher Michel Foucault's thinking and postcolonial approaches to the analysis of capitalism, authors of different backgrounds such as Kalyan Sanyal and Sandro Mezzadra each proposes a theory of postcolonial capitalism. Mezzadra emphasizes how capitalism's manifold forms of exploitation necessitate the production of social difference. Engaging with critical perspectives exploring capitalism's key links with colonialism, slavery, race, gender, and nature, his theory of postcolonial capitalism argues the histories of the production of social difference are intersected by, but go beyond, what Marx accounts for with the argument that capitalism's only form of exploitation is the appropriation of surplus value on the factory floor (Mezzadra 2011). Postcolonial approaches and theories of settler colonialism all emphasize how colonialism's need for the production of difference—not simply the will to eliminate the native—resulted in the malleability of the law. Cascading effects of power delegation that are typical of imperialism, especially ruling by proxies, and the various legal improvisations and loopholes created by colonialism are examples of how the production of difference (whether based on race, ethnicity, religion, or gender) goes hand in hand with the multiplication of labor—that is, capitalism's production of social difference in the economy.

In turn, Sanyal's theory of postcolonial capitalism focuses on the role of market for accumulation in the informal economy. In economies in the Global South showing a mix of formal and informal elements, market relations enable the appropriation of the wealth generated by labor that is not directly organized by industrial capital (Sanyal 2007). This key proposition suggests the institution of the market—not limited to labor markets—is the locus of wealth appropriation.

By looking at the intersection of South-South migration from Asia to South America and the expansion of the informal economy under global neoliberal capitalism, I build on those theories of postcolonial capitalism to draw new insights from the uneven application of legality in popular markets. My framework explains how the extraction of wealth in informal economies across the Global South necessitates the discursive and practical redefinition of legality. It contributes to understanding the mechanisms of accumulation in informal economies, such as accumulating through the institution of the market, enclosing the common resources, and using ambiguity as a tool of regulation.

Foucault's understudied theory of illegalisms, arguably his clearest engagement with Marxist thought, gives elements to theorize how legality is instrumentalized to serve as a tool of government in the popular markets. Foucault coined the neologism "illegalisms" in his 1972–1973 College de France lectures *The Punitive Society* (2015).[2] It broadly describes the myriad illegal practices that permeate society broadly, but that are also distinctively associated with specific social groups. The theory of illegalisms asserts that the law is the product of power relations, not a given or fixed category external to the totality of social relations. It goes on to say that the emergence of the liberal order resulted in a new distribution of tolerance for violations of the law. Law and enforcement, far from being uniformly applied, are much stricter on crimes against property typically attributed to the lower classes ("illegalisms of property" such as theft, property damage, idleness) than financial wrongdoings usually reserved for upper classes ("illegalisms of rights" like tax evasion, accounting irregularities, and circumvention of customs levies). The disproportionate punishment of the lower classes for their presumed economic behavior suggests the liberal order considers them social enemies not because of their acts but because of who they are (Amicelle 2013; Amicelle and Nagels 2018; Deleuze 1985; Fischer and Spire 2009; Gros 2010; Harcourt 2015; Tazzioli 2016, 2017; Valverde 2016).

The theory of illegalisms is a useful departure point to understand how the uneven application of legality in popular markets enables informality, serving special interests and hurting the majority of vendors (Hirata 2014b; Piza 2012; Telles 2009, 2010). By arguing that illegality is treated differently according to social groups—what Foucault calls the "differential management of illegalisms"—he insists legality is a field of dispute in which social and economic power are exercised based on uneven enforcement and the capacity to not just bend, but to mold the law. Thus, law is not a negative form of power that limits one's conduct, but rather an instrument of social control that modulates the conditions under which a given act can be committed, differentiating populations according to types of behavior that are socially tolerated and economically productive. Unlike traditional political economy approaches, Foucault fundamentally argues that not the law but the differential management of illegalisms shapes regimes of accumulation within and outside the wage labor relationships of production.

By shedding light on the intersection between legal and social categories, the theory of illegalisms helps explain the discursive, practical, and legal shifts that criminalize the most marginalized vendors. A central aspect is the notion of "popular illegalisms," adding a class dimension to Foucault's analysis and highlighting social conflict both in terms of class conflict and state repression. Foucault famously argued that the rise of the disciplinary society is, as *Discipline and Punish* points out, the dissemination of devices of surveillance to control and domesticate the masses, from the factory to the prison, from sedition to rebellions. In spite of the widespread dissemination of devices of surveillance, he contends, the concept of legality is not universally applied, but it is rather an instrument for the social control of the groups that are said to commit popular illegalisms.

When applied to the informal economy, the theory of illegalisms suggests that the reconfiguration of what is considered legal or illegal is used as a tool for social control. In particular, it enables wealth accumulation while keeping vendors under tight surveillance. Some illegal practices are criminalized and suppressed not to eliminate the illicit economies but to facilitate capture by illegality. In the informal economies of Ciudad del Este and São Paulo, there are three main sets of mechanisms that enable capture by illegality: exclusive trade rights and special schedules of importation, urban redevelopment concessions and the privatization of resources, and land valorization and predatory rental fees.

In popular markets, powerful private interests create exceptional measures and exclusionary legislation. In Ciudad del Este, the concession of free-trade zones and subsequent fiscal incentives allow a handful of merchants to import manufactures tariff-free through expedited lanes, supplying the popular markets and retaining higher profit margins. While concessioners and importers are exclusively apt (legally speaking) to import and distribute manufactures, most stallholders and street vendors bear the risks of operating illegally in broad daylight. This mechanism of capture reserves the rights of trade to selected groups. The proliferation of often ill-defined or contradictory legislation allows for those groups to get away with various illegal practices such as reclassifying types, quantities, and origin of imports, using ambiguous legislation in their favor.

Additionally, in Ciudad del Este and in São Paulo, the state acts as a broker for private investors who want to capitalize in the popular markets.

The state facilitates private development of the areas where the enormous economic potential of the popular markets increases the land value. With the recent shift towards the promotion of the popular markets, the state has a key role in implementing urban redevelopment concessions. As a result, vendors are pushed off the street and other public lands. This move limits access to an essential public resource—the use of public land—and privatizes the management of vending spots that were previously self-managed by vendors or managed by local governments. Developers who acquire the rights of concession of public lands charge vendors an extremely costly administrative fee for the management of common resources (such as toilet facilities, waste collection, and maintenance of parking lots) and clear out spaces to build prime retail shops that vendors cannot afford renting.

Beyond exclusive trade rights and urban redevelopment concessions, increasingly higher stall rental fees are the most direct mechanism to extract the wealth generated by vendors. As land value increased in the popular markets, importers and distributors changed businesses to become estate owners. Just like pioneer Law Kin Chong, they opened indoor markets, which are the most viable alternative to street vending for vendors who cannot comply with the stricter street vending regulations, arbitrary enforcement, and profiling. The spread of indoor markets unlocks income opportunities in a gray zone of economic activities that are partially illegal. In these shopping malls, the sales are not recorded on the books, and compliance with taxes and laws regulating the sale of counterfeits is generally lacking. Indoor markets have a mixed effect on Chinese vendors. On one hand, the management companies intervene on behalf of stallholders when municipal or federal authorities issue fines and apprehend the goods found to be in violation of ordinances. On the other hand, the terms and conditions of rentals are unstable in the indoor markets, often word-of-mouth agreements subject to situational negotiations and extortion. Thus, the spread of indoor markets is an outlet of capital expansion for developers and real estate owners who squeeze the profits of stallholders by charging increasingly unaffordable rent prices and controlling their economic activities.

The concept of capture by illegality accounts for how the economic practices predominant in popular markets are shaped by power relations that reconfigure the boundaries between legal and illegal. The redistribution of the tolerance for illegal economic practices puts powerful groups of transnational Chinese businesspeople in a position to accumulate the wealth circulating illegally in the popular markets.

AN ETHNOGRAPHY OF MOBILITIES

This book is an ethnography of how overseas Chinese vendors shaped the popular markets in Ciudad del Este and São Paulo locally and transnationally from 1957 to 2023. Rather than being a multisited ethnography that privileges breadth in detriment to depth, my investigation combines deep ethnographies of the strategic nodes in this transnational circuit (Pinheiro-Machado 2017). By analyzing this circuit together as a single case, this book is uniquely positioned to reveal the conditions under which some groups were targeted and suppressed only to enable others to amass significant wealth. The focus on the overseas Chinese individuals makes the analysis more complex because they were represented across a spectrum of positions in this economic circuit ranging from the most vulnerabilized vendors to the extremely powerful merchants, allowing for a nuanced understanding of tensions, conflicts, and power dynamics.

Investigating the mobilities of people and products in such a transnational context invites innovative ethnographic approaches. I draw from the mobilities turn in social sciences, which I define as an epistemological sensibility to how particular kinds of mobilities, displacement, and containment are interrelated and how they affect different populations and things in distinct ways (Büscher and Urry 2009; Sheller 2018; Sheller and Urry 2006). The mobilities perspective is particularly useful for the study of overseas Chinese vendors in Ciudad del Este and São Paulo because it sheds light on the articulations of the mobility of imports and migrants in transnational circuits at the fringes of legality, as well as the tools used to either enable or stop circulation.

There has been a great deal of well-founded skepticism about works that draw from the mobilities turn to offer a naïve celebration of the misleading idea that everyone is equally mobile. However, the critical application of the notion of mobility in migration studies is a productive lens for an analysis of the gross unevenness of conditions under which people are mobile. It reminds us that mobility does not equal freedom and that it can bring about new modes of confinement and exploitation (Glick-Schiller and Salazar 2013; McNevin 2014).

With over a decade of trilingual fieldwork in Portuguese, Spanish, and Mandarin Chinese, my ethnography includes a range of data collection methods that are complementary to one another, including observation, interviews, archival material, and policy documents I collected between February 2012 and September 2024. In addition to conducting ethnographic observation in sites where I was stationed, like stalls and stores, border checkpoints, and migrants' associations, I developed mobile methods such as traveling with migrant vendors along this circuit. I also conducted sixty-seven recorded interviews with migrants, representatives of migrants' associations, and state officials in Ciudad del Este, Asunción, and São Paulo. The archival and policy research I conducted includes a range of material, such as legislation, policy memos, parliamentary committee reports, and court decisions. This material ranges in topics such as tariffs and taxes, street vending regulation, smuggling, counterfeits, migration, and human trafficking. Other types of archives I analyzed include manuals, reports, brochures, and memoirs published by ethnic associations and chambers of commerce.

My use of complementary data collection methods is important for two reasons. First, it enables me to explore contradictions and tensions across sources, geographies, and temporalities. By drawing from multiple data sources, I gathered information that would not be accessible through one method alone. I used these multiple approaches to contrast narratives from a wide range of perspectives, and problematized contradictory information and competing interpretations of reality. Second, doing ethnography across borders and through multiple legal systems led to some data being inaccessible or unreportable. Appropriate research ethics limitations applied to my data collection, analysis, and reporting on illegal or illicit behavior that could potentially cause harm to the people described in the book and to myself. I needed to forgo information pertaining to individuals and situations of irregular immigration or irregular economic activity, or both. Partially because of those limitations, each chapter features a type of data source more prominently (archival material, ethnographic observation, policy analysis, and interviews), and I juxtaposed these data sources when possible.

Because of the precarious immigration status of vendors and the illegal nature of activities in the popular markets, I privileged long-term observation and spontaneous conversations over prearranged visits and recorded interviews. Being immersed in the field allowed me to observe and partake in the migrants' daily life, despite our asymmetric positions. I engaged in activities such as eating meals together in their workplace, sharing moments of leisure in public or private spaces, celebrating cultural festivities, attending religious ceremonies, and participating in demonstrations. This form of immersion is based on trust cultivated over years and respect earned with a track record of empathy, solidarity, and allyship. It exposed me to both everyday behavior and dramatic situations that I witnessed as an ethnographer and advocate, adding new information and perspectives to the data collected through interviews and archival research. Because of my gender as a man, I had easier access to spaces and moments of sociability with migrant men. I went to tea parlors and karaokes more frequently with men than with women or mixed-gender groups. In contrast, I had limited access to observing women-only groups and interviewing migrant women.

The epistemology upon which my ethnography lies is aligned with the arguments that ethnographic research can generate theory and critical knowledge through inductive, case-specific explanations that are an interpretation of reality articulated through concepts that work as building blocks for theory, with dense descriptions of rare findings (Goldman 2006). From this perspective, case-specific theory is not immediately transposable to other cases, though it can be used as a background against which new questions emerge and concepts can have distinctive analytical purchase and political valence (Roy 2005; Stoler 2022). Further, because ethnographic writings consolidate ethnographic theories, theory is both ubiquitous throughout this book and necessarily irreducible to any single section alone (Moore 1999; Strathern 2004).

ROAD MAP OF THE BOOK

In the chapters that follow I discuss the role of overseas Chinese communities in the commodity circuit between Ciudad del Este and São Paulo. Chapters 1 to 4 start with a focus on a distinct sociological unit of analysis, namely, the state (with its emphasis on legislation and policy), the market (the physical marketplaces and the regulations conditioning economic transactions in the informal economy), civil society (including the role of local and transnational diaspora groups), and the individual (with a focus on different types of perception and various levels of agency over their mobility). In reality, these domains are not entirely separated from one another, and throughout the book I crisscross those units of analysis when that crossing is appropriate and generative.

The story of this book starts in the 1960s when overseas Chinese importers opened businesses in the newly created town of Ciudad del Este. In chapter 1 "The Making of a Commercial Borderland: Overseas Chinese Importers in a Trade Outpost," I offer an account of how the founders of Ciudad del Este conceptualized the border as an opportunity for trade, a vision that was realized as the city grew into a large trade outpost and attracted overseas Chinese merchants who achieved fortune and fame. The extensive legislation that facilitated importation, exportation, and sales in Ciudad del Este counterintuitively enabled smuggling, expanding the informal economy across the border to Brazil. Taiwanese importers lobbied the Paraguayan government for exceptional tariffs that made Ciudad del Este a trade hub, whereas Chinese importers distributed imports from Ciudad del Este to São Paulo. The existence of those trade opportunities, both legal and illegal, is predicated on the meeting point between distinct regulatory systems in Paraguay and Brazil. Those regulatory systems are rooted in development models that could not be more different from one another: extreme liberalism and national developmentalism. However, trade liberalization and regional integration in the late 1990s caused the decline of Ciudad del Este and made Taiwanese importers change businesses to find new lucrative opportunities in São Paulo, where they outperformed competitors and increased their market share. This chapter explains that the Chinese expanded new market frontiers transnationally by altering legal systems and law enforcement in Paraguay and Brazil. As they relocated across borders and transformed new markets, I traveled with them.

Following Chinese importers who moved to São Paulo, I analyze in chapter 2, "Capturing Wealth: Chinese Vendors, Shifting Legality, and Shopping Tourism in São Paulo," how shifts in the enforcement of street vending regulations expanded Chinese businesses and affected Chinese newcomers in South America's newest marketplace for Asian imports. Policies designed to manage the illegal markets in São Paulo enabled powerful Chinese distributors to siphon wealth off marginalized vendors. Under the banner "from informality to entrepreneurship," City Hall changed street vending policies, enacted stricter enforcement of counterfeiting regulations, and privatized the largest public market, keeping vendors in precarious positions with the justification of modernizing the shopping tourism infrastructure. As a result, the Chinese street vendors' and stallholders' ability to work was undermined, and Chinese distributors amassed wealth, gentrified the informal economy, and got a foothold in a fiercely competitive and immensely lucrative commercial real estate market. The interdependence between Chinese businesspeople and migrant vendors contributed to those groups' overall financial growth, but it also intensified intra-ethnic exploitation. Behind this story of economic success is an organized community that lobbied for self-serving legislation and policy. It acted not just locally, but transnationally, a subject to which I turn in the next chapter.

Migrants' associations—hometown associations, kin groups, cultural clubs, mutual assistance societies, and local chapters of international diaspora associations—bridge China's diaspora policies with Chinese migrants in Ciudad del Este and São Paulo. In chapter 3 "Entrepreneurialism from Afar: Engaging Migrants' Associations and Implementing China's Trade Policies," I turn attention to the transcontinental links between migrants' associations in South America and diaspora agencies in Asia. By supporting local businesses, organizing the community's internal affairs, and participating in citywide politics, the associations facilitated state-diaspora relations, promoted international trade, and developed an entrepreneurial ethos in the overseas communities. However, as a unique kind of transnational civil society actor locally implementing the diaspora policy set in China and Taiwan, the associations played an ambivalent role. On one hand, they unlocked opportunities for migrants to work in the informal economy by subletting stalls, assisting new businesses, providing legal counsel, and representing vendors' interests in public and official affairs. On the other hand, they rigidly organized the community's affairs and exercised tight control over vendors, limiting migrants' options for jobs, trapping them in a cycle of debt, and facilitating the capture by illegality through controlling migrants' economic, social, and political activities.

In chapter 4 "Spaces of Illegality, Tactics of Legibility: Cross-Border Mobility and Translocal Emplacement," I shift focus on how marginalized Chinese vendors made themselves legible to state officials while also navigating illegality and occupying liminal positions. In this chapter, I show that migrants developed several mechanisms to respond to the crackdown on the informal economy and on irregular migration, especially in situations such as admission to the country, worksite raids, and lawsuits. To pass as entitled travelers, cosmopolitan entrepreneurs, and law-abiding migrants, vendors embodied a version of themselves that had to be legible for official gatekeepers and consistent with the norms stipulated by the state. They presented evidentiary documents to prove a unidimensional aspect of their identity, reducing it interactionally for pragmatic purposes, such as demonstrating exceptional abilities for an outstanding professional visa or showing evidence of well-founded fear of persecution when applying for asylum. On the other hand, forgery and imposture, when used, were personhood denied to these marginalized populations in situations of systemic and legal oppression. These mechanisms were not a full-fledged form of resistance but rather the tactful compromises Chinese vendors made to maintain control over their work, residence, and transnational mobility in Paraguay and Brazil. This chapter demonstrates that migrant vendors attributed new meanings to legality and made divergent uses of it to overcome myriad obstacles when gathering visa application materials, interacting with border enforcement agents, de-escalating worksite raids, and offering compelling narratives of interpersonal, family, and business ties.

In "Conclusion: Subverting Exploitation," I synthesize the book's major findings and suggest directions for further scholarly inquiry regarding emerging forms of exploitation and subversive uses of legality. By looking at the intersection of migration from Asia to South America and the expansion of the informal economy under global neoliberal capitalism, the book draws new insights from uneven development in the Global South. It also shifts the dominant paradigms developed in the Global North to talk about migration. The book's key takeaways are not limited to specific areas, and the concept of capture by illegality can be generative in various migration and informality contexts across the world, offering a new a lens on the analysis of long-standing but understudied issues at the intersections between human mobility, precarious labor, and the shifting nature of legality.

1 THE MAKING OF A COMMERCIAL BORDERLAND

Overseas Chinese Importers in a Trade Outpost

"**FOLLOW ME.** If you want to understand this city, you have to meet someone." With these words, Hsu, a Taiwanese importer, rushed me to leave his office and walked me down the alleys of Ciudad del Este. He insisted I interview one of the pioneer migrants with the reputation of a most determined importer. We stopped in front of a business center, where I was told to wait for him to bring his friend. Given his reputation of a highly admired importer and leader of the Taiwanese community, I was not surprised to see Kao step out of the building. Kao looked kind and smiled as he approached, politely saying he remembered me from Taiwan's national day celebration a few weeks earlier.

His smile, calm and welcoming, did not stop as he proudly spoke of a glorious time of bonanza for the Taiwanese community in Ciudad del Este. Kao lived in the city for four decades and saw it develop from the moments dirty roads were being cleared and the first shopping mall opened. Every Taiwanese shopkeeper I met in Ciudad del Este spoke highly of him. Kao understood early on that commerce in Ciudad del Este is dependent on price differentials that are not naturally existing. Kao was a fierce advocate for Paraguay's deliberate choice to keep liberalizing trade, deepening price gaps with Brazil's once highly protectionist economy. When trade liberalization was implemented in Brazil and regional economic integration affected both countries' economies in the 1990s, Ciudad del Este's importers and shopkeepers like Kao and Hsu pushed the Paraguayan government to fight against the imminent closing of price gaps. They demanded that the government find loopholes and create exceptional measures to save commerce in the city. With the importers' luck, the strategy worked well, at least for a few more years.

This chapter explores how Ciudad del Este emerged as the most important trade hub in the commodity circuit between China, Taiwan, Paraguay, and Brazil where overseas Chinese importers supplied the Brazilian market with imports. By exploring the origins, consolidation, and transformation of the tariff and tax policies, this chapter reveals how trade regulation in Ciudad del Este boosted legal and illegal flows of imports across the border. The predominant view about the city attributes deregulation, lawlessness, and chaos to Ciudad del Este's informal economy. Rather, I show that the border market of Ciudad del Este is a product of complex, extensive, and contradictory legislation that creates opportunities for overseas Chinese importers and shopkeepers to capture the wealth that circulates transnationally in the informal economy.

In Ciudad del Este, the concession of free-trade zones and additional fiscal incentives allowed a handful of merchants to import manufactures tariff-free through expedited lanes. While concessioners and importers have exclusive rights to import and distribute manufactures through the free-trade zones to the popular markets in Brazil, the vast majority of Chinese stallholders, Paraguayan street vendors, and Brazilian resellers bear the risks of operating illegally at a significantly lower profit margin while subject to selective enforcement. Using the exceptional legislation of the free-trade zones and convoluted tariff and fiscal regulations, not only did overseas Chinese importers operating in Ciudad del Este and São Paulo grow their market share of official importation, but they also expanded illegal practices such as reclassifying types and quantities and adulterating certificates of the origin of imports. Overseas Chinese importers benefited from the uneven application of legality in this transnational economic space predicated on increased mobility, ubiquitous illegality, and ambiguous regulation of economic activities. Rather than eliminating the informal economy, changes in legislation, loopholes in the law, and selective enforcement enabled a few importers and businesspeople to capture the wealth that circulates in the popular markets.

In Ciudad del Este, the border determines the chances of profiting from economic arbitrage and profiteering from smuggling of goods. But those possibilities are not naturally there—they are the product of exceptional legislation and controversial policy. In this chapter, I analyze the vision of the founders of Ciudad del Este for the city, established in 1957, to become a trade hub and a tourist destination. They conceived of the border as an opportunity to explore price differentials at the meeting point of Paraguay's and Brazil's very different economic development models. The sociopolitical history of trade in Ciudad del Este evolved from such vision and conceptualization, culminating in granting exclusive rights of free trade to overseas Chinese and other foreign concessioners starting in the 1960s, and from Paraguay's complicated fiscal and trade policies that unilaterally reduced tariffs and taxes across the board from the 1970s to the 1990s. These policies increased the price gap between imports in Paraguay and Brazil and kept prices competitive in Ciudad del Este even at a moment of economic liberalization in Brazil, making the city even more attractive for overseas Chinese importers and real estate developers like Hsu, Kao, and the Law family, who not only helped Ciudad del Este become a trade hub but also later expanded their businesses to São Paulo.

DEVELOPMENT, DIFFERENCE, AND TRADE IN THE BORDERLANDS

The border trade in Ciudad del Este is an importation system in Paraguay that caters to foreign buyers. Known as *comercio de triangulación* or "triangle commerce," it originated from a particular conceptualization of the border profoundly shaped by the vision of the founders of Ciudad del Este for the future development of the city. They understood the border as the meeting point of different development models, the Brazilian and the Paraguayan. Their pragmatic conceptualization reveals that the border is not simply a line, rather, it is a social relation. Understanding the border as a social relation recognizes the difference and the interdependence a border creates between distinct social realities predicated on the very existence of the border (Balibar 2002; Hage 1998; Meddeb 2015; Mezzadra and Neilson 2013; Stoler 2022). The social relation in question at these borderlands is the economic inequality created by distinct development models. Conceptualizing the border that way was a prerequisite to formulating the Paraguayan government's achievable vision of large social transformations. Consistent with their concept of the border, the founders of Ciudad del Este envisioned a city to serve as an outward-looking zone of passage. They saw the price gaps between two distinctively regulated economies as an opportunity to be seized, not a challenge to be overcome.

The Fate of an Emporium of Wealth and Progress
The establishment of Ciudad del Este in the late 1950s represents a break in regional geopolitics. It shifts away from the tendency prevalent in Brazil and Argentina of inward-oriented, state-led occupation of the borderlands with military posts and national parks of protected natural areas (Brito 2005; Freitas 2021; Sbardelotto 2010; Silva 2010). Instead, the creation of Ciudad del Este moves towards a notion of regional and international integration through shared infrastructure and trade. Without an exit to the sea, navigation on rivers crossing Argentinian territory was the only way for Paraguay to trade with the world until the 1940s. Paraguay's economic dependence and political subjugation were symbolically and practically enacted by Argentina's control over the flow of goods to and from Paraguay. As part of a plan to create an alternative access to maritime trade, Paraguay and Brazil signed agreements in 1941 and 1956 by which Paraguay uses the ports of Santos and Paranaguá in Brazil as an extension of its national customs territory. Such agreements, still valid to this day, allow imports to disembark at those ports without inspection by Brazilian customs authorities, and then to cross a thousand miles into Brazilian territory before following the "Dry Port" on the Paraguayan side.

In the 1940s and 1950s, Brazilian and Paraguayan policymakers had an aspiration for economic development that indelibly informed their vision for the borderlands. This aspiration was based on the idea of developing vast swaths of borderlands by expanding the frontiers of agriculture and building the logistical infrastructure for commodity exportation. Such expansion concretizes the Brazilian government's desire to extend its geopolitical influence over Paraguay at the height of the Brazilian "march to the west," epitomized by Brazilian dictator Getúlio Vargas's visit to Asunción in 1941 when the first port agreement was signed.

In turn, the rise of Colorado Party's General Alfredo Stroessner[1] to power in Paraguay through a military coup in 1954 marks the beginning of the country's "march to the east." It also consolidated the diplomatic rapprochement with Brazil, including the signing of the second port agreement and the colonization of land for Brazilian farmers, making the borderlands dependent on foreign economies ever since. In the wake of the 1956 agreement, both countries agreed to build highways to link the Paraguayan capital Asunción to the port of Paranaguá. The point where Ciudad del Este is located was the physical and figurative point of encounter between Brazil's march to the west and Paraguay's march to the east.

Stroessner issued an executive order establishing Ciudad del Este in 1957. Originally called Puerto Flor de Lis and shortly renamed Puerto Presidente Stroessner, the city was officially founded as Paraguay's newest gate for the imports needed to supply a low-industrialized country. The words proffered by the appointed administrator in the foundational act that established the city exemplify the expectation of progress this new trade route via Brazil would bring about: "May this new city represent, today and forever, our relations as brother peoples, becoming a place of rest in our transit towards the ocean, and emporium of wealth and progress for those who inhabit it" (Núñez de Báez 2003, 67).

The city founders had a very specific understanding of wealth and progress. Being at the borders, they envisioned that the city's destiny was to be forged in the intertwinement of commerce and tourism. The first buildings erected in Ciudad del Este, the customs house and Hotel Acaray, are telling of this attributed double *vocación* (vocation). The construction of the customs house began in 1959, predictably located right next to where the International Friendship Bridge would be built. Hotel Acaray is a luxury casino hotel that embodied the expectations of tourism in Ciudad del Este: Paraguayan elites could now escape Asunción to enjoy rest, talk politics, and do business. Humberto Dominguez Dibb, a descendent of Christian Syrians escaping the Ottoman rule to Asunción, pioneered the luxury hotel business in Ciudad del Este. More than a fortune was needed for Dominguez to be the first entrepreneur in the tourism sector in the city. Dominguez was Stroessner's son-in-law, which made it easier for him to buy prime state land for a cheaper price before the process of selling, conceding, and colonizing land started (Karam 2013).

The commissioning of the city appears in the articulation of political power and economic interests. Stroessner appointed his confidant and Minister of Interior Edgar Ynsfrán as the official in charge of the Administration Commission of Puerto Presidente Stroessner, which planned and ruled over the city for two decades. Elaborating on the task of designing the new city to achieve its attributed double "vocation," Ynsfrán writes in his memoirs: "Basically it is about fixing a point in the country map which is presumed of geopolitical interest, whose possible communications with other points confirm the reasonable prediction of its future importance, and then, all required formalities met, declare the city founded." Bureaucratic formalities were evidently not sufficient to develop this imagined city, and he goes on to defend the need for a city plan under his responsibility: "But the city is not there, this city has yet to appear. And how is it going to appear? What is the plan that can be executed to make the city appear there where one believes the meridian of progress passes?" (Núñez de Báez 2003, 85).

The development of Ciudad del Este is symptomatic of Paraguay's extreme liberalism combining an open economy, deep-seated corruption, and a strong defense of sectoral interests. Paraguay's defense of the liberal ideology at that time is in sharp contrast with the economic development model adopted in Brazil. The economies of Brazil and Paraguay could not be more different. Unlike Paraguay, Brazil implemented a national development ideology and policies of "Import Substituting Industrialization" centered on protectionist tariffs and the growth of domestic markets. For its part, Paraguay embraced its choice for international trade and private foreign investment (Menezes 1987). Ciudad del Este's development attests to this. The city planners insisted that market speculation and real estate profits were necessary to bring about economic growth and urban development (Schuster 2015).

In the following years, larger issues than the tourism business were playing out in Ciudad del Este's casinos. Stroessner bet on domestic alliance building and distributed political power and economic privileges to establish or coopt local powerholders. He appointed high-ranking army officers, and later civilians, to strategic positions in the borderlands, allowing them to rule the area with few constraints in exchange for their support for his sector of the Colorado Party. Unsurprisingly, the regime turned a blind eye to smuggling in the ally-controlled borderlands, and it even incentivized it unofficially (Ruiz Díaz and Ons 2013). In an infamous interview in 1965, Stroessner said that the military control of the growing contraband trade was "the price of peace," suggesting that military discontent was lessened by the prospect of easy money to be gained through illicit activities (Nickson 1997). In a city of contraband and gambling, his appointees would soon become or support local politicians, creating political clan lineages that remained in power in the borderlands even decades after the fall of Stroessner (Miranda 2009). The dice were loaded.

Exclusivity and the Distribution of Officialness

Since the conception of Ciudad del Este, there have been arguments in favor of a tax-reduced importation regime to create a market for imports catering to foreigner buyers. As early as 1960, the Administration Commission led by Ynsfrán made a deal with foreign investors and importers in the name of developing the city: an agreement with the Foreign Markets Trading Corporation that conceded exclusive rights over a thirty-six-hectare free-trade zone for ten years. The company, registered in New York, was allowed to import and reexport tariff-free, and to export items manufactured in the zone with reduced taxes. In exchange, it had the obligation to develop industrial and trade activities, and the facilities developed by the company were to be transferred to the commission upon the return of the land at the end of the contract.

Despite the façade of legality, the free-trade zone concession in Ciudad del Este quickly opened the way for smuggling. As early as 1961, just one year after the concession agreement, the free-trade zone was the subject of attention of Brazilian diplomats in Paraguay. In a classified communication, the diplomatic mission in Asunción alerted the minister of foreign affairs in Brasília to the harms of what it understood was a "smuggling hub of an unprecedented scale," under the purview of "Paraguayan border authorities" and with "the complicity of residents in the [Brazilian] national territory" (Cervo 2001, 213). Diplomats announced that, despite the official goal of fomenting industrialization, the Foreign Markets Trading Corporation was engaged in the trade and smuggling of whiskey, American cigarettes, tape players, and other items.

When the concession period ended, a group that included overseas Chinese traders challenged its renewal and lobbied for favorable legislation. The transnational imports firm Business Company SRL, owned by Singaporean Chinese, Brazilians, and Argentinians, pushed Paraguayan lawmakers to propose legislation implementing a new free-trade zone. In December of 1970, when the Paraguayan senate discussed the matter during what was scheduled to be a holiday recession, opposing senators questioned the bill's sponsor about the international composition of investors, to which he replied that "capital does not have nationality." The opposing senators feared that the bill would facilitate illicit business practices and raised concerns about the Paraguayan politicians and foreign investors who were behind Ciudad del Este's commercial dynamism (Schuster 2015, 43).

The proposal eventually passed in the Paraguayan Congress in 1971. Similar to what the 1960 act established, the 1971 act stipulates a ten-year lease to a single company that would enjoy reduced tariffs, with the possibility of renewal. However, during the 1970s, the question about the free-trade zone remained unresolved. Pressure from Taiwanese and Lebanese traders brought the issue to a stalemate as they questioned the exclusive rights of the free-trade zone and the restrictive powers of the newly created regional office of the Association of Customs Brokers of Paraguay—a private entity to which the Paraguayan government delegated the exclusive mandate to vet applications and give accreditation for new customs brokers. They saw the free-trade zone and the regional office as the centers of clandestine operations, especially because the leadership of the office consisted of former customs officers who had been involved in an illegal international trade scandal not long before (Miranda 2009). Only in 1979 did Paraguay grant the Business Company SRL exclusive rights to explore the free-trade zone. Having overseas Chinese on the board of executives, Business Company SRL quickly capitalized on the cultural and legal ability of its leadership to do business in emerging Asian Tigers, particularly Taiwan, Hong Kong, and Singapore.

Overseas Chinese traders and other investors of Business Company SRL enjoyed the rights to explore the free-trade zone. Those legal rights are a type of exclusive benefit granted in the form of concessions that set strict conditions enabling specific actors to perform certain lucrative economic activities and to restrict competitors' benefits. The legality of this exclusive right does not serve justice, fairness or social legitimacy. Yet, it still shapes the conditions for wealth accumulation, putting into sharp relief how legality is a product of arbitrary officialness. It also shows how illegality operates not only through simple violations but also through an alchemy transforming the distribution of officialness: influential actors use their powers to receive exclusive prerogatives, transforming what was illegal into a legal exception. Social and political power determine the contours of legality, which is evident with the notion that an act is illegal when committed by certain social groups, but the very same act is considered legal when committed by a specific actor to whom exceptional rights apply (Foucault 1995). When one social group exercises power over others, their privileges move from the register of illegality to be legally and socially encoded as an exemption. The Stroessner regime sanctioned contraband in Ciudad del Este as an exemption given to overseas Chinese and other foreign businesspeople for a profitable return to his political allies controlling the borderlands.

The convergence between policies friendly to foreign capital and the distribution of officialness that privileges exclusiveness is not at odds with capitalist forms of wealth accumulation. As the French historian Fernand Braudel (2008) argues in his historical analysis of monopoly rights and the concessions granted to long-distance traders, sovereignly instituted markets are the roots of capitalist primitive accumulation. A similar phenomenon is evident today in special economic zones, where ordinary regulations are suspended and substituted with legal exemptions that grant exclusive rights of economic exploitation at the expense of social development benefiting the masses (Banerjea 2011; Keshavarzian 2010; Levien 2011, 2018).

In the nearly decade between the passing of the bill in 1971 and the 1979 decree that finally established the free-trade zone concession, overseas Chinese importers established businesses in Ciudad del Este. In an interview he gave me, Taiwanese importer Alex Woo spoke of the trading company his father established in 1978, saying, "Our company had an advantage: my father and my uncle spoke the language and had business connections in Asia." The overseas Chinese individuals connected to Business Company SRL opened trading houses in Foz do Iguaçu on the Brazilian side of the border, linking trade with São Paulo–based Chinese and Hong Kongese migrants through formal reexportation and smuggling. Ironically, as Hsu puts it, "The imports crossed hundreds of miles in the Brazilian territory" from the ports of Santos and Paranaguá only to "make their way back to São Paulo tariff-free."

The period between the end of one free-trade zone concession and the beginning of the other did not mean a decrease in triangle commerce—quite the contrary. A series of new legislation adopted in the 1970s reduced tariffs across the board in Paraguay, boosting triangle commerce in Ciudad del Este.

IN TRANSIT

While far-right nationalist populism promotes the idea that borders should stop people and goods, the predominant assumption in the mainstream liberal view asserts that borders should expedite goods, but not people. However, critical border scholarship shows that neither is true. Instead, borders modulate and channel the flows of people, things, and capital. In Ciudad del Este, exclusive trade rights were paradoxically followed by extensive and contradictory legislation that enabled the use of indeterminacy as a tool for governing transborder economic practices.

Indeterminacy as a Tool of Government

Throughout the 1960s, Ciudad del Este was living up to its founders' vision of a zone of economic potentialities in the way they anticipated. These borderlands became liminal spaces of a plethora of exceptional regulations and a laboratory of evolving legislation, the result of which was normative indeterminacy. Contrary to the commonsensical idea that lack of regulation and gaps in legislation cause informality, it was the proliferation of contradictory norms that expanded the illegal trade. In Ciudad del Este, shifting policy, ambiguous regulation, and the discretionary application of divergent codes facilitated profiteering (Tucker 2020).

Beginning in 1972, Paraguay established two special importation regimes that were used to disguise illegalities in trade: the Border Clearance Regime and the In-Transit Customs Clearance Regime. The Border Clearance Regime contributed to an unprecedented level of smuggling. This regime officially sought to solve issues of goods shortages for populations living in Paraguay's borderlands and aimed at regulating the importation of grains and processed foods in areas that were more easily connected to Brazilian or Argentinian providers. The assumption was that these Paraguayan border populations were disconnected from the domestic producing areas, resulting in being penalized by tariffs meant to protect national producers unable to provide for these populations. However, the Border Clearance Regime allowed for the smuggling of goods in proportions never seen before through the use of false invoices and misrepresented clearance reports (Ruiz Díaz 2006).

The Border Clearance Regime expanded convoluted illegal operations that combined smuggling and legal importation. An example is the Brazil-Paraguay-Brazil smuggling of coffee beans. Such a maneuver was intended to evade the high export taxes and other levies applicable in Brazil. Upon proof of exportation clearance from Brazil and importation in Paraguay, Brazilian exporters received tax credits that compensated for these levies. This practice reached an absurd point in the 1960s and 1970s, when Paraguay became one of the main coffee exporters to Brazil, even though Brazil is one of the world's top coffee producers and exporters, and Paraguay does not cultivate coffee at all. On the Brazilian side, rigid measures were adopted and more discretionary power was given to border agents who effectively seized a gigantic number of trucks smuggling coffee back into Brazil in the 1970s. The Brazilian Coffee Institute lobbied Brazilian lawmakers who passed legislation with more severe penalties, and the government adopted stricter law enforcement guidelines. However, in the 1980s, the decline of the coffee business in Brazil and changes in "export taxes" decreased the industry's interest to keep pushing the government for stricter enforcement, bringing the number of people criminally implicated in smuggling coffee to nearly zero in the following decades (Fiorotti 2015; Miranda 2009). This is not because of a change in legislation or policy, but because the coffee industry's interests shifted over time due to changes in global trade.

Another example is cigarettes. Brazilian producers exported to Paraguay to avoid the 70% tax rate applied in Brazil, only to have cigarettes smuggled back through backroads or exported to Brazil with false certificates of origin. From 1989 to 1994, cigarettes exported from Brazil to Paraguay jumped from 655 million to 2.3 billion—much higher than the demand in Paraguay. Similar to the case of coffee beans, Brazil's fight against cigarette smuggling in the 1980s and 1990s resulted from a fierce lobby from the tobacco industry, revealing that political and social power of influential business groups effected changes in legislation and shifts in enforcement (Rabossi 2010).

In the 2000s, the focus of enforcement on the borders near Ciudad del Este shifted again, this time to manufactured goods and counterfeits at the heart of the city's triangle commerce. Unlike coffee beans and cigarettes, these goods are not made in Brazil. The crackdown on counterfeits, too, is affected by a transnational lobby, this time linked to the global discourse on intellectual property rights protection (Pinheiro-Machado 2017). Brazil's crackdown on the smuggling of coffee, cigarettes, and counterfeits shows that enforcement priorities are not purely a matter of application of the law, but rather are contingent on power relations grounded in vested interests of private businesses and political pressure of the industry.

Also adopted in 1972, the In-Transit Customs Clearance Regime is the special importation regime that was most clearly intended to benefit triangle commerce. This regime was put in place in response to the end of the concession period of Ciudad del Este's first free-trade zone. It reduced to 22% the tariff rates applicable to imported goods that enter the Paraguayan territory provided that they are sold to foreigners. That tariff rate is less than half of the one applied in the rest of Paraguay and much less than the rates applied in Brazil.

At the same time, on the Brazilian side, two policies that aimed to increase the reserve of foreign currencies in response to the 1973 global oil price surge had the unintended consequence of boosting triangle commerce. The first policy was an increase of the tariffs on luxury goods of 100% in 1974 and 200% in 1981. The second policy, implemented by Brazil's Central Bank between 1976 and 1979, stipulated that Brazilians traveling abroad were required to make a mandatory deposit payment in dollars, except for travel to neighboring countries. This disincentivized travel to countries outside of South America and bolstered domestic tourism. The Iguazu Falls soon became a popular tourist destination for middle-class Brazilians. Quickly, Paraguay lifted the requirement of a visa for Brazilians staying under eight hours in Ciudad del Este, which immediately caused a vertiginous growth in shoppers and resellers (Freire da Silva 2014a; Rabossi 2004). In Kao's view, "the visa lift clearly was a game changer" for the Taiwanese importers in Ciudad del Este, a community that was growing fast in the late 1970s and early 1980s. He thinks the Paraguayan government adopted the right policies to seize an opportunity created by global economic volatility and Brazil's protectionist measures: "It is funny how a global crisis can be an opportunity if the government acts quickly: the informal economy thrives when people have less money in their pockets."

The flow of Brazilian shoppers kept growing from the late 1970s to its peak in the mid-1990s. For instance, in 1987, Brazilian customs authorities reported approximately one hundred buses daily, that is, roughly five thousand shoppers who traveled overnight to buy in Ciudad del Este and resell in Brazil (Rabossi 2010, 5–6). The following year, shoppers tripled to more than fifteen thousand daily, leading customs officers to complain that the high volume simply could not be feasibly inspected. The growth of excursion buses shows that not only middle-class travelers were buying fine imports in Ciudad del Este, but also that many working-class people turned to the informal economy to earn an income as long-distance peddlers reselling imports they bought in Paraguay across all corners of Brazil.

In this period, what the Brazilian officers call petty smuggling was largely tolerated on the Brazilian side of the border, and practically was not enforceable. The chief of the Federal Police of Brazil in Foz do Iguaçu reported that between US$15 million and US$20 million in goods were smuggled monthly from Ciudad del Este in 1989. He went on to say that enforcement agencies were not capable of eliminating such widespread smuggling: "This trade can be inconvenient to Brazil, but we tolerate it. The role of the Federal Police is to modulate it" (Rabossi 2010, 5). Enforcement of smuggling on both sides of the borders was malleable. It shows that legality does not merely equal adherence to regulatory norms but rather to the situational morality that determines a state official's permissiveness for illegal practices (Kalir, Sur, and Van Schendel 2012; Van Schendel and Abraham 2005).

As triangle commerce was gradually consolidating, many domestic and international migrants flocked to Ciudad del Este seeking economic opportunities. Ciudad del Este's population grew from 26,485 in 1972 to 62,326 in 1982, and it kept growing exponentially in the decades to follow, reaching 223,350 residents in 2002. Domestically, the construction of the Itaipú Dam, a binational project of Brazil and Paraguay, contributed to pull labor forces. Once laid off, many workers became street vendors or found jobs in the imports warehouses of Ciudad del Este. International migrants like the Taiwanese, in turn, were attracted by the In-Transit Customs Clearance Regime and contributed significantly to the increase in investments in downtown, especially imports shops and shopping malls.

Taiwanese are the second largest international migrant group in Ciudad del Este, with the peak in migration being in the late 1970s and early 1980s. This migration was motivated both by trade opportunities in Ciudad del Este and political turmoil in Taiwan. Many left the island due to the fear of annexation by China after the end of the Mutual Defense Treaty between the United States and the Taiwan in 1979, a year after the United States recognized Beijing's government. Most Taiwanese migrants hailed from the city of Taichung in the early 1980s and became shopkeepers specializing in selling imports to Brazilian shoppers. Kao says the situation in Taiwan and Paraguay was "a perfect storm" of push and pull factors, with "the lack of freedom, economic and political freedom in Taiwan at the [Chinese] Communist Party's doorstep, and the prospect of rich pickings in Ciudad del Este." In a sector dominated by the Lebanese community locally and the Cantonese migrants operating from São Paulo, Taiwanese importers gradually increased and outnumbered other groups.

Migrants' associations played a crucial role in the socioeconomic integration of Taiwanese migrants, being instrumental in helping them set up businesses and acquire credit for building malls. The oldest of these associations is the Chinese Association of Ciudad del Este, founded in 1982 by migrants like the Kao and Hsu's father. That same year, the association initiated the construction of the six-story shopping mall Lai-Lai, named after the most famous hotel in their hometown of Taichung. According to Kao, the Taiwanese migrants' plan "was to build a mixed-use building with import shops on the first floor and hotel rooms on the upper floors," which converges with the founders of Ciudad del Este's vision for the city's double "vocation" for commerce and tourism. However, realizing that, as Hsu explained, "Brazilian shoppers would not spend the night in Ciudad del Este" because they traveled with organized excursions returning at twilight, the association eventually decided to use all the building space for commercial leasing. In the following years, the association helped Taiwanese migrants build at least seven additional shopping centers.

With the end of the ten-year lease period of the free-trade zone concession in 1989, the Chinese Association of Ciudad del Este-Paraguay was an influential advocate for changes in the fiscal legislation to "keep benefiting triangle commerce," as Hsu said. The association pushed for lowering the tariffs even further and cutting other taxes. It sponsored the creation of a unified sales tax for imports "in transit," which was eventually set at a reduced rate of 7% by the Paraguayan administration that followed the deposition of Stroessner in 1989.

FIGURE 1.1. Lai-Lai Center in Ciudad del Este, 2015. Photograph by Douglas de Toledo Piza.

The price gap in imports sold in Paraguay and Brazil is a crucial element for the success of Ciudad del Este's triangle commerce, attracting migrants like the Taiwanese. The "clearest threat" that can put an end to triangle commerce is, as Hsu puts it, the lowering of tariffs and taxes in Brazil. Anticipating the imminent trade liberalization in Brazil in the 1990s, Hsu and other leaders of the Taiwanese community put pressure on the Paraguayan government to keep triangle commerce alive in Ciudad del Este.

The Paradoxes of Triangle Commerce
The Paraguayan government answered the call of Ciudad del Este's Taiwanese business community to further liberalize trade. Even before joining the General Agreement on Tariffs and Trade in 1994 and the U.S.-led push for trade liberalization globally, Paraguay's first democratic government following the deposition of Stroessner ceded to the pressure of interest groups and unilaterally adopted a comprehensive trade policy reform, lowering tariffs across the board and abolishing tariffs on a series of goods. Eventually, nearly all imports in Paraguay were tariffed at a maximum rate of 10% or lower.

Tax cuts were even more drastic when, conceding to the continuous push of Ciudad del Este's businesses groups like the Chinese association, the legislature passed a major fiscal reform in 1991 and empowered the executive branch of government to lower the taxes on imported items. The government issued decrees that created what was later called the Special Tax Regime, popularly known as the "Special Tourism Regime." The Special Tourism Regime further reduced tariffs of goods considered to be "in transit" to Brazil and also lowered sales taxes of these imports such as the value-added tax, sales tax, corporation tax, and selected goods tax.

This favorable legislation led to the peak of triangle commerce in the mid-1990s. Incentivized by its successful lobbying, the Taiwanese importers and shopkeepers formed new associations to represent their business interests in lowering tariffs and taxes. The most important of these associations are the Taiwanese Chamber of Commerce-Paraguay and the Federation of Chinese Businesspeople of Paraguay, established in 1995 and 1997 respectively. Hsu, who has held leadership positions in both, proudly says that they "do crucial advocacy work for policies to support triangle commerce" and that "without our pressure, the government would not adopt the right policies, and this city's economy would be neglected." Like the Chinese Association of Ciudad del Este-Paraguay, these associations help Taiwanese migrants capitalize on their position as brokers who can navigate the cultural, language, legal, and bureaucratic systems of exporting countries like Taiwan and China. As a result, Taiwanese importers outcompeted traditional importers in Ciudad del Este, altering the trade routes from reexportation via Miami to exports from Taiwan and China.

Ciudad del Este and Foz do Iguaçu were no exception to the new 1990s migration from China that increased the overseas population in destinations across South America. The Chinese migrants in Ciudad del Este were lured by the idea of economic prosperity as importers. However, they lacked the start-up capital and faced almost insurmountable linguistic, diplomatic, and legal barriers. Arriving in a market where Taiwanese migrants had already consolidated a strong position, the Chinese migrants found abundant income opportunities in Taiwanese businesses, but limited alternatives. Reflecting on how easy it was to find a job as a stallholder, Chinese migrant Sandra also emphasized how vulnerable she felt for not finding employment options outside the Taiwanese community: "Finding a job was not the problem, any Taiwanese importer would take me when I got here.... But the problem is that we [Chinese migrants] were at their mercy. If they like you, fine. If they don't, you get laid off and they will tell the others, so no Taiwanese boss will take you. That is very dangerous. You have to make them like you. And, like, me, I didn't know Portuguese or Spanish. Where else could I find a job?" Like Sandra, most Chinese migrants work as stallholders in Taiwanese shops. Many do not live in Paraguay because it is more difficult for them to obtain documentation and maintain lawful immigration status in a country that recognizes Taipei's government as the legitimate representative of the Chinese state.

Not only did Paraguay's Special Tourism Regime save triangle commerce, but it actually boomed. As advantageous prices attracted even more Brazilian shoppers to Ciudad del Este, Paraguay's internal revenue increased steadily in the first half of the 1990s. Between 1988 and 1995, imports grew from US$1 billion to US$3 billion, and the customs tax revenues increased, astoundingly, 1,648%. The peak in sales was in 1994, when Brazil

FIGURE 1.2. Ciudad del Este skyline, 2018. Source: Cmasi.

adopted the *real* as its currency, which initially exchanged for the American dollar at a rate of 1:1. That year, nearly 3.5 million Brazilian shoppers made their way to Ciudad del Este at least once, and an astonishing number of 1,200 buses crossed to Ciudad del Este on a single day, the Saturday before Christmas night (Rabossi 2004). Experiencing an increase in purchase power for the first time since the economic stagnation and rampant inflation that characterized Brazil's economy in the last years of dictatorship in the 1980s, Brazilian consumers flocked to Ciudad del Este. Resellers found an eager local clientele ready to buy the latest imports they brought from hundreds or thousands of miles away. In Ciudad del Este, more than four thousand importers and distributors obtained a license to operate under the Special Tourism Regime just in 1994.

As Ciudad del Este supplied a growing demand for imported goods in Brazil, importation in Paraguay achieved record numbers in the 1990s. Smuggling to Brazil increased even more dramatically. Nearly half of all imports consumed in Brazil in the early 1990s were smuggled from Paraguay, according to the former head of the Paraguayan Central Bank

(Penner 2006). In the late 1990s, the Brazilian ambassador to Paraguay, Bernardo Pericás Neto, expressed concerns with Ciudad del Este. His preoccupation was similar to what the diplomatic mission in Asunción had expressed nearly four decades earlier, but the number was remarkably higher. He alerted the Ministry of Foreign Affairs that the spike in smuggling was "flooding the Brazilian markets" at an unprecedented level: an estimated US$12 million annually of smuggled imports and other illicit goods (Miranda 2000).

The political and economic consequences of the economic development model adopted under Stroessner outlasted his regime. Paraguayan analysts call this "Stroessnerism without Stroessner" (Rojas Villagra 2014). The primary goal of the Special Tourism Regime is to sustain triangle commerce that emerged out of Stroessner's economic and political ambitions. Triangle commerce and contraband diverted trade policy goals and caused negative economic consequences for Paraguay, resulting in an astonishing paradox: Paraguay is an extremely open economy and, yet, it shows high levels of smuggling.

SAVING TRIANGLE COMMERCE, AGAIN

When faced with regional integration under the Southern Common Market (MERCOSUR)—a free-trade agreement between several countries in South America—Paraguay used trade liberalization to benefit a class of merchants including the overseas Chinese. Paraguay's use of trade policy instruments has been consequential for its economy and contradicts the development model adopted in the country. Given the country's dependence on agricultural exports, it would be expected that Paraguay would use MERCOSUR instruments to gain unrestricted access to the major consumer markets of other members of the bloc. Moreover, contrary to what the proponents of economic integration expect from a small economy under regional integration, Paraguay chose not to temporarily protect or develop strategic manufacturing sectors while gradually promoting its participation in regional and global commodity chains.

Triangle Commerce Under Regional Integration

In the early 1990s, Paraguay was under enormous pressure from Brazil and Argentina to engage in regional integration through MERCOSUR. Founded by the Treaty of Asunción in 1991, MERCOSUR aimed at eliminating all tariffs and non-tariff barriers among members—initially Brazil, Argentina, Uruguay, and Paraguay—by the end of 1994. However, capital-intensive manufacturing sectors were a contentious and unresolved issue between the two most industrialized countries of the bloc, and the original goal proved unachievable. Adopted in December 1994, the Protocol of Ouro Preto resets MERCOSUR's goal to be a customs union with the application of a Common External Tariff on imports from outside the bloc, in a gradual transition to a common market. By seeking to eliminate tariffs among members and impose a shared tariff for imports from outside the bloc, MERCOSUR represents, at least in principle, the end of triangle commerce.

As soon as MERCOSUR started being negotiated, Paraguay and Taiwan sought to establish new free-trade zones in an attempt to remedy Ciudad del Este's inevitable economic decline and protect the Taiwanese importers from setbacks. The Taiwanese government immediately obtained approval from Paraguay to establish the Parque Industrial Oriente (Orient Industrial Park) on the outskirts of Ciudad del Este, with the hope that Taiwanese importers could assemble goods in Paraguay and keep a strong share of the Brazilian and Argentinian markets. Against that backdrop, Taiwan secured an Agreement of Mutual Protection and Promotion of Investments with Paraguay in 1992. The Taiwanese government granted US$9.5million to a Taiwanese businessman who represented Taiwan in the acquisition of a forty-hectare lot and became the executive director of the industrial park after its establishment in 1994.

In turn, the Paraguayan government passed legislation in 1995 that set the legal framework for establishing new free-trade zones, with the intention to grant the Orient Industrial Park a concession. The Paraguayan government approved the fiscal incentives for an industrial park in Ciudad del Este to avoid what the Paraguayan Central Bank once called the "death" of triangle commerce due to the establishment of MERCOSUR. If successful, the industrial park would allow for goods to be exported to the bloc as "Made in Paraguay." The executive director plainly said at the time of the creation of the Orient Industrial Park that its main advantage was to be able to export to members of MERCOSUR free of tariffs. Despite all efforts, the industrial park is underutilized, with only a handful of companies manufacturing goods that are popular in triangle commerce such as toys, board games, Christmas trees, wall clocks, and other souvenirs. Kao is one of the manufacturers operating in the industrial park. I was surprised to learn that a prominent Taiwanese importer in Ciudad del Este was, after all, also a manufacturer. It turns out the same factors that represent a blow to importation in Ciudad del Este are an encouragement for those willing to turn to manufacturing. So Kao did. "You don't go against the wave and let it crush you, you go along with it and ride on. I tried to convince my compatriots and importers, but they wouldn't listen to me. It's all about diversifying your business. When importation is not profitable, I have my factory that holds up for me." I finally understood why, amid so many anxious faces of his fellow Taiwanese importers, Kao's smile was indeed a lasting one.

However, the free-trade zones were a contentious issue in the negotiations of MERCOSUR in the first half of the 1990s. Paraguay's position was essentially linked to the Orient Industrial Park in Ciudad del Este. Paraguay demanded that a free-trade zone in Ciudad del Este benefit from a special customs regime like the regime being proposed for the free-trade zones already operating in Manaus (Brazil) and Tierra del Fuego (Argentina). Not only did Brazil and Argentina reject Paraguay's demand, but they objected to Paraguay's plan of establishing a free-trade zone in Ciudad del Este altogether, arguing that stronger mechanisms of control of origin were needed to certify that goods were indeed manufactured in Paraguay, not just assembled there with little value added. Pointing to Paraguay's fame for noncompliance, they feared that a free-trade zone in Ciudad del Este would undermine the customs union—or "perforate" it, as they said.

MERCOSUR eventually allowed the establishment of new free-trade zones as long as they met the requirement of being grounded in prior legislation. This was clearly a victory for the Paraguayan diplomats who maintained that the country had a long history of free-trade zones and argued that Paraguay's 1985 Customs Statute, which precedes the MERCOSUR agreements by a decade, is preexisting legislation regulating the ingress and exit of goods from the free-trade zones. On the other hand, the decision was only a partial victory for Paraguay because MERCOSUR also rejected Paraguay's demand that a special regime apply to these zones, deciding instead that only Manaus and Tierra del Fuego be exempted from the common external tariffs when exporting to MERCOSUR customs territory. In the end, Paraguay's lukewarm win did not lead to the Orient Industrial Park petitioning for a free-trade zone concession, and not until 2002 did the Paraguayan government authorize free-trade concessions, all located in Ciudad del Este.

A decade after the establishment of the Orient Industrial Park, São Paulo–based Chinese and Hong Kongese importers who were already doing business through Ciudad del Este tried in 2002 to extend control over trade by operating in the industrial park. These importers had consolidated the smuggling of goods from Paraguay to Brazil in the 1980s but were facing a crackdown on the contraband of counterfeits after the U.S.-led global "war on terror" linked Ciudad del Este's Lebanese importers with money laundering and financing of terrorism. The Chinese importers struck a deal with the executive director of the industrial park: they offered a US$4 million loan in exchange for a "donation" of portions of the industrial park. However, the deal was stopped by a 2002 investigation conducted by Paraguay's Anti-Mafia Police, Brazil's Federal Police, and Taiwan's Yuen Control that accused the executive director of colluding with Hong Kong–based criminal organizations. Kao expressed the sentiment prevalent in Ciudad del Este's Taiwanese community: "It tarnished our reputation and ruined business." After that, the Taiwanese government wanted to reassert its control over the industrial park and repair the ignominy it had fallen under. In 2006, Taiwan's International Cooperation and Development Fund took over the administration of the industrial park and renamed it Taiwan Industrial Park.

With the failure in establishing a free-trade zone in the industrial park in a timely manner, Taiwanese associations lobbied Paraguay to use two MERCOSUR transitional regimes to save triangle commerce: the Adaptation Regime and the Schedules of Exception to the Common External Tariff. Paraguay's Adaptation Regime incentivized smuggling to an unprecedented level. The MERCOSUR Adaptation Regime was specific for each member country and aimed to gradually eliminate outstanding tariffs on trade within the bloc. The main rationale for the Adaptation Regime was to provisionally protect domestic industries during the transition to regional free trade and promote the conversion of these sectors towards productive integration within the bloc.

However, Paraguay flagrantly used the Adaptation Regime, which was in effect between 1995 and 2000, to increase fiscal revenues. Paraguay raised tariffs on items that were highly imported under the Brazil-Paraguay-Brazil smuggling scheme, enabling the use of the Adaptation Regime for laundering the smuggling of cigarettes exported from Brazil to Paraguay. This is evident in the paradox that while cigarettes benefited from enormous tax reliefs in the Special Tourism Regime, they were simultaneously highly tariffed under the Adaptation Regime and were extremely profitable for Paraguay's public coffers. Between 1996 and 1999, imports in Paraguay under the Adaptation Regime totaled over US$1 billion, with a tax revenue of US$250 million. Roughly 85% of this volume was from cigarettes, 70% of which were from Brazil (Ruiz Díaz and Ons 2013). Counterintuitively, the triangle smuggling of cigarettes benefited the Brazilian tobacco industry, which endorsed it. The CEO of the most important Brazilian tobacco company at that time admitted it in an interview with a major Brazilian magazine in 1998: "Exporting [cigarettes] for illegal reentry is, unfortunately, the only protection mechanism that the tobacco industry has against the invasion of imports that flood the market" (Rabossi 2010, 17).

The use of the Adaptation Regime for the smuggling of cigarettes was obvious, and the Brazilian government demanded actions to put an end to it. Acquiescing to Brasília's mounting pressure, Paraguay moved cigarettes from the Special Tourist Regime to the general importation regime and even increased tax rates in 1998. Moreover, Brazil took unilateral measures that same year to combat smuggling by increasing taxes on cigarettes exported to South American countries to 150%. These two actions combined reduced the importation of Brazilian cigarettes in Paraguay dramatically, from US$142 million in the first half of 1998 to US$3.7 million in the same period in 1999 (Ministerio de la Hacienda de la República del Paraguay 2000).

In addition to the Adaptation Regime, Taiwanese importers in Ciudad del Este pushed Paraguay to instrumentalize another MERCOSUR special regime of importation, the Schedules of Exception to the Common External Tariff. This regime allows each MERCOSUR member country to apply tariffs different from the Common External Tariff on specific imports from outside the bloc, as long as they are in accordance with World Trade Organization agreements. Over time, MERCOSUR authorized Paraguay to apply three Schedules of Exception on selected imports. Additionally, Taiwanese importers lobbied Paraguay to reduce or eliminate tariffs on selected imports included in the schedules common to all MERCOSUR members: the Schedule of Capital Goods and the Schedule of Informatics and Telecommunication Goods. While it was expected that both the national schedules and sector schedules would eventually converge to the Common External Tariff, Paraguay managed to extend them several times. Hsu told me that "we're not experts in trade policy or fiscal policy, but we learned the trick. You can't expect the government to spontaneously act on your behalf. But you can learn new knowledge about trade policy not only in Paraguay, but in the region." Because of the push for Paraguay to use all of the different trade policy tools at its disposal, the country has exercised a considerable degree of autonomy in trade policy on imports from outside the bloc, despite MERCOSUR's institutional and political constraints.

Paraguay's Schedules of Exception served the private interests of groups that have a strong foothold in triangle commerce. As early as 1995, items like beverages, perfumes, and cosmetics totaled nearly a quarter of the country's Schedule of Exception. Ciudad del Este's chambers of commerce, including the Chinese Association of Ciudad del Este-Paraguay, the Taiwanese Chamber of Commerce-Paraguay, and the Federation of Chinese Businesspeople of Paraguay, successfully lobbied for including technology-intensive consumer goods in the country's Schedules of Exception. Throughout the 2000s, imports under Paraguay's Schedule of Exception included cameras, video games, audio devices, TVs, and data storage hardware, which were almost three-quarters of imports under the Schedule of Exception in 2008. "It was absolutely necessary to include the electronics in the Schedules of Exception, otherwise, the tariffs would raise the price to the level of Brazil, making it prohibitively high for our business to stay alive," said Hsu. Similarly, the goods imported under the Schedule of Informatics and Telecommunication Goods, which one should expect to be technology-intensive goods needed in strategic sectors of the domestic economy, are actually top sales in Ciudad del Este, with laptops, computer parts, cell phones, and computer screens making up nearly 75% of goods imported under that schedule in 2008.

The amount of technology-intensive consumer goods imported in Paraguay exceeds the country's demand by far, which is explained by Ciudad del Este's triangle commerce and smuggling to Brazil. Because of the low tariffs applied to imported electronics under the Schedules of Exception, Ciudad del Este remains a major destination for Brazilian resellers who still find better prices in Paraguay. Electronics are so important in today's triangle commerce that overseas Chinese importers and shopkeepers opened new shops dedicated to electronics in other Paraguayan border cities like Salto del Guairá, Pedro Juan Caballero, and Encarnación, replicating the business model of Ciudad del Este.

Trade liberalization and regional integration were not the only threats to Ciudad del Este's economy, which was severely affected by the after the U.S.-led "war on terror" and its crackdown on transnational organized crime in the tri-border area. The border between Ciudad del Este and Foz do Iguaçú, which local businesspeople celebrated as the epitome of free market and concretization of the neoliberal agenda, was quickly condemned under the securitizing agenda of the fight against terrorism. While Argentina and Paraguay embraced the rhetoric associating Lebanese migrants with money laundering and international terrorism funding, Brazil under the Workers' Party administration refused the hypothesis and demanded evidence from U.S. intelligence (Karam 2010; Rabossi 2013, 2014). The Brazilian government remained skeptical of the war on terror's possible hidden agenda, notably after the implementation of "assertive diplomacy" under Minister of Foreign Affairs Celso Amorim between 2003 and 2010. Brazil only accepted training from the U.S. government to combat international crimes related to counterfeits and smuggling. The Brazilian government ceded to this request to demonstrate compliance with U.S. stipulations that were hurting the Brazilian economy since the country was included in 2002 in the Office of the United States Trade Representative's property rights violation watchlist (Pinheiro-Machado 2017). The Brazilian operations to fight smuggling and counterfeits on the borders with Ciudad del Este caused a dramatic decrease in shopping excursions to that city, and shoppers now travel to São Paulo instead.

Ciudad del Este experienced a huge decrease not only in resellers but also tourists visiting the Iguazu Falls. They prefer to shop instead in the award-winner Duty Free Shop Puerto Iguazu that opened in 2002 in a state-of-art facility on the Argentinian side of the border. For the Brazilian middle-class tourist seeking to kill time and consume conspicuously, the preference for a fancy duty-free shop featuring tap beer kiosks and live DJs is obvious. These tourists tend to see Argentina as a bohemian, culture-oriented, and Europeanized society—the opposite of the image that they have of Paraguayans as lazy, uneducated, and backwards. The duty-free shop caters to a type of self-entitled shopper who is an international traveler seeking to explore local attractions such as dining in quaint restaurants or gambling in the town's casinos. The location of the duty-free shop, just after the International Fraternity Bridge that unites Brazil and Argentina but right before the immigration and customs checkpoint, is telling of the public it seeks to attract. Though located in Argentinian territory, foreigner tourists can go from Brazil to the duty-free shop without having to clear Argentina's immigration and customs. By design, it is a place where the foreigner's commitment to consumption comes before the taxpayer's economic duties to the state—the same kind of place that Ciudad del Este's founders envisioned it to be.

With fewer shoppers traveling to Ciudad del Este and most focusing on electronics, interest groups in the city lobbied the Paraguayan government to take for the first time a measure available for a MERCOSUR member country: modifying its Schedule of Exceptions for up to 20% of the items on the agreed upon list. In 2014, the Chamber of Commerce and Services of Ciudad del Este and the Federation of Chambers of Commerce of Ciudad del Este presented a report to the Paraguayan government asking to modify its Schedule of Exceptions. The proposal was adopted by the government. According to the decree that dictates the modification, the justification for it is to "react against the exchange rate policies of emerging economies in the region," a situation which "demands temporary policies to compensate for the negative impacts on sensitive sectors of the national economy, particularly border cities and regions, as it was brought to the national government's attention by trade associations and clubs from these places." The main argument of the chambers of commerce was that an increase in tariff reductions would positively boost the economy of Ciudad del Este as well as combat smuggling by incentivizing the increase in the level of formal importation. The decree makes this goal explicit, mentioning that "it is necessary to make commitments towards the formalization of commerce," which would increase the state revenue of tariffs and taxes. Coincidentally, the formalization policies of Ciudad del Este's triangle commerce followed Brazil's new focus on formalization of a few years earlier.

Attempting to Formalize Triangle Commerce

In March 2011, when a Taiwanese migrant was appointed president of the multiethnic Chamber of Commerce of Information Technology Goods in Ciudad del Este, he advocated for "formalizing Ciudad del Este" and, controversially, declared himself the "founding father of the Unified Tax Regime" (Ciudad del Este TI 2011). The Unified Tax Regime is Brazil's 2009 policy of formalization specific to the importation of goods proceeding by land from Paraguay to the border between Ciudad del Este and Foz do Iguaçu. There is no evidence in support of the claim that the Taiwanese businessman played any role in lobbying the Brazilian government to pass the law, and many dismiss his call for formalization as cynical, empty discourse. In any case, Brazil's President Luiz Inácio Lula da Silva[2] of the Workers' Party designed a formalization policy focused on increasing the income of Brazilian working-class resellers who rely on triangle commerce to earn an income.

The Unified Tax Regime changes the legal status of those resellers from a smuggler to an individual who is legally considered a "Licensed Retailer Importer Micro Company"—a convoluted, contradictory term that makes no more sense in Portuguese than it does in its English translation. Formalization under this regime is very simple at first glance. The applicant enrolls for the program online or in person at the customs checkpoint. Once enrolled, the now importer self-reports at the customs checkpoint in Foz do Iguaçu and clears customs through a "Simplified Importation Clearance," paying a unified tax that replaces all other tariffs, fees, and taxes applicable to regular importation. The Internal Revenue System of Brazil generates an importation receipt with which the importer can issue a sales receipt when the goods are sold in Brazil.

However, three main aspects of the Unified Tax Regime make it more complicated and less attractive for resellers. First, individuals are not eligible to enroll, only companies are. In fact, the law passed in the context of another bill that establishes the category of "Individual Micro-Entrepreneur." The goal of that bill was officially described as to formalize all "informal workers" in Brazil and turn them into "small business owners." The shoppers and resellers who travel to Ciudad del Este were considered a special group within these workers because of the complex regulatory systems that apply across this transnational economic circuit. Thus, their specific situation was addressed in separate legislation focused on triangle commerce. But for most resellers, becoming an Individual Micro-Entrepreneur was not desirable or possible financially or bureaucratically.

Second, the Unified Tax Regime necessitated the creation of the corresponding counterpart of export registration system on the Paraguayan side of the border. The Brazilian government negotiated with Paraguay for the establishment of the Transborder Trade Regime that mirrors the Brazilian policy. The Transborder Trade Regime creates the figure of the "Paraguayan vendor exporter," a Paraguayan company that is licensed to operate under the regime. The chambers of commerce of Ciudad del Este, beginning with the one represented by the Taiwanese migrant who declared himself the "father of the Unified Tax Regime," held workshops for importers and shopkeepers seeking to adapt to this new regime. However, because the Transborder Trade Regime represents an additional layer of recordkeeping, it raised suspicion for many shopkeepers—including Hsu and Kao, who refused to adopt it—and only a meager record of twenty-four stores had registered by 2012. For the sake of comparison, that number barely reaches 5% of the companies registered in the Special Tourism Regime that same year. However, despite the abysmal enrollment number, the most popular electronics shops did adhere to it, increasing their sales and creating an avenue for Brazilian resellers who specialize in lighter, higher value-added goods.

Lastly, the most important limit to this fictional idea of turning resellers into micro companies is that the Unified Tax Regime allows only a small volume of trade per person to formalize, all of that with tariffs and taxes that still are prohibitively high to constitute an attractive profit margin. Each micro company can only import a maximum of US$62,500 per year with unified taxes at a rate of 42.5% (later lowered to nearly half because of low enrollment). As a result, there were less than two hundred "micro importers" registered under the program in 2015. Brazilian resellers, like overseas Chinese importers who relocated to São Paulo, realized that trade liberalization in Brazil meant nearer destinations with better prices for the same imports.

Even the most generous interpretation of the Unified Tax Regime says its success is only limited. It did, however, have pernicious consequences. In the political economy of illegalities, formalization and repression are two sides of the same coin, being complementary rather than mutually exclusive. As a formalization policy, the Unified Tax Regime reworks the boundaries of legality, setting new parameters under which certain practices that were previously considered illegal are henceforth in compliance with redefined terms of legality. By creating a new categorization of formality, the Unified Tax Regime justifies the intensification of the crackdown on any practice that falls outside it, which is still considered smuggling from a purely legal perspective.

On the other hand, the Unified Tax Regime opens new ways of disguising sales/export in Paraguay as well as import/transit in Brazil. For example, "micro importers" buy goods under that regime to be able to show enforcement officers the clearance certificate if stopped on the road, hoping the officer will not bother inspecting the cargo or, if needed, accept bribery in exchange for not confiscating the merchandise. This is particularly true for laptops and other technology-intensive imports that have a high value-added tax per unit.

All in all, the Unified Tax Regime and its Paraguayan counterpart reflect an understanding that the answer to popular markets must, in the view of the policy proponents, recognize the social and economic vitality of the informal economy workers. However, while it does not offer appropriate conditions for vendors to formalize, it serves once again the interests of those expanding the informal economy of the border trade.

PALIMPSEST

Borderlands are unique spaces of encounters and passages. The border in Ciudad del Este must be understood as the signifier of a social relation characterized by economic inequality and different development models. That swath of borderland was conceptualized by the founders of the city as a site of economic opportunity in the meeting point of national economies and their distinct regulatory goals. Their vision for the city, deeply influenced by the notion that the borderland is an outward-looking infrastructural corridor to facilitate global and regional circulation of goods, attributes to Ciudad del Este the double "vocation" of commerce and tourism. Furthermore, for the Stroessner regime to effectively build alliances domestically and alter the geopolitics regionally, it necessitated Ciudad del Este to serve as a trade outpost enabling his allies to extract the border revenues. The border market of Ciudad del Este was a product of complex, extensive, and contradictory legislation that enabled, both in legal and illegal ways, the capture of the wealth in this circuit through the concession of free-trade zones and fiscal incentives. It favored a capitalist-entrepreneurial transnational class that understood the border as the determining factor to profit from economic arbitrage and profiteer from smuggling of goods.

The conceptualization of the border in Ciudad del Este was born of price differentials between the economies of Brazil and Paraguay. Yet, the price gaps did not sustain themselves naturally. Rather, they had to be maintained and widened. The history of Ciudad del Este is in this sense the history of the manipulation of price differentials through trade and fiscal policies, including the exclusive rights to explore free-trade zones and the proliferation of special regimes that reduce tariffs and taxes applicable to imports considered to be only "in transit" in Paraguay. Policies like the free-trade zone concessions of 1960 and 1979, the In-Transit Customs Clearance Regime of 1972, the Special Tourism Regime of 1990, the Adaptation Regime of 1995, the Schedules of Exception to the MERCOSUR Common External Tariff, and the Transborder Trade Regime of 2009, all of which have benefited overseas Chinese importers, shopkeepers, and stall sublessors like Law Kin Chong, Hsu, Kao, the Singaporean concessioner of the free-trade zone, and the Taiwanese president of the chamber of commerce. These policies were designed because of the border, in the name of circulation across it, and oriented to foreign economies.

The overseas Chinese importers and shopkeepers have played a unique role in the establishment and development of triangle commerce. They were free-trade zone concessioners and members of the board of importing companies that spearheaded the market as early as the 1960s. Later, they formed a robust community of importers and shopkeepers who benefited from reduction in tariffs and taxes. With the implementation of MERCOSUR, a trade governance and regional integration structure that shaped the mobility of goods in Ciudad del Este, triangle commerce became unsustainable. However, the overseas Chinese importers and shopkeepers lobbied the Paraguayan government to negotiate for the adoption and extension of exceptional measures that protected triangle commerce during the gradual implementation of regional free trade and the establishment of a customs union for goods outside the bloc. Throughout the last six decades, they have connected Asian manufactured goods with São Paulo's market.

Ciudad del Este's fate was—and continues to be—determined by price differentials resulting from the application of discrepant tariffs and taxes on each side of the border. Emerging from the encounter between two economies once oriented by very distinct development models, a dramatic divergence in tariffs and taxes now defeats the purpose of the customs union established by MERCOSUR and trade liberalization adopted both in Paraguay and Brazil. But this divergence continues to expand the informal economy and to create more opportunities for powerful actors to capture the wealth that circulates illegally. Like an old manuscript that shows past traces, Ciudad del Este became a palimpsest, a persistent outline of never-completed urban and economic development. As profit margins increasingly decreased in Ciudad del Este, a few overseas Chinese migrants like Law Kin Chong left their businesses in Ciudad del Este for São Paulo, making the Brazilian city the new epicenter of this circuit. As they moved, so did the economy.

2 CAPTURING WEALTH

Chinese Vendors, Shifting Legality, and Shopping Tourism in São Paulo

ON A MORNING IN AUGUST 2018, Chinese migrant Johnny Fong texted me on the instant messaging application WeChat: "Can you talk now?" He was devastated and enraged. Johnny and thousands of other stallholders had just lost another battle against the Shopping Circuit Consortium, a private company that took over the management of the Dawn Market in São Paulo, where they used to work. "Where can I meet you?" I asked him, knowing that his stall, our typical meeting place, had been demolished to make way for the new mall the Shopping Circuit Consortium was planning to build. He told me to meet him at the Dawn Market east gate, from where we could see the location of his stall. "Look at it," he screamed when I got there, "that is where I worked six days a week for over a decade. It's dumpster trash now."

Less than one year before, on September 12, 2017, Johnny and I attended the testimony of the head of the Consortium, Zhu Surong, to the São Paulo City Council Committee on the Dawn Market. Between June and December 2017, the committee investigated irregularities in the Shopping Circuit Project, an ambitious plan City Hall launched in 2011 in partnership with the private sector to redevelop urban infrastructure and promote popular markets in downtown. In his testimony, Zhu denied accusations of wrongdoings and said that he complied with the terms of the Shopping Circuit Project concession agreement the Consortium signed with City Hall. Zhu, a migrant and leader of the Chinese community in his mid-fifties, declared that his role in the Consortium was to recruit prospective stallholders and shopkeepers for the new mall and that he received a bonus of over five million dollars for having signed numerous sale and lease contracts (São Paulo City Council 2017). Johnny, a thin man in his late forties, was outraged by Zhu's statements. He nodded his head in disapproval and said that the Consortium charged prohibitively high rental fees from stallholders like him who, he continued, are the true generators of wealth in the popular markets.

Johnny's and nearly five thousand stalls were demolished not because City Hall wanted to eliminate the Dawn Market but, rather, for developers to expand the popular market infrastructure. In the early 2010s, policymakers and businesspeople in São Paulo shifted their discourse and actions on popular markets. In the past, they combatted the popular markets, but they eventually discovered their enormous economic potential. The promotion of the popular markets as a "shopping tourism" destination replaced the desire to eliminate them. The state's attempt to enclose common resources is not merely an effort to dispossess workers of access to public spaces where they sell goods. Rather, the desire is to keep workers generating value for capture. The informal economy, looked down upon before, is now celebrated and capitalized upon.

In this chapter, I analyze how the policies for the popular markets in São Paulo shaped the Chinese migrants' ability to accumulate wealth in this transnational commodity circuit. City Hall restricted the actors who can participate in the popular markets in three ways: changes in street-vending policies, stricter enforcement of street vending and counterfeit regulations, and the privatization of the Dawn Market, which was the main alternative to street vending. While City Hall's actions undermined the ability of Chinese stallholders and street vendors to work in the Dawn Market and on the streets, those changes also benefited Chinese businesspeople like Zhu, who were involved in the privatization of the Dawn Market and the development of malls.

In over a century, the downtown popular markets have undergone significant transformations. Some of the most important changes were caused by overseas Chinese individuals in the last few decades. City Hall has been another key actor in those shifts, implementing various policies in the 1990s and 2000s to harshly enforce regulations on street vending and counterfeits, which criminalized vendors. This chapter shows how the transformation of the Dawn Market from its inauguration to its privatization increased the ability of overseas Chinese investors and realtors to capture the wealth circulating in downtown popular markets while keeping street vendors and stallholders in a precarious position.

THE HISTORY OF POPULAR MARKETS IN DOWNTOWN SÃO PAULO

The historic economic and social development of the city of São Paulo has influenced the downtown popular markets like the 25 de Março Street district, where the Dawn Market originated, and the neighborhood of Brás, where it eventually relocated. Poor migrants have settled downtown since the turn of the twentieth century and contributed to the emergence of low-income markets in working-class and impoverished neighborhoods.

Not until the turn of the last century, a period that coincided with the arrival of international migrants of various groups, did São Paulo urbanize and see its economy boom. Intense migration from Europe, East Asia, and West Asia between the 1880s and 1920s made São Paulo ethnically diverse and turned downtown into a bustling commercial district. Migrants settled on 25 de Março Street because the rent was cheaper due to constant floods, which damaged the inventory and caused vendors to sell at discounted rates, making the street known for low wholesale pricing. Syrian-Lebanese migrants are credited with opening the first shop on 25 de Março Street in 1887, followed by Portuguese, Spanish, Italian, Armenian, and Jewish migrants (Truzzi 2008). By the early 1900s, more than five hundred store-front shops were operating on or near 25 de Março Street; most of those were migrant-run small businesses, while shopkeepers and other tenants rented rooms in the upper-floor tenement apartments (Cesarino and Castana 2017; Oliveira 2010; Truzzi 1993). The city's elites, blaming what they believed to be the "dirty" business of poor migrants, left downtown in the following decades for districts like Higienópolis ("Hygieneopolis") and Campos Elíseos ("Champs Élysées")—whose names are emblematic of the upper classes' desire for sanitization and the search for a European-oriented marker of high social status.

From the 1930s to the 1960s, rapid urbanization, industrialization, and new migration changed the city, and the popular markets were no exception. Lebanese and Jewish migrants pioneered a strong textile industry in São Paulo, favoring shopkeepers of those communities, who specialized in wholesale haberdashery items in the 25 de Março Street district. Jewish manufacturers settled in an adjacent neighborhood, making it one of Brazil's most important garment districts, later taken over by South Koreans in the 1970s and Bolivians in the 2000s (Karam 2006; Lesser 1999; Silva 2006).

Starting in the 1960s, downtown underwent a new shift in demographics with the settlement of new working-class and poor communities. Upper-class residents, upscale businesses, and government buildings all left the city center again for suburbia, opening the way for lower-class residents, workers, and consumers. Real estate developers focused on developing areas other than downtown, especially after the shifts in urban and land regulations that reduced the floor area ratio of new buildings in downtown in the 1950s. A combination of the elites' interest in moving out, novel frontiers of real estate expansion, and new urban plans caused the downtown to lose its economic centrality to other areas (Frúgoli 2000, 2001; Kara-José 2010). The upper classes' abandonment of downtown and the private and public sectors' lack of interest in preserving it caused the deterioration of the built environment and the devaluation of the land, with a greater number of residents living in tenement apartments that lacked renovation but remained connected to services and employment opportunities for the working class. The elites quickly labeled this transformation as "degradation," reproducing the idea of an assault on morality attributed to the lower classes' behavior and the socioeconomic changes in the area.

With the first groups arriving in São Paulo in the 1950s, the overseas Chinese migrants entered the popular markets in downtown in the 1970s and 1980s as wholesalers. Cantonese migrant Angelo Wong and the Taiwanese Tsai brothers are examples of those operating in these markets at that time. They filled a void left by the traditional wholesalers when a spike in prices caused by deindustrialization pushed them out of business. The Tsai brothers migrated through family migration chains in the mid-1980s stating the "number one reason we came is because our uncle's laundry was doing well and he needed help." Like their uncle, the Tsai brothers also feared the political turmoil in Taiwan, not only because of geopolitical shifts favoring Beijing's stance on Taiwan's political sovereignty, but also because of domestic signs of contestation to the Chiang Kai-shek[1] regime. Quickly, they left the taxing labor of the laundry for an opportunity in the wholesale market in downtown São Paulo. Specializing in the distribution of domestic goods, the Tsai brothers, like a few fellow Taiwanese migrants, lowered their profit margins to increase their market share, establishing themselves as key wholesalers in the 25 de Março Street district. Hong Kongese and Cantonese migrants like Angelo Wong specialized in distributing imported manufactures that were not easily available in the Brazilian market. Wong entered the downtown popular markets in 1979, just two years after he migrated from Guangzhou. Similar to other Cantonese distributors, the imports he sold included European luxury items and "Asian electronics that were traded initially via Miami . . . and later through Ciudad del Este," as he explained me.

In addition to official importation, overseas Chinese importers distributed goods smuggled from Paraguay. Pointing to the infamous Chinese traders operating through Ciudad del Este, Wong told me a story I heard repeatedly from fellow Cantonese traders: Chinese and Hong Kongese distributors also struck an illegal deal in the 1970s with Brazilian customs officers in Paranaguá Port, the main entry gate for cargo destined for Ciudad del Este. The deal consisted of diverting part of the imports so that they never reached Paraguay.

At the same time, street vending mushroomed in downtown São Paulo as the manufacturing sectors and other labor-intensive industries dwindled and no longer absorbed the growing labor force. Many street vendors traveled from São Paulo to Ciudad del Este to procure imported goods. The neighborhood of Brás was no exception to the growth of street vending. Once a major industrial area later abandoned during the postindustrial era, it then became a vibrant retail district specializing in garments produced in family-run workshops or sweatshops operated by domestic and international migrants (Freire da Silva 2008; Hirata 2014a; Itikawa 2006).

Since the 1990s, the concentration of low-income residents and workers in downtown São Paulo has intensified, such as tenement dwellers, squatters, and street vendors. Additionally, there has been an increase in international migration to downtown, where rentals are still relatively cheap and income opportunities for street vendors and stallholders continue to expand, including Chinese, Bolivians, Peruvians, Haitians, Angolans, Senegalese, and Syrians. The private sector and right-wing politicians condemned what they labeled unfair competition with street vendors and stallholders who sold cheaper imports in a moment of intensification of globalization and trade liberalization. They redeployed the ideologically charged discourse of "degradation," waging war against migrants, the homeless, substance users, and sex workers. After having abandoned downtown, the private sector and the elites drew from that old discourse, which had been used to justify hygiene policies, to create another powerful narrative that gained traction in city administration: the need to "revitalize" downtown through private investments and attracting middle-class residents, businesses, and consumers. Wanting to put an end to the popular markets, City Hall launched a few projects in the 1990s and 2000s, aligned with the interests of shopkeepers, developers, and business sectors, to keep vendors off the streets (Kara-José 2010; Moraes 2018).

However, this desire to eliminate street vending changed radically into the promotion of popular markets. The overseas Chinese communities played a key role in this transformation. They made downtown São Paulo known for a thriving economy specializing in affordable goods, attracting the interests of developers in revitalizing downtown by investing in the popular markets.

Overseas Chinese Communities in the Popular Markets of São Paulo

In the 1990s, overseas Chinese migrants achieved an even more significant share of popular markets, displacing Brazilian vendors who could not compete with a network of migrant vendors selling cheaper imports. With the end of protectionist trade policies in Brazil and the rise of export-oriented industrialization in Asia, the overseas Chinese wholesalers in São Paulo reactivated trade relationships and social ties in Hong Kong, Taiwan, and China. Many had become Brazilian citizens and had legal, cultural, and language advantages to spearhead the importation of manufactured goods from Asia to São Paulo.

The majority of overseas Chinese vendors were a significant group of new stall sublessees, contributing to changing the downtown São Paulo popular markets dramatically. Their work opportunities were created by earlier overseas Chinese migrants including those who had run shopping malls in Ciudad del Este and moved to downtown São Paulo. There, they opened the first indoor markets in the 25 de Março Street district in the mid-1990s. Law Kin Chong, the protagonist of the story that opens the book, pioneered in opening three such indoor markets with nearly two thousand stalls in 1994 and 1995. He also made a move that proved lucrative, and leased nearly half of the stores of downtown São Paulo's iconic two twelve-story towers of Galeria Pagé, a buzzing shopping center. He then subdivided those stores into small stalls and subleased them to newcomer Chinese stallholders. By the mid-1980s, Law had over a decade of experience as a distributor in São Paulo, in addition to the years he worked in his family's businesses in Ciudad del Este. After facing investigations by the Federal Police and being charged for selling smuggled goods in the 1980s, Law turned to a more profitable and less risky business that he predicted was the future of São Paulo's popular markets: commercial real estate. He summarizes his move: "I stayed with my parents at their store in Paraguay for a few years. Then, I decided to come back to 25 de Março Street because a huge change was happening in the real estate sector there" (Brazilian Congress 2004, 20).

Like Law, Zhu Surong started off as a distributor in the 1980s, before turning to real estate and subleasing stalls in the Dawn Market. Having left Qingtian county in the province of Zhejiang for São Paulo at the age of twenty-five in 1986, Zhu opened a shop in a mall within one year of his arrival with the support of his family members who were already living in the city. Zhu says he lived the modest life of a hard-working shopkeeper until he became an importer in the late 1990s. In 2008, he opened his largest imports company specializing in importing handbags from China (São Paulo City Council 2017). Zhu established himself as one of the largest importers in the Dawn Market area. He was a business partner and close ally with other importers who became disliked by many Brazilian vendors for buying stalls in cash to sublet to Chinese migrants. The influence his partners and allies exercised over stallholders was significant. They were appointed to key positions in the most influential associations of migrants, with Zhu being nominated the "Permanent Honorary President" of the Chinese Association of Brazil as soon as he became head of the Shopping Circuit Consortium in 2016.

Unlike Law and Zhu, most Chinese migrants are not importers and real estate developers, but vendors who occupy a rather precarious position in the popular markets. Having migrated from Wen Zhou in Zhejiang Province to São Paulo in 1997, Johnny Fong is representative of a new Chinese migration that started in the 1990s. This new migration is predominantly composed of Fujianese and Zhejiangese, who have difficulties finding other income opportunities due to their precarious immigration status, cultural and language barriers, limited education attainment, and lack of economic capital. Relying on Chinese wholesalers and stall sublessors to supply goods and lease a stall, these migrants work double shifts as street vendors in the early hours of the morning and as stallholders during regular business

FIGURE 2.1. Chinese vendors in a stall in an indoor market in downtown São Paulo, 2017. Photograph by Douglas de Toledo Piza.

hours. As Johnny said, they work at dawn to escape street vending enforcement and, additionally, because their clientele of overnight travelers arrives in organized bus excursions as early as 2a.m.

The spread of indoor markets owned by Chinese distributors unlocks income opportunities for undocumented migrants working in a gray zone of economic activities that are partially illegal. In the indoor markets, sales are not recorded on the books, and compliance with taxes and laws regulating the sale of counterfeits is generally lacking. Though stallholders are subjected to tax auditing and inspection of counterfeits, the management companies of the indoor markets intervene with city government and federal enforcement officials on behalf of the stallholders. Moreover, because the indoor markets are private property, vendors are not in violation of street-vending regulations, being the best alternative to the streets. Johnny Fong said that he "could not stand the constant harassment by enforcement agents, the extortion, the bribery." Losing merchandise to the municipal inspector and the police was the norm. Without a hesitation, he left the streets for a tiny stall in an indoor market, and later he and his wife were some of the first Chinese migrants to run a stall in the Dawn Market.

On the other hand, stallholders are still subjected to enforcement of counterfeits. Their position is unstable, and they must constantly negotiate the terms and conditions of their rents and inventory with the management company, the stall sublessor, and the imports distributor. The spread of indoor markets is a new outlet of capital expansion for developers and real estate owners who squeeze the profits of stallholders by charging one of the highest rent prices per square foot in São Paulo. A study by the consultancy firm Cushman & Wakefield in June 2011 suggests that the average rent price per square foot in the 25 de Março Street district and around the Dawn Market in the Brás neighborhood is higher than the high-end shopping malls and boutique retail districts in São Paulo. Besides the rent, vendors are charged an informal fee of up to US$60,000, as well as being subjected to extortion and paying illegal fees to the management company, abusive stall sublessors, and corrupt officials such as inspectors and police officers (Freire da Silva 2014a, 52).

All in all, overseas Chinese communities played a key role in profoundly altering the distribution of goods and the real estate market in downtown popular markets. While a few are importers, wholesalers, and real estate investors, the majority are newcomers who work as stallholders and street vendors. The same street-vending policies that undermined those vendors' ability to work enabled a group of investors to capture the wealth that circulates in the popular markets.

POLICIES FOR THE POPULAR MARKETS

Since the late 1980s, various policies have addressed unlicensed street vending, tax noncompliance, and sales of smuggled and counterfeit goods in downtown popular markets. As city administrations changed, so did these policies, ranging from regularization to the intensification of enforcement. However, in the early 2010s, an administration shifted policy from business-sponsored law enforcement to developer-friendly promotion of the popular markets, changing the local government's attitudes towards the popular markets irreversibly.

Regularization Policies and Dialogue with Social Movements

Unlicensed street vending was the priority issue in City Hall's management of popular markets in the late 1980s. The administration of the leftist Mayor Luiza Erundina[2] opened a dialogue with social movements and called for public hearings to address the demands of street vendors. Brazilian street vendors organized and created associations in a period of increasing democratic participation and direct action following the end of the civil-military dictatorship in Brazil. Mayor Erundina was a champion of workers' rights and incentivized the creation of unions, including the Informal Economy Workers Union and the Licensed Street Vendors Union. Despite fierce opposition in the City Council, her administration passed a bill in 1991 that created the Use of Public Space Permit, enabling City Hall to issue street vending permits for eligible applicants. The bill also stipulates the creation of the Street Vendors Permanent Councils to serve as permanent channels of communication between street vendors and public authorities.

Law Enforcement and the "Revitalization" of Downtown São Paulo

Although street vending was seen as a social rights issue in the early 1990s, it quickly transformed into a law enforcement problem during the conservative administrations of Paulo Maluf[3] and his successor Celso Pitta[4] in the mid-1990s. These administrations showed no openness to dialogue with social movements. Street vendors were not perceived as workers, but rather as "a segment of the population that combined loiterers, the unemployed and those struggling to survive," a view that made them a public order issue rather than a socioeconomic one (Hirata 2014a, 98). Both Mayors Maluf and Pitta sought to eliminate street vending in downtown São Paulo, which unintendedly favored the Chinese-owned indoor markets because it drove vendors to relocate from the streets to the private shopping malls. While most Brazilian vendors did not have the means or the desire to relocate, the indoor markets remained the main income opportunity for Chinese newcomers like Johnny Fong.

The desire to eliminate street vending was part of a push for new development projects in downtown São Paulo. During this time of intense privatization in Brazil, Mayor Maluf launched the comprehensive Downtown São Paulo Urban and Functional Revitalization Program (PROCENTRO). He had huge support from the sector of São Paulo's business community that represented speculative capital's interests in land valorization (Moraes 2018). The business community behind the plan monopolized the narrative in the media, contributing to the "satanization of street vending in downtown" and proposing to relocate vendors to remote areas (Kara-José 2010, 31). The elimination of street vending in downtown São Paulo was also aligned with the interests of international organizations like the Inter-American Development Bank, which was the major funder of PROCENTRO and actively promoted the vision that curbing street vending was needed for achieving urban revitalization.

The plan was only stopped when a scandal broke linking Mayor Pitta and his allies to a massive bribery scheme in street vending enforcement, culminating in his impeachment. A special City Council investigative committee known as the Committee on the Bribery Mafia found that inspectors extorted street vendors in exchange for lenience with noncompliance with street vending regulations. City officials used the bribery money to pay City Council members who belonged to the political parties that supported the government (Cardozo 2000). The bribes were also used to finance election campaigns, thus contributing to the maintenance of the political party power structure in the city of São Paulo. It was not until a new administration took office and proposed major changes to PROCENTRO that negotiations with the Inter-American Development Bank were finally concluded in 2004.

Negotiations with City Hall

In the early 2000s, organized labor movements pushed the center-left administration of Mayor Marta Suplicy[5] to guarantee the right to work in the streets. Social movements and civil society advocacy groups explicitly rejected the Mayor Suplicy's plan "Rebuild Downtown," her administration's twist on the PROCENTRO program. Under the pressure of social movements, Mayor Suplicy promoted democratic and direct participation of downtown residents and workers. In the first year of her administration in 2001, City Hall replaced the PROCENTRO steering committee that exclusively represented big business with a forum that included groups directly affected by the implementation of the plan like community leaders and social movements as well as advocates and academic experts.

Vendors demanded a permanent solution to what they insisted should be termed "solidarity economy" instead of "informal economy" (Fórum Centro Vivo 2001). A meager record of 891 additional licenses were eventually issued in 2002. Mayor Suplicy finally created the Street Vendors Permanent Councils, which were not meeting despite being established in the 1991 bill. At the same time, vendors' associations managed in 2003 to negotiate with City Hall for a word-of-mouth solution for unlicensed street vending. The deal they struck with the administration consisted in City Hall allowing vendors to work, even if they did not have licenses. Overseas Chinese vendors, who were not represented in the informal workers' unions, did not participate in the negotiations with City Hall.

A Return to the "Revitalization" Plan and the Unmaking of Regularization Policies

During the right-wing administration of Mayor José Serra,[6] there was a crusade against street vendors in the name of public order and urban revitalization. In his administration, enforcement of street vending regulation was part of a larger trend, supported by the business community, of interventions to "cleanse" downtown São Paulo of homeless people, substance users, and street vendors in order to attract middle-class residents and revitalize the city center for upscale services and businesses. By all accounts, his policies returned to the law-and-order approach of Mayors Maluf and Pitta. In his first weeks in office, in 2005, Mayor Serra reinstated Procentro under the same name although no longer in capitalized letters, reverting back to the same elitist vision of a decade before. He quickly dismantled the consultative forum created by the preceding administration, leaving the decision-making power exclusively for his administration. He also ended the Department of Labor's assistance programs that supported street vendors.

Additionally, Mayor Serra implemented stricter and more comprehensive policies for the popular markets that went beyond the issue of street vending. For the first time, City Hall was systematically attacking counterfeits, a global agenda pushed by the World Trade Organization and Western superpowers, amped up by the U.S.-led fight against terrorism supposedly financed by money laundered in the informal economy. Under the banner of Procentro, Mayor Serra launched Operation Revitalization, a taskforce that included the Military Police and the Civil Police, both controlled by the state governor and with more powers than the City Hall–controlled Municipal Guard. In April 2005, Mayor Serra published an evaluation of the first months of Operation Revitalization with blunt classism and a harsh law-and-order discourse: "City Hall inspected 100 establishments and confiscated 15 tons in merchandise. In partnership and harmony with the Police and the state governor, the area has been recuperated. We will continue this work, incentivizing the building of new residential buildings, repopulating downtown" (Moraes 2018, 101).

Soon, Mayor Serra's administration launched "Operation Clean." The operation name evokes the idea of cleansing downtown of the poverty and lawlessness he attributed to it. More specifically, it aimed to combat substance abuse, counterfeits, and undocumented migration. Chinese street vendors and stallholders were doubly affected as presumed sellers of counterfeits and as undocumented migrants. Mayor Serra repeatedly mentioned them as a justification for enforcement to ensure the city was complying with international intellectual property rights. For the first time, these vendors were specifically targeted on those two grounds. Before, they were indirectly affected as unlicensed street vendors, with City Hall's focus being, however, the larger group of Brazilian vendors. Furthermore, the fact that the Chinese street vendors and stallholders were not organized in any union making claims to the right to work protected them from being a target of rhetoric and policies, but this changed dramatically under Mayor Serra.

Not only was street vending enforcement tougher, but regularization policies were overturned. In 2007, Mayor Serra's successor Mayor Gilberto Kassab[7] revoked all existing 1,940 street vending permits and suspended the issuance of new ones. His administration also dissolved the Street Vendors Permanent Councils in 2011, which cut off the only permanent and institutionalized channel for dialogue with vendors' associations. In immediate response, street vendors established the Street Vendors Forum. Yet, without the protections they used to have and lacking a means to make themselves heard by City Hall, vendors remained vulnerable to Mayor Kassab's increasingly abusive use of the police to curb street vending.

ENFORCEMENT: GOVERNING STREET VENDORS AND STALLHOLDERS THROUGH FORCE

Throughout the 1990s and 2000s, São Paulo City Hall gradually increased the use of the police to enforce the law in the popular markets. The deployment of coercive force in the popular markets is not simply the implementation of a law-and-order approach. Rather, the deployment of coercive force has historically served the interests of capital accumulation in urban circuits (Freire da Silva 2014a; Piza 2012; Telles 2012; Tilly 1990). In the popular markets, enforcement was selective, disproportionately affecting street vendors and stallholders, with an uneven application of regulations regarding public space and counterfeits. By policing the streets and the Dawn Market, City Hall profoundly altered the conditions of accumulation in popular markets.

Enforcement of street vending regulations in São Paulo can be divided into three moments. In the first moment, throughout the 1980s to 1990s, municipal inspectors were the primary enforcement officers acting in the popular markets. Street vending regulations were considered purely an administrative matter, not a criminal one. Inspectors checked whether vendors held a permit and verified the payment of the appropriate fees. They also ensured that licensed street vendors only worked in their designated spots and in compliance with the regulations regarding the use of public space.

A new moment in street vending enforcement began with the creation of the Metropolitan Civil Guard in 2002. City Hall transferred the mandate to inspect street vending to the Metropolitan Civil Guard, including imposing fines, confiscating merchandise, and keeping unlicensed vendors off the street. The City Hall's decision to transfer the inspection prerogatives to the guard did not take vendors' perspective into account. The move, made by a center-left administration, officially intended to disempower inspectors and thus curb extortion schemes in the aftermath of the investigations on bribery mafias conducted in 1999 by City Council. However, this transfer of mandates made street vending no longer an administrative enforcement issue but a police matter (Hirata 2014a, 108).

The third and last moment starts with Operation Delegated in December 2009. Operation Delegated is an unprecedented agreement Mayor Kassab reached with the state governor to deploy the Military Police to enforce street vending regulation on 25 de Março Street, soon extending the operation to all popular markets in downtown. Controversially, it allows for the mayor to deploy the Military Police for a new range of issues determined by the municipality, including administrative matters unrelated to public safety. Under Operation Delegated, City Hall hires Military Police personnel on their days off, at overtime rates, to inspect licensed street vendors and impede unlicensed street vending. In its first six months, the number of Military Police officers hired under Operation Delegated jumped to 4,000.

Operation Delegated expands the mandates and the power of the police to a level that is higher than any other police force performing their usual tasks. While the Metropolitan Civil Guard is a municipal police force responsible for patrolling public properties, such as parks and squares, the Military Police undertake street patrol and response as well as tactical operations. They often work in collaboration with the Civil Police, who oversee judicial affairs such as investigating crimes and recording criminal processes. Military Police officers working in Operation Delegated have more power and serve more functions than in their ordinary duties. They combine the functions of the inspectors and Municipal Guard with the Military Police's authority to police people's behavior. More specifically, the Military

Police have exclusive powers to conduct a search of personal belongings (often used to inspect and apprehend the goods of street vendors), declare an act a criminal offense, and arrest an individual. While serving Operation Delegated, Military Police officers impose sanctions on street vendors, as a deterrent, for offenses that are unrelated to the street vending itself, such as resistance to orders, contempt of police officers, incitation to violence, and even crimes of conspiracy (Freire da Silva 2014a; Hirata 2012). As a result, street vendors were being charged more often, even though there was no change in criminal law nor the codification of a new type of criminal offense. Additionally, the power of Military Police officers emanates from their perceived and exercised extralegal authority, especially given the history of para-legal and illegal means of social control through militarized police in Brazil.

For the Chinese vendors in the popular markets of São Paulo, Operation Delegated is particularly intimidating, especially for undocumented migrants. They fear the constant stop-and-frisk, and the frequent workplace raids can jeopardize their immigration status. Having regularized his immigration status over a decade earlier, Johnny still had vivid memories of his fears as an undocumented migrant. During an informal conversation in his stall in 2012, he said, "I get why so many [undocumented migrants] are terrified of the police." He blushed in anger as his eyes became tearful, and he rushed me out of his stall. I thought he wanted to end the conversation, and to my surprise, he walked me over to his fellow Wenzhounese stallholder Xiaobo. Without any introduction, he abruptly asked him a question in a local Wenzhounese dialect that I could barely understand. Xiaobo's answer was short and his look seemed to suggest he did not want to speak anymore. Johnny returned to his stall and I followed him. He told me he asked Xiaobo what he thought of the police, and the answer was straightforward: he dislikes the officers walking around because they are "sending people back to China." Xiaobo was undocumented, and he did not show up to work a few days the week before because he was afraid of Operation Delegated.

Operation Delegated is part of a larger tendency of militarization of public administration and public spaces in the city of São Paulo. The Kassab administration appointed high-ranking reserve Military Police officers to key positions in city departments, municipal agencies, and city companies. Moreover, it appointed reserve Military Police officers to thirty out of thirty-one district prefectures, starting with the districts adjacent to 25 de Março Street and the Dawn Market. In total, nearly one hundred reserve Military Police officers were appointed to key decision-making positions during the Kassab administration, a number with no precedents in the period after the end of the civil-military dictatorship in Brazil.

The Kassab administration securitized the management of street vending; that is, it used a misleading discourse of vendors as threats to urban safety and moral order to justify taking extraordinary measures. Kassab was explicit about his strategy to use Operation Delegated to siphon vendors off the street into the Dawn Market and indoor markets. He also called chief strategists from the Military Police to draft a plan for the Dawn Market. In fact, he appointed a reserve Military Police officer to his newly created position of Dawn Market administrator. Mayor Kassab justified his appointments with "the need for technical expertise," which in this case was the military knowledge of tactics of deterrence and dispersion used to ensure public order through repressing what was perceived as "disorderliness" and even riots (Hirata 2012).

Another move by the Kassab administration to integrate the police forces into the management of popular markets was the implementation of the program City Free of Counterfeits and Illegal Commerce. Also known as City Free of Piracy, the program combined the street vending enforcement done by the Military Police with enforcement of counterfeits by the Civil Police. The program was sponsored by the Brazilian Institute of Ethics in Competition, a nonprofit that gathers national and multinational corporations as well as chambers of commerce to promote big business's interests and disincentivizes what it calls "unethical competition" by deterring fiscal evasion, informality, and falsification (Freire da Silva 2014a). The program was designed in response to the inclusion of Brazil in the Office of the United States Trade Representative's property rights violation watchlist in 2002, shifting the narratives and policies around street vending during a time when a new global discourse on intellectual property was emerging (Pinheiro-Machado 2017). In Brazil, São Paulo was the first city in the country to adopt the City Free of Piracy program in December 2009, the same month when Operation Delegated was launched, with the popular markets in downtown being considered a priority.

The adoption of the program in São Paulo empowered the Civil Police's Department of Crime Investigation, an organ controlled by the state governor, to intensify the crackdown on the selling of counterfeits. Under the program, the Civil Police discretionarily enforced the existing legislation on falsification (which relates to the production of copies, not their distribution) against street vendors and stallholders. Additionally, it deliberately decided to combat counterfeits through deterrence, particularly incriminating street vendors and stallholders for other criminal offenses such as violating consumer rights, fiscal evasion, and conspiracy as well as immigration status. Wenzhounese stallholder Xu Yuhua was fined for consumer rights issues twice in 2012. She said the Civil Police were profiling Chinese vendors. She was also charged with fiscal evasion, a process that took her over two years to clear. The Civil Police's decision to use deterrence as a means to prevent and combat counterfeits was justified by the need to take further preemptive enforcement actions to control illegal commerce, especially because the Civil Police investigators realized that, as a consequence of the lack of victim representation (the brands), vendors were seldom charged in the courts for the lawsuits originating with the confiscation of the goods. At the same time, the number of actions by the Civil Police within the scope of the program increased with growing numbers of mandates issued by judges to inspect street vendors and stallholders. This shows that the brands were not interested in receiving indemnification from vendors resulting from courts' decisions, but rather in judicializing the regulation over market competition. Control and repression of intellectual property rights violations are, in this context, mechanisms for deterrence of competition perceived as unfair (Freire da Silva 2014a).

With the deployment of both the Military Police and the Civil Police to control and deter vendors in downtown São Paulo's informal markets, street vendors and stallholders were subjected to penalties not only for administrative violations but also for criminal offenses. The City Free of Piracy program and especially Operation Delegated expanded the practice of incriminating vendors' resistance and naturalized police brutality against vendors. For instance, the Military Police said the death of a thirty-year-old street vendor who was shot by an officer serving Operation Delegated was an isolated error. Before Operation Delegated, the police were already incriminating the resistance of street vendors, but the primary targets were leadership figures and organizers, such as the leader of the Independent Street Vendors Union, who was charged with the crimes of extortion, incitation to violence, vandalism, and conspiracy after a demonstration in 2006 and sentenced to six months in prison. After organizing demonstrations against the intensification of City Free of Piracy and Operation Delegated in December 2010, the same union leader was murdered with multiple gun shots in his union headquarters, while the police investigation about the motivations for the crime was inconclusive. Thus, by increasing the likelihood of incriminating vendors, policing demobilized the resistance against street vending enforcement.

The deployment of coercive force and various deterrence practices by the police to manage the popular markets has had diverse effects on overseas Chinese individuals. Importers and distributors were negatively affected by the new focus on counterfeits and smuggling. Chinese street vendors were desperate to leave the heavily policed streets for a stall. Tougher enforcement increased the demand for stalls as it funneled street vendors to the private spaces of indoor markets. Developers and realtors benefited from valorizing commercial real estate, developing new shopping malls and building more stalls in the Dawn Market, which generated a steady revenue stream for them with the stall rental fees.

However, at the end of his administration, Mayor Kassab, who describes himself as a representative of the interests of developers and who made a professional career in Latin America's self-proclaimed largest real estate syndicate, adopted a new discourse and policies to revitalize downtown. His vision to achieve this was no longer through eliminating the popular markets, but by including them in urban redevelopment projects. The turning point was the Shopping Circuit Project, launched in 2011, which promised a privatized solution to vendors' problems by granting concessioners the right to redevelop the public infrastructure of and around the Dawn Market.

FROM THE DAWN MARKET TO THE SHOPPING CIRCUIT PROJECT

The launch of the Shopping Circuit Project in 2011 shows that City Hall's attitude towards the popular markets changed significantly: from a problem to be fixed to the poster child of shopping tourism. The Shopping Circuit Project links the five major popular markets of downtown São Paulo. Under the project, investors redeveloped the urban infrastructure of the popular markets in exchange for privatizing the management of the Dawn Market, which allowed investors to capture a large portion of the wealth that circulates in the popular markets through the collection of rents and incorporation of highly valued land. The project paved the way for capitalist devices of valorization and accumulation in the popular markets.

The Dawn Market opened in 2005, two years after a group of thirty vendors presented City Hall with a proposal to solve the challenges of unlicensed street vending. The proposal consisted of relocating vendors from the streets to a land plot of roughly 915,000 square feet. That land is public property that belongs to the Brazilian Federal Government, and at that time it was momentarily ceded to a private company, GSA Management of Fairs and Events LLC, or GSA. GSA specialized in the collection of trash from the garment sweatshops and street vending in the surrounding streets, but had not made extensive use of the plot. Because the Dawn Market is located on federally owned property, City Hall did not have the prerogatives to intervene in it on the grounds of regulating commercial activities or the use of municipally owned public spaces.

At first, few street vendors were convinced that they should move to a landfill with no consumers in sight. Yet, the Dawn Market soon boomed. For one reason, Mayor Serra took a tougher approach to street vending enforcement starting in 2005, making the Dawn Market a refuge for vendors and the only reliable marketplace for clients. For another reason, the Dawn Market is the only popular market in the overcrowded downtown that has a parking lot for the growing fleet of organized excursion buses traveling overnight with resellers from all over Brazil, becoming a prime location for vendors in search of an avid clientele. In 2008, less than three years after its opening, the Dawn Market changed from being an open-air market with thirty vendors and no bathrooms to a large tin-roofed warehouse with more than four thousand stallholders. Half of these were Chinese migrants subletting from a handful of diasporic Chinese businesspeople like Zhu Surong's business partners, who bought stalls from Brazilian vendors and subleased them. Johnny Fong was one of them and so was Xu Yuhua, who became a stallholder in the Dawn Market after over a decade of harassment by the Civil Guard and the Military Police she experienced as a street vendor and stallholder in the nearby 25 de Março Street. "It's through the associations," she explained, "that you make contacts to sublet a stall in the Dawn Market."

Initially, the Dawn Market was self-managed, with vendors being entirely responsible for administrative, operational, and logistical issues. Vendors self-organized to establish a cooperative and a management company that wrote bylaws, enforced regulations, and made decisions on a wide range of issues such as the location of vending spots, admission of new vendor members, and investments in infrastructure. However, after

FIGURE 2.2. The Dawn Market in São Paulo with its bus parking lot, 2013. Source: Portal da Prefeitura. 2013. Photograph by Henrique Boney. Reprinted with permission.

two years of self-management, GSA increased the monthly fees and became the de facto management company of the Dawn Market. As per its license, GSA was contractually obliged to pay the federal government a monthly compensation of US$76,000, while it collected an estimated total of US$1.4 million monthly in fees from stallholders, excluding the revenue of parking lot fees from every one of the 250 daily buses.

With such astonishing revenue, Mayor Kassab took aggressive steps for City Hall to take control of the Dawn Market. In 2009, the Kassab administration negotiated the use of that public land with the federal government's Department of Public Treasury. Additionally, his administration petitioned the Public Prosecutor's Office to analyze City Hall's request for the cession of the land, hoping to expedite the process. The prosecutor endorsed Mayor Kassab's plan and recommended the federal government cede the land to the municipality and call a concession bid on the rights to explore it. Further, City Hall hired the Brazilian Project Structuring Company, a company that monopolized the business of economic assessments resulting in urban concessions to private developers in state capitals in Brazil, to assess the economic viability of a public-private partnership to redevelop the Dawn Market (Freire da Silva 2014a).

In April 2010, the federal government revoked GSA's license, which led to uncertainty over the status of the land. City Hall eventually obtained the concession over the land half a year later. The land is considered municipal for the duration of the cession, and stallholders were again required to hold a permit issued by City Hall. However, though 4,574 stallholders were cataloged by a census conducted by City Hall and promised permits, nearly half of them did not, including Johnny, who "could not open for businesses for months," as he told me. Brazilian stallholders, many of whom had participated in workers' movements, mobilized to restore their right to work in the Dawn Market. The overseas Chinese stallholders took a different path and relocated to indoor markets. Most entered into a sublease agreement with a Chinese-managed shopping mall. As overseas Chinese businesspeople opened more and more indoor markets, they pushed the migrants' associations to convince the stallholders that they did not have any other solution. Johnny was one of many who did not want to relocate to a shopping mall, but he was threatened with losing his stall: "They told me the Dawn Market

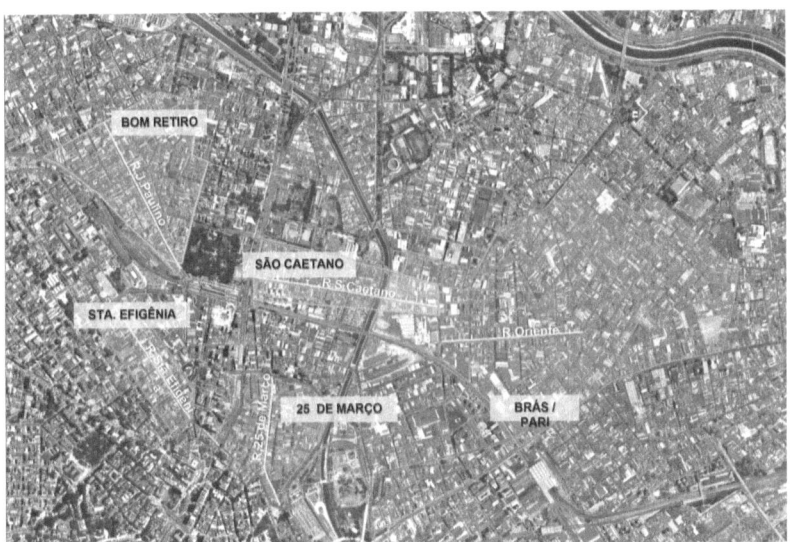

FIGURE 2.3. City Hall's map of downtown São Paulo showing five popular markets to be connected through the Shopping Circuit Project, 2011. Source: Circuito de Compras 2011. Laurindo Martins Junqueira Filho, Carlos Meira Ribeiro, and Flaminio Fishmmann / SPTrans. Reprinted with permission.

will be demolished, and I will lose everything if I don't agree with being relocated."

In February 2011, Mayor Kassab launched the Shopping Circuit Project together with his confidant, the Military Police Commander-in-Chief Álvaro Camilo. The launch of the Shopping Circuit Project implemented Mayor Kassab's vision for the Dawn Market that included privatizing its management and establishing a partnership with private investors to redevelop the urban infrastructure around the popular markets. The most contentious part of the project was the new shopping mall that replaced the demolished Dawn Market, despite over four thousand stallholders voting in assembly in February to reject it and restore self-management instead. The project was launched with an estimated cost of US$900 million, though not effective by the end of Mayor Kassab's term because the São Paulo's Accounting Court suspended it momentarily due to lack of transparency in budgeting, reporting, and oversight.

Inheriting such a controversial project, the succeeding administration was faced with a tough decision. City Hall could choose to proceed with the project without modifications, alter it within the narrow limits set by the cession agreement, or revoke the agreement and return the land to the federal government, leaving the over four thousand stallholders without a solution. The new administration decided to continue with the project, but in a new direction.

POPULAR ENTREPRENEURIALISM

The administration of center-left Mayor Fernando Haddad[8] ceased to describe popular markets as an enforcement issue. Rather, it developed an original view of the popular markets as a form of "popular entrepreneurialism," that is, the economic vitality of low-income vendors' entrepreneurial solutions despite adversities in non-hegemonic economic circuits, making do with little resources. Such an interpretation of popular markets is not exclusive to Mayor Haddad. He and his team found inspiration in President Lula's approach to the informal economy, particularly the 2009 bill that decriminalized the low-income, long-distance traders who travel to Paraguay to buy imports to resell in Brazil.

Mayor Haddad adopted the perspective that the market and consumerism unlock access to income and goods in the popular markets, facilitating the realization of citizenship rights and social welfare not fully achieved otherwise. At first glance, this perspective is in stark contrast with the classic left's ideological position, which blames the market forces and private interests for corroding the abilities of working-class populations to generate fair and sufficient income and access goods and services. Mayor Haddad's approach, in turn, shares the assumption that self-entrepreneurialism and the market are viable options to bring about economic growth in already vibrant commodities circuits of working-class vendors and shoppers. In his view, the market should serve the government's goals, not the other way around. His approach to the popular markets boldly embraced political imagination and experimentation to instrumentalize the market to lift the low-income populations out of more exploitative circuits of market capitalism.

Mayor Haddad's popular entrepreneurialism approach can be understood as the government's attempt to instrumentalize the market to achieve socioeconomic equality. The unrealized promises of developmentalism in the global economy had failed to provide opportunities for equitable socioeconomic growth in most countries, where leftist governments could no longer afford opposing the market merely on ideological grounds. American anthropologist James Ferguson (2011, 2015) urges us to move from the purely analytical critique of power to a pragmatic politics. In his view, leftist governments should privilege experimentation with the market and the pursuit of positive political programs over sterile ideological denunciation.

In the Brazil of the Workers' Party era, political experimentation with the market is a controversial component of the success of economic and social policies that lifted large populations from hunger and poverty and increased economic well-being across all classes. Regarding the popular markets, both Lula and Haddad engaged pragmatically with the market and promoted the entrepreneurial ethos of vendors to achieve the presumed goals of restoring work dignity, distributing wealth, and bringing about social justice. The promotion of popular entrepreneurialism in Brazil reflects an understanding that the answer to popular markets must necessarily recognize the social and economic vitality of the workers by bringing the market practices of disenfranchised populations to the fore. In this sense, the government's support for the popular markets is not about promoting budding capitalists, but rather, to reverse the effects of dispossession and capture by ensuring that people excluded from wage labor can sustain themselves despite the limiting conditions imposed by global capitalism.

Changes in the management of popular markets started in the first weeks of Haddad's administration. Mayor Haddad immediately cut to half the number of Military Police officers serving Operation Delegated, decreasing it to record low figures at the end of his administration. Additionally, he ordered City Hall–controlled civil guards to shadow the Military Police officers to ensure the operation was not abusive. In his first year in office, when City Hall still managed the Dawn Market, his administration issued 1,940 street vending permits—the highest number ever—primarily for stallholders working in that market. Following a tragic fire that killed hundreds of people in a night club in southern Brazil, the mayor consulted vendors and established a taskforce to adapt the infrastructure of the Dawn Market according to the Fire Department safety regulations. This allowed City Hall to spend public funds to build out the infrastructure of the Dawn Market.

Other significant changes were introduced after Mayor Haddad appointed close allies, directly aligned with the Mayor's Office, to the positions of chancellor of labor and chancellor of urban security in 2013 and 2015. The new Chancellor of Labor, Artur Henrique da Silva Santos, a prominent union advocate, resumed the dialogue with vendors and Mayor Haddad called for public hearings to draft a Street Vending Plan and pledged to establish a deliberative Street Vending Council. The Haddad administration showed other signs that City Hall was willing to increase the opportunities for street vendors in downtown popular markets by commissioning the world-renowned Gehl Architects to design a pedestrian-only project for 25 de Março Street.

Despite the huge differences with the preceding administration's position on the popular markets, Mayor Haddad continued the Shopping Circuit Project. Both the chancellor of labor and the mayor were explicit about what they believed was the project's potential for upward social mobility of street vendors through popular entrepreneurialism, especially given the Brazilian lower classes' peak in consumption power at the beginning of the 2010s. The Department of Labor was renamed the Department of Labor, Development, and Entrepreneurship, and it designed policies to promote environmentally and socially sustainable small businesses, including startup funds for slum dwellers to "become entrepreneurs," and a system of quotas and preferences in City Hall's procurement that privileged goods produced in the "solidarity economy." In this context, the Shopping Circuit Project was imagined to be an effective avenue for street vendors' economic success. In the words of Chancellor Santos, the project was aimed at "promoting business and entrepreneurship, making the popular markets more attractive to tourists, and generating employment and resources for São Paulo residents." He went on to say that "enhancements in infrastructure and services will improve the central areas of the city serving the shopping tourism" (Santos 2016).

Chancellor Santos believed he could change the concession agreement to make it more equitable, turning away from the focus of Mayor Kassab's original project, which received criticism for benefiting developers and not the vendors. He suspended the call for bids and revised it after consulting several times with the comptroller general of São Paulo. Chancellor Santos and Mayor Haddad believed that the concession bid would bring the private investment needed to achieve the project goals without City Hall having to spend public resources. Chancellor Santos told me in an interview in August 2017 that the Shopping Circuit Project had "the potential for economic inclusion of those who have been excluded for years, but City Hall needs to make sure that the essence of the Dawn Market does not change: it has to remain 'popular,' it has to remain for the people."

Chancellor Santos signed a thirty-five-year concession agreement with the bid winners, the Shopping Circuit Consortium. The Consortium is composed of three bidding companies and has combined financial assets of US$26 million. The companies, now amalgamated under the Consortium, are led by an investment banker, a developer, the manager of a popular shopping mall in other Brazilian cities, and Zhu Surong. Zhu is the only individual who had business in the Dawn Market before. The Dawn Market was demolished in 2018 and operated in an improvised facility for months until the new building opened in December 2021, renamed "Shopping Circuit—The New Dawn Market." The fancier, three-storied shopping center has over 4,000 stalls, 1,000 stores, and capacity to serve 100,000 consumers daily with a food court of 1,200 seats and parking for 315 buses and more than 2,400 vehicles (São Paulo City Council 2023).

City Hall's view was not shared by the Dawn Market stallholders or the street vendors, who organized to speak up about their issues. According to the stallholders, the concession agreement granted immense power to concessioners who unscrupulously raised the rental costs. Moreover, they argued, there was a contradiction between keeping the Dawn Market popular and the new high-end building that was built by the Shopping Circuit Consortium. The Brazilian stallholders protested in front of City Hall and demanded the City Council members of their district stop the project,

FIGURE 2.4. Shopping Circuit: The New Dawn Market, 2024. Source: Circuito de Compras SP, SPE S.A. Reprinted with permission.

eventually resulting in the creation of a special committee in 2017 that investigated irregularities committed by the Shopping Circuit Consortium (São Paulo City Council 2017). The Brazilian and Bolivian street vendors emphasized that the continuation of the project did not serve the interests of workers because, even if lease fees were affordable, it did not regularize more than a hundred thousand street vendors. Overseas Chinese stallholders did not organize or protest. They remained under the surveilling eyes of overseas Chinese businesspeople who were leaders of the migrants' associations and supported the Shopping Circuit Consortium. In Johnny's words, "Everywhere you go, every plan you make, they make sure to remind you 'they got your back' but only if you do what they say—they are so powerful!"

To make the stallholders' situation even worse, the Consortium effectively became the manager of the Dawn Market when the new administrations of João Dória and Bruno Covas[9] took office, returning to a law enforcement approach and an elitist vision for downtown. The Dória administration's campaign slogan was "Clean City," which was a set of controversial policy proposals including forcibly removing the homeless and substance users from the street as well as erasing graffiti murals and tagging. Under the banner "Clean City," popular markets were morally condemnable again. Street vending was seen once more as a law enforcement issue that was dealt with by the deployment of the Military Police. The crackdown on counterfeits intensified. Mayor Dória reinvigorated Operation Delegated by augmenting the incentives for Military Police officers serving the operation with a new benefits package and an increase in the number of posts available. Unlicensed vendors opposed to the expansion of Operation Delegated and insisted that "the use of public spaces is a social issue that has to be addressed with dialogue with vendors' associations and all other street vendors, not with threats or oppression" (Fórum dos Ambulantes 2016). Further, vendors refused "being treated as illegals" and demanded what they claim was their "right to the city." However, like prior administrations that desired to eliminate street vending due to its alleged "dirtiness," this administration understood that the vendor's only alternative to keep working in public spaces was to enter into a sublease contract with the Shopping Circuit Consortium.

The combat against popular markets was a complicated priority for Dória and Covas, one that caused a major crisis in the administration's top ranks. In 2017, when Mayor Dória's protégée and chancellor of justice controversially accepted the proposal of the largest Chinese-owned indoor market to pay a fine in exchange for clearing violations such as selling counterfeits, the chancellor of sub-prefectures denounced it as illegal quid pro quo and stepped down. Then Deputy Mayor Covas rejected it too, creating new animosity between him and Mayor Dória. Deputy Mayor Covas wrote op-eds emphasizing the administration's commitment to put an end to irregular commerce and stepped in as acting chancellor of sub-prefectures to personally handle the matter. As soon as Covas was sworn in as mayor, he fired the chancellor of justice.

Throughout the last four decades, the management of the popular markets in São Paulo has shifted in many directions. Pro-worker administrations privileged dialogue with street vendors, whereas conservative administrations dealt with street vending as an enforcement matter. Despite the stark contrast between different administrations' ideological and political positions, street vending and popular markets were seen as a problem to be solved throughout the 1990s and the 2000s. However, starting in 2011, popular markets have been promoted and rebranded with the Shopping Circuit Project, though each administration had a radically distinct vision for the project. The project's initial goal was to "revitalize" downtown not in opposition to the popular markets, but through them. Despite this, the desire to promote popular markets was not centered on the vendors' best interest. Rather, popular markets represented the new frontier of capital expansion among the working class and the urban poor.

CAPITALIZED UPON

As communitarian forms of social cooperation are now recognized as a major economic force, the popular markets in downtown São Paulo have been targeted by capitalist devices of valorization and exploitation. The shifts in policies for downtown São Paulo popular markets—from formalization to increased enforcement and privatization—enabled capture by illegality by restricting the actors who can participate in the popular markets and facilitating dispossession and the extraction of the wealth that circulates in the informal economy. While City Hall's actions undermined the ability of overseas Chinese stallholders and street vendors to work in the Dawn Market and on the streets, those same policies enabled overseas Chinese investors and realtors to capture the wealth that circulates partially in illegal ways in the popular markets. Not merely illegality but, rather, the flexible application of legality transformed the political economy of the popular markets, exacerbating the constant dispute over determining what is permissible, what legal parameters can be changed, and how to use loopholes in the law.

City Hall's approach to the popular markets has varied dramatically since the late 1980s, from regularization policies to enforcement of regulations on street vending and counterfeits. However, a clear turning point is the Shopping Circuit Project, which marks a departure from the desire to eliminate popular markets to their promotion and was launched within a little over one year of Operation Delegated and the City Free of Piracy programs. These policies effectively criminalized vendors to deter street vending and increased their risk of being penalized for selling counterfeits, while simultaneously promoting popular markets as shopping tourism destinations, privatizing the Dawn Market, and funneling vendors to the private spaces of indoor markets. The spread of indoor markets, though it unlocks income opportunities for stallholders, is an outlet of capital expansion for developers and real estate owners who squeeze the profits of stallholders by charging unaffordable rent prices.

The goals of the Shopping Circuit Project changed too. City Hall acted as a broker for the private interests of investors who capitalized in the popular markets and developed the areas where land value increased due to the economic potential of the popular markets. City Hall implemented urban redevelopment concessions, pushed vendors off the street, and privatized an essential public resource—the use of public land. Under privatized management, urban developers charged vendors a higher administrative fee for common resources (such as toilet facilities, compliance with safety regulations, and waste collection) and cleared out vending spaces to build prime retail spaces that vendors cannot afford to rent. These changes were not successfully reversed even when a new City Hall administration contended the popular markets should remain "for the people" and promoted popular entrepreneurialism as a way to ensure vendors retain a fair share of their revenue.

When I met with Johnny Fong in front of the demolished Dawn Market, he said he did not want to sign a lease agreement with the Shopping Circuit Consortium. "I don't have to sweat my body off for their profit," he said with anger. After a long breath, he concluded with desolation: "Well, what can I do? It is not like I have other options." His search for the alternatives a Chinese stallholder like him has to access income-generating opportunities points out the challenges Chinese migrants face to achieve their migration goals. To overcome those challenges, many engage in the highly transnational associational life of the Chinese diasporas to connect with economic opportunities for success in the informal economies of South America. That opens up a new and globalized world of opportunities—and challenges.

3 | ENTREPRENEURIALISM FROM AFAR

Engaging Migrants' Associations and Implementing China's Trade Policies

"FOR CHINESE MIGRANTS, BRAZIL IS the new destination of choice," said the president of the Chinese Association of Brazil in 2012. Her quote hit the headlines of one of the largest newspapers in Brazil (*O Estado de S. Paulo* 2012). The quote attests to the fact that Brazil has become a popular destination for Chinese migrants with limited financial resources. This view suggests that Brazil is a country where the life chances of low-income migrants will improve because of the opportunities for economic success in the informal economy. Contrary to most media coverage that uncritically reproduces the stereotypical idea of a "Chinese takeover" in sectors of the economy like manufacturing, finance, energy, mining, and agriculture, the quote refers to the growing presence of Chinese migrants in Brazil's popular markets.

Thirty years before, the president of the Chinese Association of Ciudad del Este-Paraguay had similarly said in his inaugural speech that Ciudad del Este was an ideal "place for overseas Chinese to do business and raise their offspring" (Taiwanese Chamber of Commerce-Paraguay and Chinese Association of Ciudad del Este-Paraguay 2015, 12). The association, established to support the Taiwanese community in Ciudad del Este, actively promoted the city as an attractive destination for those seeking opportunities to invest and live abroad. In the early 1980s, the association created favorable conditions for the economic success of migrants, played an active role in promoting businesses in the city, and assisted migrants in becoming importers, distributors, and shopkeepers.

Both in Ciudad del Este and in São Paulo, the associations implemented the diaspora policies of the Chinese and Taiwanese governments, continuing a long, transnational history of business and trade promotion among overseas Chinese communities. How did migrants' associations in Ciudad del Este and São Paulo bridge Taiwan's and China's engagement with the overseas Chinese populations? In this chapter, I show that, by engaging with the diaspora, participating in citywide politics, and organizing the community's internal affairs, the associations facilitated state-diaspora relations, promoted international trade, and developed an entrepreneurial ethos in the overseas communities.

By adapting and implementing the diaspora policy of the Chinese and Taiwanese governments, the associations supported business and boosted triangle commerce in Ciudad del Este and the popular markets in São Paulo. They lobbied for exclusive trade rights and lower taxation, rewarded the businesspeople involved in the privatization of the Dawn Market and the development of indoor markets with honorary titles and top decision-making positions, and strengthened ties with elected officials and the police. As a unique kind of local and transnational civil society actor, the associations played an ambivalent role. On one hand, they unlocked opportunities for migrants to work in the informal economy by assisting new businesses to grow, providing legal counseling, and representing vendors' interests in public and official affairs. On the other hand, they rigidly organized the community's affairs and exercised tight control over vendors, limiting migrants' options for jobs, trapping them in a cycle of debt, and hindering their ability to find housing arrangements. The migrants' associations enabled migrants' access to income-generating activities, and simultaneously they facilitated the capture of the wealth they generated. The associations represented a system of control over migrants' economic activities and contributed to siphoning off a significant portion of the vendors' revenue in the form of rental fees.

The Foucauldian concept of governmentality is useful to explain how multiple actors shape diaspora engagement extraterritorially. Foucault coined the neologism "governmentality" to refer to political rationalities by which states take the body of the population as their primary object of government (Foucault 2009). He argued neoliberal governmentality is a kind of power exercised by states and other actors through the promotion of self-realizing subjects in the markets (Foucault 2008). In other words, neoliberal governmentality fosters the market by cultivating entrepreneurial subjectivities and reorienting state institutions towards a market-friendly attitude. When applied to the analysis of state-diaspora relations, the concept of neoliberal governmentality emphasizes how governments promote an entrepreneurial ethos among diasporic populations and privilege subjects abroad who are seen as well-positioned brokers in today's globalized economy (Délano and Gamlen 2014; Hickey et al. 2015; Ho et al. 2015; Ho and Boyle 2015; Larner 2007; Liu and van Dongen 2016; Mullings 2012; Ong 1999; Ragazzi 2009).

Migrants' associations are crucial actors engaging in local, national, and transnational practices of neoliberal governmentality. This chapter explains the role of the Chinese diaspora associations in Ciudad del Este and São Paulo in linking the Taiwanese and Chinese governments with the overseas Chinese vendors. The associations in Ciudad del Este and São Paulo developed ties with places of origin, strengthening links with various overseas Chinese affairs agencies in Asia. Migrants' associations connected trade promotion in China and Taiwan with the expansion of popular markets in South America by acting in five major areas: supporting migrants' businesses, brokering for Chinese governments in the area of international trade promotion, fostering new migration destinations in cities where popular markets were mushrooming, organizing community responses to the crackdown on popular markets, and representing vendors and businesspeople in public affairs.

MIGRANTS' ASSOCIATIONS, TIES WITH THE HOMELAND, AND DIASPORA POLICY AGENCIES

Starting in the late nineteenth century, overseas Chinese groups developed an intense social, cultural, and political life around migrants' associations (*huìguǎn*). These associations can be divided into three major types: native-place associations, surname or kin associations, and trade or business associations. The most important of these are the native-place associations (*tóngxiānghuì*) because the feelings for one's hometown and the idea of returning to that place unite diaspora policy goals and foreign entrepreneurs of Chinese ancestry. Within this group, hometown associations (*qiáoxiānghuì*) are the ones that facilitate the most cultivation of ties between overseas Chinese populations and their hometowns or the counties of their ancestors. The cultivation of ties with the hometown (*qiáoxiāng*) is integral to the Chinese culture of establishing relationships of mutual obligation between individuals (*guānxì*) (Chan 2000, 2005; Chan and Chan 2011; Douw 1999a, 1999b; González 2017; Liu 1999; Tracy and Lever-Tracy 2002).

The cultivation of ties with the homeland is not just spontaneous. Rather, what can be translated as "overseas Chinese affairs" (*qiáowù*) includes a broad range of diaspora institutions and policies that draw from the feeling of shared belonging and instrumentalize migrants' associations for various strategic purposes. Overseas Chinese affairs have been a crucial issue of Chinese foreign policy since China's imperial government. They have also changed substantially over time. Starting in the late Qing dynasty, with a spike in emigration from southern provinces to southeast Asia, China adopted policies aimed at increasing economic, cultural, and political ties with the overseas Chinese populations. The Chinese state gradually consolidated the discourse that the overseas Chinese individuals belonged to the Chinese culture and nation. This issue was so important in the making of the modern Chinese state that the Republic of China established the Bureau of Diaspora Affairs in 1921 and its successor, the Overseas Chinese Affairs Commission (OCAC), in 1926.

Following the retreat of the nationalist government to Taiwan in 1949, the governments in Taipei and Beijing took distinct attitudes towards overseas Chinese affairs. The Republic of China claimed the continuity of the Overseas Chinese Affairs Commission. In 1949, OCAC was transferred to Taipei. However, shifts in foreign policy in Taiwan resulted in changes in the agency's terminology. Notably, when the Democratic Progressive Party defeated the Kuomintang in national elections in Taiwan for the first time in 2006, it changed the English name to Overseas Compatriot Affairs Commission, though the English acronym OCAC and the Chinese name remained the same. This reflects the Democratic Progressive Party's de-Sinicization policies that privileged the term "Taiwanese" over "Chinese." With the new Kuomintang administration in 2012, the government changed the official English name back to the original. The Kuomintang government was not a majority in the legislative house and, later that same year, relented to the opposition's demand to rename it the "Overseas Community Affairs Council, Republic of China (Taiwan)" and elevate it to the cabinet level. The name changes suggest that the conflicting views of the two parties put overseas affairs in the middle of an unresolved question of self-identification as Chinese or Taiwanese, and of the disputes around Taiwan's legitimacy as an independent state and a distinct nation. The dilemma is reflected in the official OCAC documents, which commonly use the phrase "Taiwanese residing abroad and those of Chinese/Taiwanese descent" (To 2014).

In turn, the Beijing government established its own Overseas Chinese Affairs Commission as early as 1949, adding "People's Republic of China" to the name five years later. However, the Chinese Communist Party soon adopted a strict policy on emigration, return, and citizens abroad, abolishing the Overseas Chinese Affairs Commission in 1969, at the height of the Cultural Revolution. The PRC practically cut off ties with the diaspora between the 1950s and the 1970s, impacting the migrants' relationship with their locality of origin. During that period, hometown associations convened their members annually in Singapore and Hong Kong. It was only with Deng Xiaoping's economic reform and Beijing's adoption of the Open-Door Policy in 1978 that the Overseas Chinese Affairs Office of the State Council (OCAO), a cabinet-level agency, was created with the mandate to liaise China's central and local governments with overseas Chinese populations, and to design and implement diaspora policies. Starting in the 1990s, conventions were held again in the hometowns in China, attracting high-level local political authorities who were strategically networking with the diaspora previously left abandoned (Zhou and Liu 2016).

While the government in Taipei continually tapped native-place associations around the world to connect with its diaspora, the revival of overseas Chinese affairs in China in the late twentieth century necessitated the empowerment or creation of a range of semiofficial agencies and state bodies at multiple levels of government. These institutions were responsible for designing and implementing policies related to migrants, returnees, and family members of overseas Chinese. Additional diaspora institutions gained prominence in China, including the United Front Work Department and Federation of Returned Overseas Chinese. Still, the OCAO remained a paramount institution until the late 2010s, expanding in size, scope, and power. A significant shift in the early 1990s was OCAO's new influence on the China Travel Service for the first time since its creation in 1949, making it more involved in the economic diplomacy targeted at the diaspora. Further, OCAO supported provinces to establish their own local offices and was key both in creating the China Overseas Exchange Association in 1992 and establishing local branches in the provinces. Even before that, the provinces with the highest numbers of migrant-sending towns developed a comprehensive framework of agencies dedicated to overseas Chinese affairs. In Fujian, the local OCAO was established in 1978, the same year the national office was created, and in Guangdong, just two years later, in 1980. In total, more than a thousand agencies and offices were created at the county level and above as early as the 1990s (Cheng and Ngok 1999).

Associations in Ciudad del Este

In Ciudad del Este, the most active diaspora association is the Chinese Association of Ciudad del Este-Paraguay. Established in 1982 and accredited by OCAC soon after, this association welcomed any migrant who self-identified as "ethnic Chinese." It created three additional chapters in Paraguay, in the capital Asunción and the border cities of Encarnación and Pedro Juan Caballero. The Chinese government is far less present in the lives of diaspora communities in this borderland and no OCAO-recognized associations exist in Ciudad del Este or Foz do Iguaçu, the Brazilian city that shares borders with Paraguay.

Other important diaspora associations include the Taiwanese Chamber of Commerce-Paraguay and the Federation of Chinese Businesspeople of

Paraguay established in 1995 and 1997, respectively. The Taiwanese government played an important role in establishing those associations. In 1994, representatives of the OCAC visited the Chinese Association of Ciudad del Este-Paraguay to help found the Taiwanese Chamber of Commerce-Paraguay. In Paraguay, OCAC replicates the model it follows internationally of supporting a national chapter of an umbrella organization that congregates the various hometown associations accredited with the office in Taiwan, the Overseas Chinese Association-Paraguay Chapter. Just like in fellow diaspora communities, hometown associations in Paraguay cultivated cultural and economic ties because of the shared identity of being connected to the same native place, a networking opportunity developed in Ciudad del Este by the Paraguay Chinese Club of Hometown Associations.

By the time these associations were established in the 1980s and 1990s, Taiwan and Paraguay had a solid tradition of diplomatic relations, which was essential for the success of the associations. A particular focus of the Overseas Chinese Association-Paraguay Chapter was on diplomatic and foreign affairs. With the creation of Ciudad del Este in 1957 in the background, Paraguay and Taiwan signed the Trade and Economic Cooperation Treaty in 1962, followed by a Friendship Treaty in 1968, and the Conventions of Tourism and Investment in 1975. The latter was adopted after the special importation regimes implemented in Paraguay in the early 1970s, and it created protections for Taiwanese migrants and investors moving to Ciudad del Este. Since then, Paraguay and Taiwan have held annual meetings for negotiation of the priority areas for bilateral relations. More than seventy agreements between the two countries were signed in areas such as trade, foreign aid, and scientific or academic cooperation.

Due to geopolitical shifts in Asia and South America, diplomatic relations between Paraguay and Taiwan started late but have lasted longer. It was only in 1957 that President Generals Chiang Kai-Shek and Alfredo Stroessner established diplomatic relations, within three years of the latter coming into power. The rapprochement was based on the ideological similarities between the two regimes, which were both army-ruled, U.S.-backed, and anti-communist. Paraguay remains one of the few countries that has maintained diplomatic relations with Taipei after the replacement of Taipei's government by Beijing's in the United Nations in 1971. This contrasts with Brazil, which was the first country to recognize the Republic of China in 1912 but switched to the People's Republic of China in 1974.

Associations in São Paulo

The largest association in São Paulo is the Chinese Association of Brazil, originally founded in 1980 as the Chinese Cultural Association of Brazil and renamed in 1982. Created only two years after the establishment of OCAO in China and recognized by that office, the Chinese Association of Brazil has a history of infra-diplomatic assistance to the Chinese community in São Paulo. Its original mandate was to deliver cultural and social services at a time when there was no consulate in the city. Today, it gathers nearly sixty associations, mainly of four types: native-place associations (hometown and province of origin), age- and gender-based associations (such as the youth, retired people, or women), occupation-related associations (vendors, traders, and businesspeople), and one-China groups. The Chinese Association of Brazil describes itself as a "patriotic Chinese community," and though it welcomes a broad membership, its political agenda alienates certain groups, particularly Chinese of the 1949 migration and anti-Chinese Communist Party Taiwanese as well as overseas Chinese populations that left Southeast Asia fearing annexation during the Cultural Revolution, like Hong Kongese, Singaporeans, and Indonesians (Stenberg 2012).

Other associations have opposing political agendas. One important example is the Chinese Social Center of Brazil in São Paulo. It was founded in the 1970s as a chapter of the first Chinese association established in Brazil by Cantonese migrants in Rio de Janeiro in the 1920s (Shu 2023). The Chinese Social Center was originally focused on cultural and social activities, however, it later became a pro-independence hub, as both previous migrants and newcomers disavowed the Chinese Communist Party regime. Likewise, the membership of the Hakka Social Center of Brazil in São Paulo includes the Hakka community and others who oppose the Chinese Communist Party. The Taiwanese Association of Brazil—a chapter of the International Federation of Taiwanese Associations—helped the Taiwanese agency OCAC establish a Culture Center of Taipei Economic and Cultural Office in in São Paulo in 2005, one of only sixteen offices of its kind that serve as de facto consulates in countries that do not recognize Taipei's government.

While the major functions of native-place associations were initially to provide social and educational support for fellow regionals, the commercial role of the native-place associations should not be overlooked. Regional groupings are closely linked to specific types of commercial activities, and many regional associations were established to promote business networks among their fellow members both within and beyond national boundaries (Liu 1999; Qu 2016).

The Chinese Association of Brazil underwent a major shift in its convergence with the OCAO's agenda set in Beijing, placing greater emphasis on economic issues like the promotion of international trade and entrepreneurialism. By extension, most associations affiliated with it realigned with the shift in focus towards importation, business mentality, and self-employment. Examples include the native-place associations of the largest groups of Chinese migrants, such as the Association of the Cantonese of Brazil and the Qingtian Association of Brazil, both founded in the early 1990s. Other native-place associations in São Paulo include the Wenzhou Association of Brazil and the Min Nan Association of South America, which gathers migrants from the Fujian Province, though there is also the Association of Fujianese in Brazil that precedes those two associations.

In São Paulo, the associations' focus on the promotion of entrepreneurialism and importations expanded the overseas Chinese migrants' businesses in the popular markets mainly in three ways. First, the associations supported business. They facilitated opening firms, subleasing stalls, supplying goods, managing inventory, and representing vendors in lawsuits and negotiations with various government agencies. Associations and leaders acted as the management company for commercial and residential buildings where migrant vendors worked and lived, tying together migrants' personal, social, and economic activities. This had an ambiguous effect on migrants, who, on one hand, had access to opportunities to succeed as vendors, but, on the other hand, were subjected to everyday forms of control over their livelihoods and business. Even when migrants' businesses were thriving, the associations facilitated the extraction of an unfair share of their revenue in the form of high stall rental prices and other sublease fees.

Second, associations supported the migration of newcomers who worked as stallholders and street vendors selling manufactures imported from China. The associations' role in supporting access opportunities for Chinese vendors helped expand Chinese businesses in the popular markets and diversify migration routes to cities where the popular markets were booming. The native-place associations based in São Paulo are national in name and grew quickly to represent a membership beyond the residents of that city. Those associations exercised influence in migrants relocating to various cities across Brazil and supported establishing local chapters which remained connected to the national headquarters. Not only did the associations offer various kinds of assistance to newcomers, but they also sustained migration by liaising with travel agencies in the migrant-sending counties in China. This controversially raised suspicion of an illegal industry around irregular Chinese migration, reproducing the idea that Chinese migrants are trafficked in to distribute counterfeits and smuggled goods.

Lastly, the associations helped implement locally the Chinese government's trade policies. An important part of the activity of the native-place associations revolved around receiving delegations from China who represented the agendas of the Chinese central or subnational government and the business community. The associations prominently highlighted this area of action on their websites and advertised this service in Chinese-language newspapers as a membership benefit (Stenberg 2016).

In addition to native-place associations, other types of associations were established with the specific goal of creating economic opportunities in downtown São Paulo popular markets. For instance, both the Overseas Chinese Youth Federation of Brazil and the General Association of the Chinese Businesspeople of Brazil, established in 2002 and 2007 respectively, assisted with services like import brokerage, business coaching, legal counseling, and accounting. While the trade and business associations were not directly connected with migrants' native place, they nevertheless established and maintained indirect links with the hometowns. A feeling of fellowship underlies these business associations, and many trade guilds were formed predominantly by merchants from the same locality. Additionally, even the cultural associations founded in the 2000s in São Paulo understood that support for business is a central aspect of the work that they do. The president of both the Beijing Cultural Exchange Association of Brazil and the Union of the Chinese Women of Brazil told me in an interview in

2017 that "whether Chinese migrants are struggling in their stalls or succeeding financially, business is an integral part of our cultural identity here, so business is an important area of activity of our organizations."

By focusing on overseas Chinese individuals and their integration into the popular markets, trade associations diverged from other business organizations and chambers of commerce that are devoted to large-scale economic projects and promoted trade and investment between Chinese and Brazilian businesses. The clearest example of the latter is the Chinese Chamber of Commerce of Brazil, which is closely affiliated with the Chinese consulate in São Paulo. Other examples include the Brazil-China Economic Development Chamber, China-Brazil Chamber of Commerce, Brazil-China Social and Cultural Institute, Brazil-China Business Council, and Brazil-China Chamber.

GREAT EMISSARIES: THE NEXUS BETWEEN TRADE AND MIGRATION

When I first interviewed the founding director of the Overseas Chinese Youth Federation of Brazil, I walked into a small office on the busiest street of a popular market and noticed that the room had nothing but a desk, a chair, a telephone, a computer, and a calendar on the wall. The calendar pictured a container ship, and the red and gold text was written entirely in Mandarin Chinese, except for a few words in English that stood out because of the large font and bold black letters: "Great Emissaries of China: trading since times immemorial." Together, the text and imagery suggest that Chinese trade is being revived due to a dispersed network of diaspora communities, who are seen as emissaries connecting goods made in China with markets around the globe. Furthermore, it implies that, unlike the past, when China was forced to open its ports to international trade, today's China is not just an entrepôt for foreign traders of imperial powers, but a center from which its emissaries disperse to create and reactivate proper Chinese commercial circuits.

In the interview, he pointed to the calendar and told me that "two things are in the Chinese blood: a concern to accumulate substantial savings for when you are old and a particular ability to trade. All Chinese have that in their veins." As a migrant and an importer, the director embodies the figure of the emissary that the calendar evokes, embracing his perceived mission to succeed as a businessperson who trades with China from afar, and making this an integral part of the display of his Chinese identity. He construes a narrative that fuses migration and trade to justify simultaneously his migration trajectory and his occupation, in which market-based notions of excellence inform his perceptions about Chinese-ness, belonging, and selfhood. His self-identification as a Chinese businessperson overseas is shaped by China's efforts to form a particular kind of subjectivity among its diaspora population—a type of subjectivity that includes the inculcation of an entrepreneurial self and the creation of mobile market subjects. In this sense, he is a product of the kind of neoliberal governmentality exercised through diaspora policies that aim to achieve extraterritorial processes of subjectivation, particularly discourses and policies that reclaim the diaspora to promote market-based notions of selfhood, peoplehood, and national identity (Zhou and Lee 2013).

The focus on developing entrepreneurial selves and creating mobile market subjects was present in the discursive ways that China engages with the overseas population in São Paulo. For instance, the Chinese consulate in São Paulo, in partnership with the Chinese Association of Brazil, promoted Chinese cultural festivities at which speeches by Chinese diplomatic authorities reinforced the idea that the homeland is "proud of the overseas Chinese who bravely explore the world and persist in the search for the best conditions to fulfill their aspirations here, in China, or elsewhere," as the vice-consul general said during the 2017 Chinese New Year celebration in São Paulo. Representatives of associations echoed ideas of success (in the popular markets) and courage (to migrate), propagating the notion that, at least for these Chinese in São Paulo, Chineseness is tied to economic success as a vendor abroad.

Helping Migrants to Succeed in Popular Markets

One of the major goals of the associations is to help migrants to succeed in the popular markets. For instance, in 2015, the Qingtian Association of Brazil revised its mission to make this goal, which had always been an important feature of the association, even more front and center. In addition to seeing itself as the meeting point for social activities and cultural celebrations of the Qingtianese in São Paulo, the association understood itself to be a beneficial society of mutual help that provides assistance for fellow Qingtianese who are struggling in their businesses, whether as stallholders or shopkeepers. Moreover, the association claims the role of the main mediator of conflicts in the community. According to the association director, if in the past conflicts used to be about family issues such as divorces or fights between family members, the major source of conflict between migrant vendors now is defaulting on informal loans.

Another major change in the Qingtian Association of Brazil was the creation of a dedicated Department of Migrant Support. The department primarily helps migrants with a range of everyday activities related to their businesses, like subletting stalls and filing paperwork to apply for a Brazilian social security card or open a bank account. The department also runs a legal clinic specializing in how to respond to consumer protection lawsuits. In partnership with the Chinese Association of Brazil, it established the São Paulo Overseas Chinese Center, which was recognized by OCAO in 2015. Under the slogan "By, with, and for the overseas Chinese," the center extends support to all Chinese migrants, irrespective of place of origin. It has committees on policy and legal aid, safety, education, and charity. Information about this service is disseminated in the OCAO-sponsored *South America Newspaper*, on channels in the instant messaging application WeChat, and in printed materials like brochures and flyers. According to the president of the Qingtian Association of Brazil, "because the biggest challenge of overseas Chinese in Brazil is to prosper in business," the center is primarily focused on "building entrepreneurial skills among migrant vendors and importers." These changes have been implemented with the support of OCAO, which shares best practices of hometown associations in other countries that successfully established support centers geared towards importers and vendors.

Other associations, too, support the services provided by the center. The Overseas Chinese Youth Federation of Brazil is a major funder of new services, hiring two permanent lawyers as well as covering most of the center's running costs. The former president of the federation, who stepped down to serve as the first director of the center, told me that "the association sees the decision to divert funds and personnel to the center as a natural and positive change." In an interview he gave me in 2011, he said the federation's main goal was to facilitate young migrants' integration into the job market, specifically helping them find jobs as clerks in stalls or submitting the paperwork to obtain municipal licenses as stallholders. His vision for the federation was "to make it a center for people who endure hardship in the commercial districts." This vision is communicated to Chinese vendors, who accept the idea of being a vendor struggling in the popular market but reject the presumed similarity between their trajectory and that of the president of the federation.

The General Association of the Chinese Businesspeople of Brazil was established with "the single and simple goal of providing the means for Chinese vendors to succeed in downtown São Paulo," as the president of the association told me in an interview. Its name is suggestive because it frames the Chinese stallholders as businesspeople, not just vendors, elevating their occupational status. This association provides services like translations, legal workshops, and the counsel of attorneys for commercial or immigration issues. It provides free support to its members thanks to the assistance of the Overseas Chinese Service Center, an office based in China that is OCAO's designated center for worldwide overseas Chinese business service providers. In only five years between 2012 and 2017, the General Association of the Chinese Businesspeople of Brazil helped stallholders and shopkeepers to open more than 3,300 businesses. Further, the president of the association said that given the increase in robbery and physical assault against the Chinese stallholders, a new area of focus is "promoting a stable work environment for vendors, particularly regarding the cooperation with state agencies to ensure public order and prevent crimes in the markets." The association cosponsored the creation of a Community Safety Council dedicated to crime prevention in the area, establishing a durable partnership with municipal authorities and public safety agencies.

To a large extent, the work of the associations in São Paulo and Ciudad del Este aligns with the trade promotion goals of diaspora policies designed in Asia. The strongest feature of the engagement with the diaspora in these cities is not promoting integration into the host society, protecting migrants' rights, or sponsoring cultural events. Rather, their most significant role is to foster trade and activate new commercial routes in globalized circuits of wealth circulation. For example, a high-level representative of the

Chinese Association of Ciudad del Este-Paraguay told me in an interview in 2015 that "since day one, the association has placed economic mutual assistance at the center of the activities we do, which is what the Taiwanese government wants the migrants' associations to do around the world." He continued to say that "while cultural issues like festivities and education are important, no Taiwanese would have moved to Paraguay had the road not been paved for them to do well financially."

Another example in Ciudad del Este is the Chamber of Commerce's advocacy work to improve the Taiwanese traders' position in Paraguay. In a special report prepared for the visit of the OCAC chairman in 2015, the Taiwanese Chamber of Commerce-Paraguay and the Chinese Association of Ciudad del Este-Paraguay emphasized the work of the Chamber of Commerce is aligned with Taipei's goals of promoting trade through the diaspora communities and increasing the connections among migrants around the world:

> The president of the Chamber of Commerce, its directors, supervisors, and consultants upheld the general goal of making all efforts to improve the status of Taiwanese merchants in Paraguay, strengthening ties between the Taiwanese executive authorities on trade matters and local chambers of commerce, studying the correspondent legal affairs, and protecting the rights and interests of Taiwanese merchants. The objective was to promote cooperation with Taiwanese merchants in any country in the world, exploring business opportunities and seeking mutual interests in developing commerce. This converged with the view of fostering ties with Taiwanese merchants worldwide, promoting solidarity and friendship among these fellow compatriots, and exchanging experiences in business management. The generation of people who founded the Chamber of Commerce planted trees for today's generation to enjoy the cool of the shadows, repaying their predecessors for their hard work. (Taiwanese Chamber of Commerce-Paraguay and Chinese Association of Ciudad del Este-Paraguay 2015, 12)

A major difference between the associations in the two cities, however, is that while the ones in Ciudad del Este focus predominantly on advocating for importers, distributors, and shopkeepers, the ones in São Paulo support a larger group of migrants who hold more precarious occupations, especially stallholders and street vendors. However, the assistance that the associations in São Paulo give to the migrants who are in more precarious positions is ambiguous in purpose and effect. Migrants I interviewed have a rather critical view of that assistance, which they said keeps them dependent on the stall sublessors, many of whom occupy high-level positions in the associations.

Brokering for Chinese Governments

A key strategy of the overseas Chinese affairs agencies in China and Taiwan to connect with associations abroad when establishing and strengthening ties with the diaspora is "reaching out" (*zǒuchūqù*, which can also be translated as "going out") (Cheng and Ngok 1999; Thunø 2001). This strategy run in parallel to China's "Go Out Policy" (*zǒuchūqù zhànlüè*), also known as "Going Global Strategy," announced in March 2000 with signature projects where China expanded its construction companies abroad and later serving as a blueprint for more ambitious foreign policy projects, including the famous Belt and Road Initiative. "Reaching out" was a strategy to connect with the diasporas, marking a significant shift from the earlier thinking of the 1970s of migrants as disloyal and even from the more transnational approach of the early 1990s of returning to help China grow. The government replaced the slogan "return and serve the country" (*huíguó fúwù*) with "serve the country" (*wèi guó fúwù*), suggesting that physical return no longer is a requirement for the display of patriotism and that diasporas are a strategic asset abroad (Liu 2016; Xiang 2007). In Ciudad del Este and São Paulo, OCAC and local OCAOs sent representatives to the overseas community on official travel from the 1990s to the mid-2010s.

Interestingly, municipal governments and public companies in China's industrialized southeast coast instrumentalized associations to reach out to the diaspora in South America. Even though these cities are not the native places of the diasporas in Ciudad del Este and São Paulo, they viewed them as privileged business partners and strategic traders. In 2014 alone, nine representatives of city or province governments visited São Paulo to showcase their exports portfolio. Both the Chinese Association of Brazil and the Qingtian Association of Brazil held workshops for overseas Chinese importers and vendors during these visits. This contrasts with the chambers of commerce in São Paulo, which liaised predominantly with Brazilian businesspeople.

Other visits exclusively targeted the overseas Chinese community. For instance, the LED Manufacturers Association of Shenzhen, whose business trip was sponsored by the OCAO in Guangzhou, met only with overseas Chinese individuals. Similarly, the representatives of gift manufacturers on a business trip in 2015 did not meet a single Brazilian businessperson. The president of the General Association of the Chinese Businesspeople of Brazil explained to me that representatives expected that after the visit they would be in a better position to understand these vendors' needs and customize orders to match the needs of Brazilian low-income buyers. Representatives also partnered with local associations to facilitate pool sales for migrant vendors who are not big enough buyers or lack expertise in customs clearance procedures.

The governments that reached out to the associations in São Paulo and Ciudad del Este represent industrial cities that specialize in specific goods, from pottery to light bulbs, from sportswear to toys, and so on. Many goods found in the popular markets in South America—like religious articles, carnival masks, or souvenirs with sayings in Portuguese or Spanish—are only marketable if customized and adapted for language and culture. For instance, according to the president of the General Association of the Chinese Businesspeople of Brazil, a manufacturer representative visiting São Paulo found out that the reason for low sales was that action figures had sayings written in incorrect Portuguese and that religious icons with the face of Jesus Christ were painted in red, which is the most common color of deities in Chinese culture.

The industrialization plan implemented in China after Deng Xiaoping's reforms produced geographical specialization by type of manufactured goods. The city of Yiwu in Zhejiang province is known as a "global supermarket" because the Yiwu China Commodities City Group, a state company controlled by the local government, organizes the world's largest commodities wholesale market, the Futian Market. When the company learned that nearly 90% of what is sold in São Paulo was supplied by Yiwu it organized business trips to São Paulo with high-level political representatives, including the governor and the mayor who traveled all the way from China (Freire da Silva 2014a; Pliez 2010). The company also deepened its ties with the Chinese Association of Brazil to do a market analysis and expand trade with Chinese importers based in Brazil. Interestingly, it sponsored the travels of representatives of four Taiwanese associations and chambers of commerce from Ciudad del Este, which shows the market potential of triangle commerce was more important to those representatives than political and ideological tensions over national identity.

As in the distant past, when the Chinese government maximized the economic benefits of the ethnic link between China and its migrants and their descendants abroad, OCAC and OCAO recently tapped the associations to reach out to the diaspora with the goal of increasing trade. By reaching out to them, the Asian agencies connect with a population that is not necessarily from the native locality.

Additionally, a major focus of the Taiwanese government's reaching out to the diaspora in Ciudad del Este was to garner support on the ground for foreign affairs. Because Taiwan has struggled to keep Paraguay's recognition of Taipei's government after China's economic and political rise in the last few decades, OCAC repeatedly tapped the associations to exhort the community to pledge support. For instance, the celebration of the 108th National Day of the Republic of China was held jointly with the Overseas Chinese Festival in Ciudad del Este on October 12, 2019. An OCAC representative was sent from Taiwan to deepen the ties with the organizers, the Paraguay Chapter of the Overseas Chinese Association. The OCAC representative said that the "overseas Chinese have played a very important role in all stages of the history of the Republic of China," and they must "work together to assist the embassy and the consulate in promoting diplomacy and overseas Chinese affairs" (Baxi Huaren Xun Wang Zi 2019).

Creating New Destinations

Associations played yet another important role at the intersections of migration routes and commercial circuits, facilitating the making of new migration destinations where popular markets were booming. Brazil is now an established destination for Chinese migrants, which the president of the Qingtian Association of Brazil attributes to Brazil's relatively relaxed immigration system. The increase in the Brazilian lower classes' consumption power, a growing demand for imports, and the mushrooming of popular markets throughout the country, all made Brazil a place where Chinese migrants can thrive. One of the major attractions would-be migrants find in the idea of moving to Brazil is the opportunity to become a self-employed entrepreneur, even if that means going through hardships as a stallholder or street vendor.

In addition to "reaching out" to the associations, the diaspora agencies in China and Taiwan deployed another strategy to connect with the overseas Chinese communities: "inviting in" (*qǐngjìnlái*, which can also be translated as "welcoming in" or "bringing in") (Cheng and Ngok 1999; Thunø 2001). Like "reaching out," the overseas Chinese affairs strategy of "inviting in" runs in parallel to China's broader foreign policy directions. While attracting foreign investment especially of the diasporas is a strategy that was initiated with Deng Xiaoping's opening up policies, president Xi Jinping's[1] new era in Chinese foreign policy greatly shaped diaspora policy, intensifying the "inviting in" strategies. He is a long-standing proponent of "large overseas Chinese affairs" (*dàqiáowù*), calling for broad and deep cooperation between China and the diaspora. Currently, this concept is an integral part of the "Chinese Dream" (*Zhōngguó mèng*)—the central pillar of the government's political ideology that combines economic modernization, technological innovation, and cultural revival (Liu 2016). Additionally, in 2018, China rolled out a major restructuring of diaspora institutions. OCAO, a government apparatus, was absorbed by two party apparatuses, the Federation of Returned Overseas Chinese and the United Front Work Department, an institution of the Chinese Communist Party tasked with co-opting political forces outside the party. With this restructuring, China instrumentalized diaspora politics for geopolitical purposes, moving from the purely economic support of the diasporas towards expanding China's soft power abroad (Liu 2022).

When it comes to China's diaspora agencies bringing the South American diasporas in, OCAO invited the Chinese Association of Brazil to participate in their annual meetings in China gathering worldwide overseas associations. Local OCAOs from migrant-sending provinces like Guangdong, Zhejiang, and Fujian also invited leaders of native-place associations. Inviting association leaders aimed to increase networking opportunities, learn about the development plans of major business groups controlled by overseas Chinese communities, and attract foreign investments or receive donations. Similarly, OCAC sponsored the travel of representatives from both the Taiwanese Chamber of Commerce-Paraguay and the Chinese Association of Ciudad del Este-Paraguay.

The former president of the Chinese Association of Brazil told me in an interview in 2017 that the native-place associations visited China at the request of OCAO. In these visits, it promoted a positive image of Brazil as a destination for Chinese migrants, a view disseminated in migrant-sending counties. Other associations also offered workshops in China about Brazilian immigration and commercial law in partnership with OCAO province offices, attracting an eager audience of travel agents and migration intermediaries.

All this effort aimed at not only growing migration to Brazil, but directing migration to new destinations. During her tenure, the former president of the Chinese Association of Brazil implemented her vision of opening up new markets in the north and northeast of Brazil. Her plan, shared with the representatives of the Yiwu wholesale company, was to start new popular markets in Brazil's northeast. She assessed that the popular markets in São Paulo were saturated because too many vendors compete for clients, nearly a third of whom were resellers who travel overnight to São Paulo from the northeast of Brazil (Freire da Silva 2014a).

Many cities in Brazil became popular destinations for Chinese migrants. Migrants are partly motivated by a desire to escape stricter enforcement in São Paulo, especially after City Hall launched Operation Delegated and the City Free of Piracy programs in 2009 and 2010. The former president of the Chinese Association of Brazil proudly said in an interview she accomplished her plans to make popular markets across the country more attractive than São Paulo. Many leaders of native-place associations shared her vision. Representatives of various associations suggested that the migrants in São Paulo relocate to the Brazilian northeast, including Recife's São José market and the street fairs in Caruaru and Sulanca (Silva 2008; Rabossi 2010). Commenting on the opening of a Chinese consulate in a major city in that area in 2016, the president of the Qingtian Association of Brazil told me in an interview that "opening a consulate there was vital to support our community where they have better chances to succeed in business. The market is saturated in São Paulo. A stallholder in the northeast makes twice as much, pays less in rent, and has a better life."

Taiwanese associations are similarly facilitating migrants' relocation to new marketplaces in Paraguay where they have better opportunities for economic success. According to the director of the Chinese Association of Ciudad del Este-Paraguay in an interview he gave me in 2015, "there is a disincentive to remain in Ciudad del Este's declining economy and, at the same time, an incentive to open businesses in the border towns" of Encarnación, Salto del Guayrá, and Pedro Juan Caballero. While Ciudad del Este still attracts Brazilian shoppers, the price gap between imports in Ciudad del Este and Brazilian cities is closing because of trade liberalization in Brazil and regional economic integration under MERCOSUR. However, the associations realized that opening shopping malls in other border cities in Paraguay is profitable because these malls attract shoppers who do not travel as far to Ciudad del Este. The Chinese Association of Ciudad del Este-Paraguay established local chapters in Encarnación and Pedro Juan Caballero, and new ones were created like the Encarnación Chapter of the Taiwanese Fellows' Solidarity and Aid Association. The associations negotiated with the province governments to receive tax subsidies for shopping malls in exchange for the promise that they would create jobs.

Local governments in China and Taiwan are actively collecting information about migration from native-place associations in Brazil and Paraguay. The Taichung government in Taiwan says that it has a responsibility to support the overseas Chinese in Ciudad del Este. Likewise, the OCAO of Guangdong Province designed a booklet with relevant information about Brazilian cities, including the size of the diaspora population, contact information for local associations and clubs, and economic highlights including a list of import/export offices. The booklet was distributed through the Network of the Overseas Chinese in Brazil, which is a privileged channel promoted by the Chinese Association of Brazil and all major associations.

Mobilizing Against Crackdown on Illegal or Irregular Commerce

From behind the counter of his stall in Shopping 25 de Março, Qian, a migrant from Qingtian, watched a demonstration of nearly four hundred protesters on June 30, 2011. The protest demanded the end of Operation Delegated, the City Free of Piracy program, and the so-called mega-operations to combat illegal or irregular commerce, all of which directly affected the Chinese vendors in downtown São Paulo. Protesters included a majority of Brazilians and a significant number of international migrants, especially Bolivians and Peruvians. However, Chinese vendors like Qian did not join the rally. Instead, the following day, Qian and over seven hundred Chinese vendors protested the shutdown of five indoor markets. In April and May 2011, each of these indoor markets was closed for approximately ten days during crackdown operations on counterfeits and smuggled imports. In one of those markets alone, 780,000 imported goods were confiscated, worth $110 million at that time (Piza 2015). This all-Chinese demonstration was called for by native-place associations that marched with vendors. Compared to Brazilians and other international migrants who work in the same popular markets, Chinese vendors participated much less in public demonstrations. Very few Chinese vendors joined multiethnic protests like the ones that Qian watched from his stall. Rather, they joined demonstrations organized by the associations.

Native-place associations and other associations played a crucial role in organizing Chinese vendors in mobilizations against the crackdown on illegal or irregular commerce in São Paulo and represented them in institutional channels of participatory citizenship in São Paulo and Ciudad del Este. Chinese migrants in downtown São Paulo organized for issues directly related to their economic activities. The primary goal of their mobilization was to ensure that they retained the ability to keep running businesses. This differs from earlier groups of Chinese and Taiwanese migrants in São Paulo, who mobilized politically along ideological, national, and party lines, especially around issues that pertained to the homeland. It is also distinct from other migrant groups who organized in the last few decades for migrants' access to services and rights. Overseas Chinese vendors, in contrast, saw an increase in associations that claimed to represent their business interests and act as political brokers doing advocacy with governments and state institutions.

Six years after that demonstration, Qian was one of nearly a thousand Chinese stallholders affected again by the shutdown of two indoor markets. On September 11, 2017, São Paulo City Hall revoked the business licenses of those indoor markets and ordered the doors be literally walled over. The Ershiwu Jie channel of the WeChat application, a popular channel among migrant vendors for the real-time translation of relevant local news into Mandarin Chinese, was flooded with news about the shutdown, official notifications from City Hall, and questions and complaints from Chinese stallholders. Qian kept his eyes on his phone, waiting for a message with the decision of the associations on which course of action to take.

The shutdown was part of the Internal Revenue System's operation against illicit commerce in São Paulo, in partnership with City Hall. Dubbed Operation September due to its atypical duration of more than a month, it was self-described as the largest operation in the state of São Paulo to crack down on goods smuggled into the country. The operation included 105 tax auditors who confiscated 880 tons of goods, transported in 68 fully loaded trucks (*Folha de S. Paulo* 2017).

Operation September was the first action of City Hall's newest program to curb piracy, the Legality Movement, launched that week. The program was a partnership with the Movement in Defense of the Brazilian Legal Market, which is sponsored by the Brazilian Institute of Ethics in Competition and the Brazilian Forum against Piracy and Illegality. On the occasion of the launch of the Legality Movement, Bruno Covas (then deputy mayor and chancellor of sub-prefectures) wrote an op-ed entitled "São Paulo without Illegality" for a major São Paulo newspaper, in which he justified the closing of indoor markets he called "notorious spaces of illegal commerce" (Covas 2017). He emphasized that his administration was closing indoor markets to combat the selling of counterfeits and smuggled goods in São Paulo. He also recognized the root cause of this issue was the tax disparity between Brazil and Paraguay, which, he concluded, incentivized smuggling.

Native-place associations and other types of associations reacted against the shutdown and called for a demonstration that Qian and more than five hundred stallholders joined. The Min Nan Association South America and the Overseas Chinese Youth Federation of Brazil held extraordinary meetings to discuss the issue. The General Association of Chinese Businesspeople of Brazil went one step further and took action on behalf of vendors. This association protested to the Human Rights Committee of the São Paulo Bar Association that the operation violated laws requiring search warrants and seized items without prior authorization, including transaction receipts, balance sheets, pay stubs, money in cash, and other personal items. The association's president said Buddhist icons were destroyed by auditors, which he sees as evidence that the operation was motivated by anti-Chinese hatred. The association also requested that the Chinese consulate in São Paulo act on the case and called on stallholders to hold another demonstration.

The associations helped the two indoor markets affected strike a deal with City Hall to put an end to the shutdown. The lawyer that represented these indoor markets, Thomas Law, is the son of the owner of both establishments, Law Kin Chong, who was imprisoned for bribery in a corruption scandal following the investigation of smuggling and counterfeits. Thomas Law signed a Memorandum of Adjustment of Conduct, stipulating that a fine of US$9,500 be billed to approximately nine hundred stallholders and that his father's management company commit to not allowing the sales of illegal goods.

Representing the Overseas Chinese Communities

Migrants' associations claim to represent the interests of the overseas Chinese communities in public and official affairs. In São Paulo, the associations sought to make an impact in local politics, given that the issues most affecting the vendors were all municipal affairs, including unlicensed street vending, the crackdown on counterfeits, and the deployment of police force to enforce regulations related to the popular markets.

The most direct way that the associations found to achieve that goal was to support community leaders running for local boards, official committees, and positions in the city government. When the Hong Kongese migrant Heida Li[2] became a member of City Council in 2010, the Chinese Association of Brazil immediately appointed her president of the association. Li was a running mate and substitute to a seasoned Brazilian politician who had been reelected for City Council a few times. Li took office when her running mate unexpectedly stepped down. However, after her term in City Hall ended, the associations realized that, despite the economic force that the community represents, it did not have a strong enough electoral basis to reelect her because most migrants did not become naturalized citizens. Instead, the associations funded incumbent council members running for reelection in districts of downtown São Paulo in exchange for a commitment to support the overseas Chinese business.

This strategy was successful and the community had a say in municipal affairs. A few association leaders were appointed to serve in the offices of those council members and city agencies controlled by them. Additionally, the associations accomplished symbolic wins that help paint a more positive image of the overseas Chinese community, such as instituting the Day of the Chinese Migrant and the promise to introduce a bill recognizing the district as São Paulo's first official Chinatown. The associations lobbied council members to bestow key leaders of the associations the highest honor a civilian can receive, which was seen, on some occasions, as a form of political protection for those leaders accused of committing illegal activities in the popular markets, such as distributing counterfeits or smuggled goods, or involvement in bribery scandals.

The most well-known Brazilian politician of Chinese heritage, William Boss Woo,[3] is a unique case of migrants' political representation. He was a Civil Police officer born to a Chinese father who had migrated to Taiwan previously and a Japanese mother, and he is married to a Korean-Brazilian woman. His personal background puts him in the self-described position of the political voice of Asian Brazilians. He successfully translated his municipal career as a two-term member of the São Paulo City Council into election to the state congress in 2006 and again in 2014. Though Woo is more closely associated with the Japanese-Brazilian community, a much larger electoral basis, he established strategic ties with the overseas Chinese associations. He campaigned on bringing about the Regularization Bill of 2009 that granted amnesty to undocumented migrants, an issue of no concern to the Japanese-Brazilian community but deeply important for the Chinese-Brazilian community. Another reason for the support he received from the associations was his hard-on-crime approach, which promised to address growing concerns of the community about issues of personal safety in a high-crime nation. This approach aligns with the double focus of the associations to combat the criminality affecting vendors while it simultaneously smoothens out strategic relationships with the various police agencies intervening in the popular markets.

In addition to securing a stronghold in electoral politics, the associations in São Paulo engaged in other types of representative politics. The associations demanded the creation in 2016 of a local chapter of the Community

Safety Council. The council is a national program establishing local forums for participatory citizenship and collective deliberation on issues of public safety. That particular chapter played a crucial role in the interaction between Chinese vendors and state institutions, especially the various branches of the police, with the goals of ensuring safety in popular markets and creating a permanent channel of communication with enforcement agencies. The council gathers citizens, residents, workers, and other interested parties to discuss monthly issues of public order and safety with the responsible state institutions.

Chinese associations were the most influential proponents of this chapter and were overrepresented. All but one of the civil society members of the chapter were Chinese associations. Furthermore, the board of directors of the chapter was composed of leaders of the overseas Chinese associations, who set the council's agenda and instrumentalized it to strengthen strategic relationship with enforcement agencies.

It was not obvious that overseas Chinese associations would privilege the Community Safety Council as a space for negotiation with City Hall and enforcement agencies. There was not a preexisting council chapter in that district, and not even the Brazilian shopkeeper syndicates showed interest in this otherwise forgotten space of civil society's participation. However, the associations were motivated to find durable solutions to Chinese vendors' most important safety issues, especially with the spike in thefts from stalls and burglary of their homes in 2015. Gangs targeted Chinese migrants because of the widespread idea that they are unbanked vendors who operate mainly in cash. These crimes were seldom reported because many vendors were undocumented migrants who feared interacting with the police and lacked relevant information (Freire da Silva 2018).

Yet, the associations quickly instrumentalized this council to implement a self-serving vision of public order in the popular markets. By having a direct communication channel with representatives of various City Hall departments and police departments, associations negotiated their priorities such as areas of increased policing activities. The associations supported City Hall's stricter enforcement of laws regulating street vending in exchange for a more relaxed enforcement of laws prohibiting illegal commerce in the indoor markets, where they demanded policing focus on theft and other crimes affecting the Chinese vendors.

In Ciudad del Este, too, associations played the important role of representing the Taiwanese community. Native-place associations and business associations were vocal about their issues and advocated for importers and shopkeepers at the local and national levels. The priority focus was lobbying for lower tariffs and taxes. Additionally, the associations centered on engagement with the homeland, influencing Taiwan's areas of priority in international affairs to benefit business in Ciudad del Este. In particular, the Taiwanese Chamber of Commerce-Paraguay acted as the spokesperson voicing the concerns of importers and shopkeepers to OCAC, which in turn shaped the Taiwanese government's agenda regarding Paraguay.

Having a significant influence on the community, the Taiwanese associations in Ciudad del Este acted as an intermediary between the Taipei government and the diaspora. When Taiwan wanted to regain control over the Orient Industrial Park in the outskirts of the city, the government used OCAC to reach out to the diaspora associations and communicate a strong message for migrants to utilize the industrial park as a strategy to create a new positive reputation for it. From the Taiwanese migrants' perspective, responding positively to this call was an ethical obligation. Migrants I interviewed said that they felt it was their duty to help the Taiwanese government achieve its goals because it represents the nation's interests. For them, their support for a goal that is not directly beneficial to them but is a collective imperative shows they understand the broader impact of keeping connected to Taiwanese society even from afar. Still, this is not purely the spontaneous behavior of individuals out of altruism. The associations ensure the social costs of membership to the Taiwanese community in Ciudad del Este are distributed across members and enforce social norms by deploying a variety of strategies that force community members to cooperate, such as naming and shaming, cultural and social alienation, penalization in economic and political opportunities, and even reportedly threats to moral and physical integrity. Like in other migrant communities, refusing to abide by the social expectations of behavior imposed by the associations can result in several degrees of exclusion from the community (Nee and Sanders 1987; Rosales 2020).

MOBILE TRADERS AND BROKERS IN THE GLOBAL ECONOMY

Years after my first interview with the president of the Overseas Chinese Youth Federation of Brazil, I interviewed him again in 2017. I asked if he remembered our conversation about the calendar in his office containing the phrase "Great Emissaries of China: trading since times immemorial." He said he did not and asked me to retell what it was about. He then smiled and reassured me: "As long as I am in this business of importation here or somewhere else, it does not matter, I will be one of those emissaries."

Migrants' associations articulated a complex migration-trade nexus, connecting diaspora-specialized agencies and homeland governments with vendors and importers in Ciudad del Este and São Paulo. The associations implemented a form of neoliberal diaspora governmentality in areas of activity as different as supporting migrants' businesses, brokering for Chinese governments in the area of international trade promotion, fostering new migration destinations, organizing community responses to the crackdown on popular markets, and representing vendors and businesspeople in public affairs. By articulating the relations between not only one but two states and a diverse diaspora, partaking in citywide politics, and organizing the community's internal affairs, the associations fused diaspora engagement with international trade promotion and the inculcation of an entrepreneur mentality. Their work helped reposition migrants as mobile traders whose migration destination is shaped by opportunities in the popular markets and who are well-positioned brokers in today's globalized economy.

By helping to implement the diaspora policy priorities of the Taiwanese and Chinese governments, migrants' associations in Ciudad del Este and São Paulo adapted to the local contexts a long, transnational history of business and trade promotion among overseas Chinese populations. The associations mobilized and represented migrants. They also lobbied for exclusive trade rights and special schedules of importation in Ciudad del Este and rewarded businesspeople involved in the privatization of the Dawn Markets and development of indoor markets in São Paulo. In their external functions, the associations strategically changed the relations with the police and elected officials. Internally, the associations acted as the main powerholder organizing the social affairs of the community and incentivized migration to cities where the popular markets were thriving. Their support for migrant business was double-sided as it provided economic opportunities for migrants in the popular markets but, at the same time, it affected their options for jobs and limited their ability to find housing and even maintain immigration status. Although the associations enabled migrants' access to income-generating activities in the informal economy, they simultaneously facilitated the process of capture by illegality through a system of control over migrants' economic activities, siphoning off the vendors' revenue in the form of rental fees.

Homeland governments at the local and national levels instrumentalize diaspora engagement to concretize the economic benefits of the migration-trade nexus. Beyond the traditional view on the migration-development nexus that looks at economic aspects of international migration—like remittances, foreign investment, and investments in human capital—international trade and exports promotion are areas of diaspora policies on the rise that need more attention. Homelands seek to foster entrepreneurialism among the diaspora populations, uncritically assumed to be an origin country's development asset. The role of migrants' associations in Ciudad del Este and São Paulo in engaging overseas Chinese populations shows that the engagement with the diaspora fosters transnational business communities to maximize trade opportunities.

Like the president of the Overseas Chinese Youth Federation of Brazil, migrant vendors showed a sense that they too are emissaries and traders. However, their ability to move across borders and stay in the places they want to live, work, and love was imperiled. Despite all odds, they succeeded.

4 SPACES OF ILLEGALITY, TACTICS OF LEGIBILITY

Cross-Border Mobility and Translocal Emplacement

CHINESE VENDOR JOHNNY FONG ARRIVED in Ciudad del Este in 1997, in the heyday of the city's economic boom. He did not stay there, however. Rather, he was in transit to his destination, São Paulo, where his uncle had arranged a job as a stallholder for him. Having landed in South America first at Argentina's capital Buenos Aires, he was driven over a thousand miles to Ciudad del Este. After crossing the border to Paraguay, Johnny was given a forged identification document under the name of a Taiwanese migrant. His shaking hands slipped the document into his wallet, he recalled, putting all his faith in that piece of paper but hoping it was not needed. He was told to show the document to the border agent if he was stopped at the Brazilian checkpoint. Near the International Friendship Bridge uniting Paraguay and Brazil, the anxious Johnny did not understand a word the driver said while looking into the eyes of a man he would never see again. Hesitantly, he stepped out of the car to meet a Brazilian man who drove him across the border and then another thousand miles to São Paulo. The following day, Johnny was dropped off near his uncle's stall. It was no surprise that his successful border crossing was only the beginning of the undocumented migrant's struggles in a place that was entirely new to him.

Johnny quickly left São Paulo for a farm in the countryside. Being an undocumented migrant was risky enough and he did not want to take any additional chance of getting in trouble with law enforcement working in the informal economy.

Fast-forward a dozen years. In March 2009, the Federal Police of Brazil intercepted four Chinese migrants and a Paraguayan woman after entering the country from Ciudad del Este—the same migration route Johnny had taken not too long before. The Federal Police believed, as the official version goes, a transnational criminal organization was smuggling Chinese migrants from Paraguay to Brazil to keep them in modern slavery. The Paraguayan woman was arrested on the count of being a leader of the organization. The Chinese migrants, in turn, were considered "victims of human smuggling" since the Brazilian legislation about human trafficking was too narrow and did not apply. Paradoxically, however, the Federal Police simultaneously saw migrants as agents of the very illegal act of their own entry and, thus, culpable for this violation. Having received orders of departure, the migrants were left with no options to remain in Brazil lawfully.

The contrast between these two stories reveals dramatic changes in law enforcement and border crossing that have characterized overseas Chinese migration across Paraguay and Brazil in the last three decades. Undocumented migrants who work in the popular markets experience a situation of double vulnerability: illegalization of their precarious immigration status and criminalization of their economic activities. Migrant vendors cope with this double vulnerability by deploying tactics to achieve their mobility across international borders and to secure opportunities to live and work in the places where popular markets are booming. Albeit limited, their tactics are examples of their everyday agency to resist the systemic violence of border enforcement, immigration systems, and criminalization of the informal economy.

Mobility and emplacement are mutually constitutive and should be analyzed together. While the vernacular meaning of "emplacement" means the location of someone, I define emplacement as the migrant's ability to be in their place of choice, whether temporarily or permanently, after crossing international borders. Thus, emplacement does not equal the demand for citizenship and adoption of a new national identity. Rather, emplacement is the migrant's ability to be where they want to pursue the opportunities to fully flourish as human beings—or, as some migrant activists say, to "live, love, and work anywhere you please" (Fernandez and Olson 2011). My definition of emplacement interrogates the international system's deep-seated assumptions that international mobility and the right to stay are naturally derived from national citizenship, the prerogatives of which are imagined to lie in the nation-state's unquestioned sovereign power. Migrants' struggles for mobility and emplacement challenge the structural violence of what citizenship scholar Ayelet Shachar (2009) describes as the "birthright lottery," that is, the accidental fact that birth location remains a determinant of one's life chances.

By intentionally shifting focus onto emplacement, I join a growing perspective in critical migration studies to move away from theorizing migrant integration. The mainstream migration studies' emphasis on integration is problematic. The notion of integration is rooted in old ideas of assimilation presupposing migrants and their descendants must lose their culture in order to incorporate into the "host" society (Alba and Nee 2003; Alba et al. 2018; Alba et al. 2011; Waters et al. 2010). Even the term "assimilation" has been resurrected recently despite intense criticism in academia and public discourse. Citizenship, once celebrated as the panacea to all problems of political exclusion, also warrants further scrutiny. Citizenship has functioned as a sorting tool of political inclusion, failing to include certain members of a community into the polity and to ensure equality of access to rights for far too many who are treated as second-class citizens. Instead, some migrants are demanding mobility and emplacement before citizenship and integration. They are demanding "locomotion," a word whose etymology implies both place and movement (Cabrera 2010; Chu 2010; Fernandez and Olson 2011; McNevin 2011).

In this chapter, I take this book's research question about informality and illegality into a new direction. How did overseas Chinese migrants deploy tactics to enter, transit, and stay in Paraguay and Brazil in reaction to the intensification of border enforcement and the crackdown on popular markets? Overseas Chinese vendors performed different personas to make themselves legible (rather than illegible, as often assumed) to official gatekeepers and state record keepers. These migrants made pragmatic decisions about the course of action that they perceived as the most effective given the limited range of possibilities at their disposal. By closely examining these tactics, this chapter sheds light on the relation between legibility and legality, showing how the political economy of illegality intersects in the popular markets with both the modes of extraction that depend on the illegalization of the migrant labor force, on the one hand, and migrants' ingenuity in their struggles for mobility and emplacement, on the other hand.

My focus on migrants' tactics responds to the call by critical migration and border scholars to shift from "seeing like a state" to "seeing like a migrant." States make populations legible in order to govern them. In his book *Seeing Like a State*, James Scott (1998) proposes a methodological shift to analyze an issue of government from the conceptual and practical lenses that state branches and officers use to act on it. When applied to migration and border studies, this approach lends itself to a critical analysis of the "securitization" of human mobility across borders and how nativism and White nationalism exclude and racialize some groups of citizens in their own countries. In this context, securitization means the discursive shift labeling migration as an aspect of national security, moving it from the realm of ordinary politics to the less democratic and less accountable realm of emergency, over which the sovereign nation-state claims to have absolute prerogatives. Paraphrasing Scott's book title, Didier Bigo (2002) argues that, as migration is increasingly subjected to stricter control and surveillance, states make migrant populations legible in order to govern their mobility. A growing number of state bureaucracies and supranational institutions were created or reoriented to securitize migration, identifying, distinguishing, and managing human mobility considered "suspicious" or "menacing." This approach presupposes migrants want to make themselves illegible to the state, which is understood as a form of resistance.

In turn, scholars of the autonomy of migration school move away from the state gaze and toward the migrant gaze. Shifting the focus onto "seeing like a migrant" reveals that migrants purposefully and actively deploy the state grammar and lexicon to construct versions of themselves, even if pragmatically and momentarily, that have higher chances of moving across international borders and staying in the places of their choice. Those scholars argue migrant experiences are shaped temporally and spatially by transformations in the sovereignty, discipline, and governmentality that states use to exercise sociopolitical control of human mobility (Garelli and Tazzioli 2017; Mezzadra 2016; Mezzadra and Neilson 2013). Thus, "seeing like a migrant" is an approach that can be located in the spaces of individual lived experiences and collective action, and yet it necessarily accounts for the ways that human mobility and subjectivities are increasingly shaped by encounters with particular forms of state power. This approach stresses the unjust nature of immigration and border policies that are embedded in the normalized but problematic assumptions of the function and legitimacy of state sovereignty and citizenship.

This chapter analyzes the tactics migrants use in regular migration channels for obtaining and displaying travel and immigration documents in tandem with the forgery of official documents as a practice of limited, pragmatic resistance. The chapter also shows how migrants question the immigration regularization policies and reinterpret them as vindication and freedom, while navigating complex amnesty programs, asylum policies, and citizenship acquisition.

MANAGING IMPRESSIONS IN REGULAR MIGRATION CHANNELS

Migrant mobility depends, at least in part, on the ability to navigate systems of control and authorization of movement. Obtaining travel and immigration documents is a necessary preparatory step in migration trajectories, whether through regular or irregular channels. For most overseas Chinese migrants in the popular markets in Paraguay and Brazil, the eligibility for applying for immigration documents is tied to work opportunities or family reunification, and the burden to prove that one is eligible for a visa falls on the applicant. International migrants have to make themselves legible to official checkers and gatekeepers, provisionally reducing their identity to the single aspect accepted as the ground for their request for authorization to migrate, like an employment offer or reunification with authorized family members. Overseas Chinese migrants in Ciudad del Este and São Paulo perform what American anthropologist Julie Chu (2010) calls "paper selves," that is, the file version of one's self that is embodied and displayed to pass as an entitled traveler and cosmopolitan international migrant.

Mastery over the "paper self" is key for a successful migration trajectory because it helps to persuasively present oneself as a desirable, upstanding migrant in the terms set by the state. In order for a migrant to succeed in their migration trajectory, there cannot be a mismatch between the version of the self as described in the documents and the impression of a truthful self that the migrant gives to the officer. Otherwise, the migrant might jeopardize the whole migration enterprise due to a lack of convincing performance, not necessarily a lack of documents or an objective assessment of the migrant's truth claim. In *The Presentations of Self in Everyday Life*, Canadian-American sociologist Irvin Goffman (1962) established a new paradigm in social theory by arguing that one's self is formed through spontaneous but reiterative situations of everyday face-to-face behavior. As these everyday situations are multiple, one can present oneself as distinct personas in different ordinary interactions. Applying that framework to migration suggests the migrant's task when entering a foreign country is to manage the impression an immigration officer has of the persona being displayed (Scheel 2019).

The making of and convincing display of the persona described in official papers include several complex steps: gathering various records and proofs to obtain the required documents, provisionally negotiating one's identity to spotlight the biographical requirements of the particular claim of eligibility to a document, embodying the version of the self that is described in the documents being used, displaying the attributes that an officer understands as necessary to prove that the self is legitimate, and managing the impression that gatekeepers and state agents have of one's performance during specific ritual interactions of border control and interior immigration enforcement. Take the example of Chan, who migrated from a village near Qingtian to São Paulo in 2012. He did not want to repeat the journey of his cousin, who entered Brazil unlawfully from Paraguay in 1999 and remained undocumented for seven years, during which he worked two off-the-book jobs in São Paulo before he decided to return to China. Chan initially thought he could ask his cousin's former employer, a Taiwanese-Brazilian, to sponsor his visa application. But the process of sponsoring a work visa is lengthy and expensive, and employers shy away from it because the employer can be subjected to civil liability if the migrant violates the terms of the visa. Even without a visa sponsor, Chan was still eligible for work authorization in Brazil, and he decided to hire a travel agency in Qingtian to help prepare his visa application. That increased substantially the already high costs of his travel, delaying his plans as family members were strained because they had also committed to contributing sums to other relatives who migrated or were planning to leave. The assistance of a travel agency was no guarantee of success. Chan was also aware of scam travel agencies in Qingtian, which, he was told, "promise a work visa for employment in São Paulo" but deliver "paperwork for a tourist visa and flight tickets to the Iguazu Falls" near the borderlands between Paraguay and Brazil.

After long months of interactions with an intermediary at a travel agency in Qingtian, Chan collected all the necessary paperwork that would presumably make him look on paper like an indispensable "asset for an importing company" due to "unique skills of prospecting trading partners in China," he told me in an interview in 2017. The travel agent persuaded him to attend an online business course and submit the diploma to make his application look compelling. Per the agent's recommendation, Chan also obtained letters from former employers emphasizing his ability to process paperwork related to international cargo and customs clearance. He tried to memorize this information—all of which was true but not the most decisive aspects of his educational and professional careers in his own assessment—to talk about it confidently in the visa interview. Chan was nervous during the interview. He thought his visa would be denied after he could not successfully explain how to apply the skills he learned in the online business course to his career in Brazil. The anxious Chan sighed in relief when he received the visa approval notice.

Obtaining the visa was only one step in a long migration journey. Chan panicked about not being able to reproduce the visa application information when he landed in São Paulo. At the port of entry, the officer prescreened Chan's visa and sent him to a more detailed interview with an immigration supervisor. Chan had trouble understanding the interview questions in Portuguese and needed the assistance of an interpreter. The interviewer went over a long questionnaire that felt like an inquisition. Having found no evidence that Chan's intention to migrate was illegitimate nor that his documents had been altered or forged as new guidelines demanded immigration officers to verify, the interviewer insistently questioned why Chan was still nervous, which can be interpreted as a strategy of migration deterrence. Chan was traumatized by this experience, and he was paralyzed every time he reentered Brazil.

Chan's case speaks directly against the assumption shared by Brazilian media and ordinary people that the Chinese migrants in the popular markets are all undocumented. Work visa options, though limited, are available for migrants like Chan who rely on services provided by a growing migration industry that matches applicants with sponsors or that prepare applications for those lacking a sponsor. By establishing an employment relationship or demonstrating valuable professional skills, migrants who hold a work visa make themselves legible within the parameters of legality to achieve mobility and emplacement. Yet, their legibility does not yield to greater confidence in making themselves more visible in public life outside of work, especially because the ritual interactions with state officers are rather tense moments that migrants want to get past. Furthermore, because work visa holders have to display a persona that is necessarily tied to a career opportunity, their embodiment and performance of the paper self has an ambiguous effect on their selfhood: on the one hand, their multifaceted identity is pragmatically reduced to that work opportunity they claim to be uniquely suited to take on, and, on the other hand, their identity as both a migrant and a worker reinforces their subjectivity as a mobile, cosmopolitan entrepreneur whose success in migration and business is indissociable from one another.

Chan's experience is indicative of the variety of immigration statuses of those who work in popular markets. Brazil's official numbers around Chinese migration have limitations in explaining the reality of vendors in the popular markets. These figures exclude undocumented migrants, naturalized citizens, and the Brazilian-born offspring who work in the informal economy. They also include investors and workers in other industries, who are a growing group of migrants in Brazil. Still, some figures are worth mentioning. Overall, the majority of Chinese visa holders in most years during the last decade are in the category of "commerce and related occupations," differing from the majority agriculture-related occupations among the pool of all migrants (Sprandel et al. 2013). Broadly speaking, the participation of Chinese migrants in the formal workforce was steadily high between 2013 and 2023, averaging more than three thousand individuals yearly and featured on the top 12 migrant group chart. Family migration and family reunification is evidenced by the fact that China was among the top four countries of birth of migrant children and adolescents eighteen years old and younger during the same period (Cavalcanti et al. 2023).

Other figures, while similarly insufficient to capture the nuances of Chinese migration in the popular markets, speak to the absolute and relative growth in work visas as well as tourist visas for Chinese, arguably used for admission to the country with the intention of overstaying the visa period. According to data from Brazil's Ministry of Labor and the Brazilian Council of Immigration, Chinese were the largest number of work authorizations (which is a requirement to apply for a work visa in Brazil) made by citizens of developing countries from 1993 to 2008 (International Organization for Migration 2010). Chinese ranked similarly high between 2011 and 2016, and totaled 11,992 additional work permits in this time period, predominantly in the category "professionals without an employment contract" (Quintino and Tonhati 2017). With 4,677 visas received in 2021, Chinese migrants consistently ranked third in the number of Brazilian visas granted (73.2% of those visas fell in the category "visit" and 22.4% were "work" visas). Chinese individuals rose to second in recipients of Brazilian visas in 2022 with 8,818 visas, and to the top of the chart in the first nine months of 2023 with 29,335 visas granted in that period, with a consistent majority of men across those years (Cavalcanti et al. 2023). Although there are specific challenges in estimating the number of Chinese migrants in São Paulo popular markets who hold work visas, my ethnographic observation corroborates the tendencies above.

It's not Brazil, but wealthier Western countries that are the preferred destinations of migrants. Many interviewees stated that migration is an investment with returns to the whole family, which includes remittances, family reunification visas, and transmission of citizenship to the next generations. The decision to migrate to Paraguay and Brazil is the result of several factors, among which two are particularly important: first, the migrant's ineligibility for, or inability to afford, migration to preferred destinations in North America, Europe, or Oceania; and second, the social and migration networks that connect would-be-migrants with income opportunities in the popular markets. In contrast to the growing barriers of migration to wealthier countries, poor and rural migrants from Zhejiang or Fujian had a greater opportunity to migrate to Brazil rather than the United States, Canada, or Australia (Stenberg 2012). Chan makes sense of his decision to migrate to São Paulo in terms of intergenerational investment in the long run. In his words, he articulates his hopes that migration to Brazil will afford his family and himself opportunities to travel or move internationally in the future: "I want to retire and live in the U.S., so I'll send my kid to college there, where quality of life and opportunities are better than here. I can't afford it now, but I hope I will have the means to do that in the future."

Likewise, Paraguay is not the most obvious choice for overseas Chinese migrants. However, Taiwanese migrants had incentives to migrate to Ciudad del Este because of the economic opportunities of commerce with Brazil and favorable immigration policies. The Taiwanese government lobbied the Paraguayan government to adopt a more flexible visa policy for Taiwanese migrants in exchange for public and private investments. For instance, Taiwanese migrant Hsu, who migrated to Ciudad del Este in 1979 at the age of eight, told me in an interview in 2015 that although his extended family included shopkeepers in São Paulo, his parents decided to migrate to Ciudad del Este because "getting the Paraguayan visa was easier than any other country in the world."

In turn, latecomer Chinese migrants have difficulties obtaining a Paraguayan visa. Instead, they obtain Brazilian visas and live in Foz do Iguaçu, commuting to work across borders in Ciudad del Este. The case of Sandra is exemplary: a Chinese migrant, she left her hometown Beijing for Brazil in 1996 at the age of twenty-four and worked as a stallholder in Ciudad del Este. She said in an interview in 2015 that commuting internationally everyday was troublesome, but as a Chinese person, it was hard to obtain a visa in Paraguay.

The stories of Chan, Hsu, and Sandra show that migration through regular channels involves the construction of a paper self. However, the systemic constraints significantly limit the options for overseas Chinese migrants, a great number of whom experience a prolonged period with precarious immigration status. In response, many of those migrants forge a paper self as a tactic for mobility and emplacement.

FORGED SELVES

Obtaining official and valid immigration papers is a privilege that not all overseas Chinese migrants have in Paraguay and Brazil. Whether at the moment of entry into the country or at some point during their presence in Paraguay and Brazil, many commit violations of the law. Yet, even unlawful border crossers and overstayers who enter with a valid visa still need to show their official and valid documentation at various steps of their migration trajectory. The only option left for migrants who do not have the resources and abilities to obtain official documentation is to use forged documents, constructed narratives, and embodied knowledge to manage the impression an officer has of the presentation of that fabricated self (Scheel 2019).

Over the Chinese vendors in Paraguay and Brazil looms large a stigmatizing narrative of document forgery. But that narrative casts a shadow on the perspective that imposture in the context of structural violence and global inequalities can be a search for personhood that was objectively denied to marginalized populations (Comaroff and Comaroff 2016). Some Chinese migrants who would otherwise be denied entry into their country of intended residence go on a longer, more complex travel itinerary, using forged documents on the way. A common route into Brazil includes flying to Paraguay and using Paraguayan documents to cross the border. "Can you imagine I was given a Taiwanese person's ID? I mean I don't even know if this person exists or if everything is made up," said Chinese migrant Zhou in an interview he gave me in 2015. Like Johnny, Zhou carried a forged document he could show if stopped by a highway patrol in Brazil. In such a case, the match of a document's visual and written information with the corresponding attributes of its bearer is the ultimate sign of legitimacy, though a thorough inspection may also include checks against other official datasets, especially biometrics, to further assess one's claim over a self. Migrants have to be unequivocally identified as the person to whom the document belongs.

Others emphasized how heightened enforcement made forgery more expensive and riskier. Comparing his trajectory with other undocumented Chinese vendors, Fujianese migrant Lin said this in an interview he gave me in São Paulo in 2015: "I don't think any cop would believe this driver's license if I got stopped. My friend's cousin, years after me, made his way up here along the same highway I did. He had a driver's license that looks more credible than the one I had. But the highway cops didn't believe him. He was sent back to China and lost money and face." In cases like this, the material properties of the document are called on to index its legitimacy: its appearance, the type of paper of which it is made, and unfalsifiable watermarks or stamps. The suspicion over illegality arises directly from the perceived illegitimacy of the document whose material itself is dubious.

On the other end of the forgery spectrum are the valid documents of a unique and proper bearer that are nonetheless obtained illegally. Chinese migrants say that bribed state authorities turn a blind eye to the fact that they do not meet eligibility criteria, and illegally issue official and valid documents. For instance, I was shown a driver's license that Jing Jing, an undocumented migrant from Zhejiang, obtained without having ever gone to driving school in São Paulo. She said in an interview in 2016 that "it is valid, not fake, though of course I don't have a Brazilian document or anything like that. If I wanted to go the Department of Vehicles to get a driver's license, I would not be able to apply." After a short pause, she went on to say "actually, this is my opinion: there is something fake, and it is not my driver's license, so what is fake is the bureaucracy that says 'you qualify, you don't.'" By emphasizing the legitimacy of the official document obtained through an officer's usurpation of the authority invested by the state's sovereign power, Jing Jing calls into question the taken-for-granted assumption that proper documentation equates with legality. Both the materiality of the document and the unfalsifiable correspondence to its bearer attest to the legitimacy of the document precisely because it does not show any trace of the illegal means by which it was obtained. Thus, it produces the same effects of legibility and acceptance that all official and properly issued documentation does.

Forgery of official documents is simultaneously a tactic for rendering a true self illegible to the state and a way to inhabit another self that is either a fabricated version of one's self or a legitimate version of someone else. Some undocumented migrants rely on fake documents in parts of their international travel and certain domains of their everyday lives in Brazil and Paraguay such as renting apartments, issuing receipts for commercial activities, or opening a bank account. For them, legibility lies in the credible materiality of the documentation, whose officialness and legitimacy will have to stand up under scrutiny.

In addition to embodiment of a paper self and the materiality of a document, the legitimacy of a migrant's claim lies in the credibility of the very relationship attested by certain documents. In the case of overseas Chinese migrants in Paraguay and Brazil, this is particularly true in the ever-present suspicion of marriages of convenience and birth certificate forgery. Examples of these quickly made headlines with dramatic photos of individuals being arrested, but the narrative constructed around this issue focuses on the attributed criminal behavior, leaving no room for a discussion of global economic or mobility inequalities that drive this behavior. It normalizes the idea that immigration systems are needed and perhaps even fair because they derive from the state's unquestionable sovereign power to regulate society and "protect" the nation, whatever this is said to mean. This view naturalizes the systemic violence of the birthright lottery. Stories about marriages of convenience and birth certificate forgery are overrepresented in the media, being far more common than the accounts of hardships and success of migrants or sensible discussions of immigration reform and global inequalities. Those two types of forgery have different consequences for migrants. Unlike marriages of convenience, in which only one migrant can benefit directly from the visa sponsorship of an eligible partner, forged birth certificates can extend the visa eligibility to migrant couples who can pass as parents of a Paraguayan- or Brazilian-born child. Both in the cases of marriages of convenience and forged birth certificates, the documents are valid, but the relationship declared in the certificate is fabricated; that is, an individual uses the state's acceptable grammar of validation to fabricate a self that is entitled to the right to stay.

Undoubtedly illegal and risky, forgery of official documents can be an autonomous praxis of liberation in a world of global inequalities, particularly economic inequalities that drive migration and inequalities in the freedom of international travel (Keshavarz 2018; Khosravi 2010; Zhang, Sanchez, and Achilli 2018). However, it also generates new relations of exploitation based on the asymmetry between migrants and networks of paper forgers. For obvious reasons, the industry around irregular migration operates at the margins of the law, which creates power relations between those in need of forged documents and those who have the (illegal) means of providing them (Gammeltoft-Hansen and Sorensen 2013; Morris 2017). In particular, many undocumented Chinese migrants are in a vulnerable situation because their precarious immigration status compounds with the control that employers, stall sublessors, and imports distributors exercise over them.

From the undocumented Chinese migrants' perspective, particularly stallholders and street vendors, their precarious immigration status creates fears and directly affects their autonomy over the means of work. Even their housing arrangements are tied to their employer. As Jing Jing said, "Some people got used to it, but every day I fear for my future, and I cannot speak out because if my boss retaliates against me, I lose my job and my income." Many undocumented vendors blame the migrants' associations for exercising control over their lives and reproducing a form of oppression that, though rooted in their condition as undocumented, affects their entire livelihood. The internalization of that fear shapes the migrant's self, who has difficulties living up to the expectation they once had of a better life that comes with the income opportunities of the popular markets. Rather, they feel that they are on the verge of entering a cycle in which their labor does not pay the meager income they get, and yet they cannot simply quit the migration plan and return to China because they have accrued migration debts they have to repay.

By deploying various tactics such as forgery of documents and imposture, undocumented Chinese migrants present a persona that is legible to state gatekeepers. They revert the presumed illegality looming large over them by using illegal means to obtain or display a forged paper self that passes as legal. In so doing, they advance both a practical critique of the state's bordering techniques and a material form of dissent that exposes the inequalities in global mobility and unjust immigration policies enacted by the ingrained power of sovereign states. However, they are not immune to forms of exploitation, economic and otherwise, as they are the weakest link in a chain of illegalities that afford them opportunities to work while also enabling the capture of the wealth they generate.

AGAINST THE STATE GAZE: BORDER ENFORCEMENT INTERSECTS WITH THE POPULAR MARKETS

The state's perspective on undocumented Chinese vendors in the informal economy across Paraguay and Brazil is informed by a binary view typical of a legal perspective, drawing a clear line between lawful immigration status and illegal migration. That view is both reductionist and contradictory. It purports migrants have agency over violations they are said to commit while simultaneously labeling them victims of human trafficking. The clearest example is Operation Da Shan, a border enforcement operation which began in 2008 to dismantle what the Federal Police of Brazil said was "a stable and permanent criminal organization, which was infiltrated in various states of Brazil and abroad to bring Chinese people from Fujian to the city of São Paulo" (Ministério Público Federal 2009b). Operation Da Shan's largest action was on May 22, 2009, when the Federal Police raided two apartment buildings near 25 de Março Street and took more than ninety Chinese migrants to the Federal Police station to check their immigration status. The police also arrested a Fujianese migrant accused of being the leader of the criminal organization, as well as thirteen Brazilians near the border with Bolivia, suspects in human smuggling and forgery.

The Federal Police traced two long and complex routes used to facilitate the entry of Chinese individuals into Brazil. From Fuzhou, the capital city of the Fujian Province, Chinese migrants entered Brazil through the border between Ciudad del Este and Foz do Iguaçu. However, the arrest of a Paraguayan woman accused of smuggling four Fujianese migrants in 2009 caused a change in the route used by the group. In the new route, migrants took a commercial flight from Pudong Airport in Shanghai to Guayaquil in Ecuador, via Amsterdam. They held Ecuadorian investor visas, travel documentation that was easier to obtain thanks to an agreement signed between China and Ecuador in 2007. From Guayaquil, they went to Peru by bus, and finally to Bolivia, where they hid for a few days preparing to cross the border on foot into the Brazilian Amazon. From the country's borderland forest, migrants took six-hour flights or were driven some two thousand miles to São Paulo. While more effective, the strategy of transiting through multiple countries both lawfully and unlawfully before reaching an intended destination increases the human and monetary costs of smuggling on different continents—migrants meanwhile face increased xenophobia under the disguise of ostensibly benevolent suspicion of human trafficking (Chu 2010, Pieke 2007; Pieke et al. 2004; Thunø 2007).

The Brazilian legislation at the time defined "human trafficking" in narrow terms that did not apply to the situation of those Chinese individuals. The crime of trafficking was defined as human trafficking with the purpose of forcing the victim to become a sex worker. A 2016 bill adapted the Brazilian legislation to the 2000 Protocol to Prevent, Suppress and Punish Trafficking in Persons, Especially Women and Children, a protocol to the United Nations Convention against Transnational Organized Crime, also known as the Palermo Protocol. The 2016 bill makes a clear distinction between human smuggling and human trafficking, the definition of which includes inhumane labor conditions characterizing modern-day slavery. Before 2016, perpetrators of crimes in Brazil that are considered human trafficking under the Palermo Protocol were charged with human smuggling. However, the enforcement of human smuggling in lieu of human trafficking accentuated the criminalization of unlawful entry and of services for border crossers, which is a common resort for many undocumented migrants, victimizing them and presupposing they lack agency entirely.

The Federal Police used tapped phone calls as evidence suggesting the unlawful entry of Fujianese individuals into the Brazilian Amazon, but many questioned whether the police collected unequivocal evidence of human trafficking. Additional evidence collected on site includes business cards of hotels in Ecuador found in raids on the apartment of the Fujianese migrant accused of trafficking, where two orders of departure addressed to Chinese individuals were also found. Citing information obtained through a breach of bank and tax confidentiality of the Fujianese migrant, the Public Prosecutor's Office of Brazil argued the accused trafficker's reported income was incompatible with the standard of life he displayed, raising suspicion of the source of nonreported income (Ministério Público Federal 2009a). The explanation for this incompatibility was, according to the prosecutors, the illicit income he supposedly earned through the distribution of counterfeits, which would explain, that version goes on, the primary occupation of most Chinese migrants taking that route to São Paulo.

Operation Da Shan was not just an anti-trafficking operation, but a crackdown on counterfeits. The title of operation Da Shan suggests the Federal Police believed early on that the allegation of smuggling of Chinese individuals was intrinsically related to the distribution of counterfeits and smuggled imports. Da Shan (*dàshān*) translates to "great mountain," which the Federal Police said was a reference to the province of Fujian, "famous for having some of the world's largest counterfeit factories . . . some of them hidden inside mountains" (Ministério Público Federal 2009b). After all, the focus of Operation Da Shan was counterfeits, not trafficking. The Federal Police and prosecutors took unlawful border crossing as human trafficking (charging the accused with smuggling as it was the category applicable given the legislation at the time), which, in turn, was assumed to be the reason vendors were forced to work in the popular markets selling imports.

Operation Da Shan had a simplistic view of Chinese migrants' attributed victimhood and symbolic capital. In the beginning of Operation Da Shan, Brazil's Federal Highway Police concluded that "these migrants lacked education, didn't speak Portuguese, and had almost no luggage or money, therefore, they would be subjected to low-paid and menial jobs when they arrive in São Paulo" (G1 2008). The Chinese migrants were at once seen as autonomous agents of illegal conduct—for which they were arrested, fined, and received orders of departure—and, at the same time, vulnerable victims of a transnational crime that would keep them in bondage in São Paulo. Similarly, the Federal Police superintendent, who coordinated the investigations from his office on the borderlands, made assumptions about the economic activities of Chinese vendors in São Paulo, saying that "the Chinese migrants have various occupations related to commerce in São Paulo, but there is an agreement between them to not speak about it to the police" (*O Estado de S. Paulo* 2009). The superintendent linked the Chinese workers' putative secrecy about their commercial activities, and its presumed illicitness, to paper forgery and human smuggling, concluding that the irregular entry of Chinese migrants constituted modern-day slavery. Operation Da Shan shows that the mobility and emplacement of Chinese migrants is limited by the Brazilian state's view of border enforcement. However, Operation Da Shan apparently did not conclusively substantiate its claim that the motivation for the presumed bondage of Chinese migrants was the selling of counterfeits and smuggled goods in the popular markets.

Operation Da Shan is not the only one that focuses on the human smuggling of Chinese migrants into Brazil, but it makes evident the spurious association between human trafficking and the selling of counterfeits. In contrast, Operation Yulin, which started in 2013, is not focused on border enforcement nor does it target the popular markets, but is illustrative of an approach that seeks to protect victims and combat abusive behavior of traffickers. Operation Yulin's mandate focuses on the combat of modern-day slavery of Chinese individuals in Chinese-operated restaurants in Rio de Janeiro. Because the first round of investigations found that dog meat was being used in the restaurants, the operation was named after the city of Yulin in China that is famous for the summer solstice Dog Meat Festival. Unlike Operation Da Shan, which was carried out exclusively by the Federal Police and was focused on Fujianese migrants' unlawful entry, Operation Yulin approaches Chinese individuals from the perspective of human rights protection, bringing together a task force composed of members of the Ministry of Labor and Employment, the Brazilian Social Security Institute, the Consumer Protection Foundation of Rio de Janeiro, and the Brazilian Health Regulatory Agency, in addition to the Federal Police. Operation Da Shan had a major impact on Chinese individuals' ability to move across Brazilian borders and into the countryside. The Federal Police used Operation Da Shan as the template for other border enforcement operations, such as Operation Sentinel, the largest ever done, which investigated Chinese distributors in São Paulo accused of smuggling Chinese migrants in and out of Brazil.

My critical view of anti-trafficking neither sides with trafficking nor does it assume a form of a naïve relativism that is complicit with harmful, criminal behavior against migrants. Rather, it problematizes the implicit motivations and unintended consequences of anti-trafficking by refusing a simplistic perspective that reproduces the binarism of legality. It upends the widespread logic of harm, and instead it interrogates the forces that have detrimental consequences to migrants despite stated goals of protecting victims of violations of restrictive, if not unjust, laws. As anti-trafficking responds to domestic and international political agendas, it reproduces notions of victimhood, vulnerability, and protection that serve those agendas and are infused with ideas of morality and cultural values. It hardly ever addresses the structural problems such as domestic and global inequalities, restrictions to international mobility, or stricter immigration systems that make people choose to migrate through illegal channels (Berman 2003; Ceccagno 2015 and 2017; Lindquist 2013). Anti-trafficking follows a dichotomous view presupposing a clear line between legal and illegal, making prevention and containment of "illegal movements" an end goal in itself and leaving no room for questioning when, how, and why human mobility is illegalized (McNevin et al. 2016, 235). However, legality does not have natural, interest-free, and nonarbitrary qualities. In the case of Brazil, Operation Da Shan did not adequately address structural problems of human mobility, nor did it consider the best interests of Chinese migrants to discern the blurred lines between human trafficking and the facilitation of unlawful entry (Dias and Sprandel 2010; Zhang et al. 2018). The crackdown on human trafficking was not able to simultaneously protect those considered victims and guarantee the conditions to remain in Brazil if they wanted, but it did facilitate the clamp down on irregular border crossings.

AMNESTY AND FREEDOM

The Chinese migrants' understanding of legibility and illegality has changed through time. While many Chinese migrants were undocumented, especially among the newly arrived, the number of those who are lawfully in São Paulo has grown. A major factor in this was Brazil's regularization programs in 1981, 1988, 1998, and 2009, which together had nearly 147,000 applicants who had entered the country illegally or accrued unlawful presence. Chinese were either the first or second largest number of applicants in each regulation program, totaling nearly 25,000. Beneficiaries who proved to be in violation of their immigration status were granted temporary visas that converted into permanent visas after a certain period of time (typically two years), allowing for family members to apply for reunification visas and eventually making them eligible for naturalization (Milesi 2011; Xavier, 2010).

Take the example of the couple Johnny Fong and Ming. Johnny is originally from Zhejiang Province's major city of Wen Zhou and was smuggled into Brazil from Ciudad del Este in 1997, while Ming overstayed her tourist visa after leaving the Min Nan region in Fujian Province for São Paulo in

1994. Ming, who ignored an order of departure she received during a raid on her workplace in 1996, has bitter memories of her experiences as an undocumented migrant in São Paulo. Johnny confided to me that "she could not sleep at night after a close friend of hers was taken to the Federal Police and received an order of departure. She was constantly afraid of being sent back to China like her friend was." In the second half of the 1990s, raids tackling the smuggling of imported goods were frequent in the popular markets in São Paulo. Though these were not immigration raids, checks on immigration status intensified to further deter illegal commerce. Ironically, she later used the same departure order to prove (unlawful) residence as part of the evidentiary documentation she submitted with her status regularization application in 1998. Ming's application was approved, eventually granting her the right to stay and a path to citizenship. As a spouse, Johnny, too, became eligible for a visa and, later, citizenship, based on their marital status. By making the unlawful lawful, immigration regularization policies bring individuals from the farthest margins of citizenship to its possible center (Bosniak 2013).

However, many migrants did not want to or could not apply for regularization. Reasons for not applying included lack of trust in the institutions, fear of retaliation, lack of knowledge of how to properly fill out applications, application fees, excessive required documentation, and a short application period. For instance, application requirements included obtaining criminal records from their country of citizenship, which is a complex, expensive, and long bureaucratic process that was not feasible in the application time window. Migrants, activists, advocacy groups, and charity organizations fought to end this criminal record requirement, which eventually happened after the 1998 policy was launched. Additionally, migrants did not receive accurate and actionable information about regularization programs or policies, and a lack of knowledge of the eligibility criteria prevented many undocumented migrants from applying. Brazil's most recent immigration reform bill of 2017 included a new regularization program, which was approved by Congress but revoked by President Michel Temer.[1] Unlike previous legislation, this migration bill no longer requires that a foreigner seeking to regularize their immigration status leave the country and apply for a new visa abroad. None of the Chinese migrants I interviewed in between 2017 and 2022 knew that under this bill they were eligible to regularize their immigration situation upon obtaining formal employment in Brazil.

As in other countries, the regularization of undocumented migrants is popularly known in Brazil as amnesty. As American legal scholar Linda Bosniak (2013) points out, advocates and critics vigorously debate whether amnesty is fair and just to those in violation of immigration status and border enforcement, as well as to those who migrate lawfully and to residents of the country, especially citizens. Many critics argue that there must be no clemency for lawbreakers, and that it would encourage more irregular migration. From the perspective of the state, as well as of some regularization advocates, amnesty is framed as a pardoning of past violations, which both accepts the law's justness and recognizes migrants' guilt.

Yet, some Chinese migrants articulate the regularization in rather different terms, contending they had been victims of an unjust immigration system. In an interview she gave me in 2017, Ming stressed that "we are not criminals, we did not commit any crime. I was considered 'illegal.' OK. Then nothing has changed in my particular situation and yet I was overnight no longer 'illegal.' So why was I called illegal before? The law needs to change, we shouldn't need to have amnesties anymore, we should have a legislation that respects people's rights and dignity." By emphasizing the arbitrary nature of legality and the need for the law to adjust to social realities and new values, Ming challenges the common notion that amnesty is a settlement based on beneficence.

Amnesty is typically associated with pardoning (to forgive the violations), and it can also imply erasure (to achieve feasibility when records of violations are widespread and unmanageable). However, a critical approach suggests amnesty is vindication. This understanding of amnesty aims to achieve migrants' freedom by accomplishing a triple effect of protecting the purported transgressors, acknowledging that the violated rule or the applicable penalty is not justifiable, and replacing the accountability calculation "pursuant to which the original offender turns out to have behaved in a way that now appears comprehensible, excusable and, perhaps, justifiable" (Bosniak 2013, 349).

Like Ming's argument, this way of conceiving of—and making political claims about—amnesty inverts the notion of accountability by positing the state as the perpetrator of injustices committed against undocumented migrants. Ming's interrogation of migration regularization shows discontent with immigration policies in Brazil. She went on to ask, "Why did the Brazilian authorities make me go through it all? It is the immigration system that is broken. While this persists, more people will be illegal. We did nothing wrong. You know, before I just accepted that violating immigration law was wrong but necessary, but now I think I did nothing wrong. The government did."

While many undocumented migrants use visibility as a tactic to demand rights and change the narrative about migration, others live in fear and do not want to come out. What the regularization policies do by using legality as a tool to remove prior administrative violations of immigration status is to make a behavior that was illegal no longer be. In doing so, it allows for migrants to make themselves legible to the state in order to be counted in and eligible for the policy. Because migrants have the burden to prove prior violation of immigration status, they necessarily have to revisit the past behavior with a new lens, and unearth a track record of illegality that most wanted or needed to hide before, when remaining illegible was used as a tactic for emplacement.

Ming's account shows the limits of a strict system of regular migration in terms of exclusion of those who are not able to collect, embody, and display the properly accepted proofs of being an entitled subject. It challenges the assumptions and biases about who can enjoy freedom of international mobility and residence abroad in an international system still based on state sovereignty and national citizenship.

SEEKING REFUGE

Regular migration is more desired because it tends to be safer and yield greater degrees of autonomy in international travels, border crossings, and residence abroad. However, it is not available to many, causing them to resort to unlawful entry or violation of immigration status. Similarly, another legal option that is not available to many and requires a narrower understanding of one's self is applying for refugee status protection.

When I first met Yu in 2017 in the stall where he worked as a clerk in São Paulo, he proudly showed me his employment record book. In Brazil, the employment record book is a registration document which has records of each formal employment one has had, and it is a symbol of stable employment and social security benefits. Most informal economy workers do not have formal employment. However, increasingly more stallholders in the popular markets in São Paulo ensure their employees are formally registered on the books to avoid legal complications. Given the intensified crackdown on counterfeits and increased government enforcement in the workplace, stallholders can no longer afford the risk of being fined or having the business shut down. In over a decade of fieldwork, I encountered many Chinese migrants, particularly stallholders, who showed me their employment record books. However, undocumented newcomers have difficulties obtaining the documentation needed to receive an employment record book and be formally employed.

Yu's employment record book was rather a novelty for many of his Chinese newcomer friends. Having just arrived in Brazil, he submitted a refugee status application.[2] While the refugee application is pending, applicants can access social services such as the free public health or education systems. Further, applicants can obtain an employment record book, seek employment, and remain lawful in the country while the application is pending. They can also apply for a Natural Persons Register, an identification document required for opening bank accounts and establishing a business. Neither illegal entry nor unlawful presence makes an individual ineligible to apply for refugee status. Forgery of official documents does not make an applicant ineligible either, though it may initiate criminal proceedings against the applicant in a separate court trial.

Like Yu, many other Chinese migrants applied recently for refugee status in Brazil. A spike in the number of Chinese asylum seekers in Brazil in 2017 surprised practitioners and human rights advocates. From 2017 to 2023, Chinese were among the top five nationalities of applicants, with over 6,500 applications in that period, a number that can be higher because over 1,000 Chinese-born applicants and Chinese nationals are not included (Secretaria Nacional de Justiça 2018; DataMigra BI n.d.). Yu thinks of himself as someone who "could be described as a refugee" because "it is impossible to live in China . . . I don't have rights in the city, and I don't have any relationship with someone that could help me succeed there." In the interview he gave me in 2017, Yu said that he feared he would fail if put to a test: he did not believe he was able to memorize the version of the paper self that is described in the application completed with the assistance of a hired attorney. He was not entirely cognizant of what constitutes grounds for refugee status, and he struggled to present himself convincingly as someone who is entitled to it.

Meanwhile, according to official data from the Brazilian government, only seventeen Chinese asylum seekers were granted asylum between 2017 and 2023, despite the fact that Chinese applicants were among the top six nationalities with the largest number of cases adjudicated from 2021 to 2023 (DataMigra BI n.d.). Hysteria about bogus Chinese refugees was widespread, citing the idea that "real refugees" are not found in China, but in poorer countries with an authoritarian government. However, in 2022 for example, only one Chinese asylum seeker was granted asylum in Brazil while three German asylum seekers were granted asylum that same year—and Germany is not considered a country that produces refugees. With a large number of applicants and low success rates, favorable adjudication of Chinese asylum seekers is not only low in absolute numbers but also abysmal when compared to the spike in applications in the late 2010s and early 2020s.

During the longer period between 1985 and 2022, only fifty-five applications of Chinese individuals were adjudicated fully on their merits. Out of these, a meager twenty-three were granted status (one for persecution based on political opinion, six for religious persecution, and ten for membership to a particular social group, with the rest of cases lacking information). Of the rejected cases, twenty-nine were rejected because eligibility was denied and one case because the extension request was denied. The average processing time for those fifty-five cases was 3.2 years. Many more applications of Chinese seeking asylum—4,287 to be exact—expired or were archived without merit analysis.

The conundrum between Yu's understanding that he could be described as a refugee and his lack of knowledge of the refugee status eligibility criteria shows that asylum has multiple understandings in everyday life, beyond the legal terms that define it. Despite the sharp line in the legal definition of asylum, migrants have flexible understandings of the social categories of migration in Brazil. This coincides with many authors' refusal to approach migration and refugee movements as separate fields of research. Rather, they argue the category of refugee strategically essentializes migrants who are making claims to their right to presence on the grounds of this administrative category (De Genova et al. 2018; Hamlin 2021; Machado 2020).

Refugee applicants have to specifically demonstrate that they qualify for status of protection exclusively granted to individuals with a credible fear of persecution on narrowly defined grounds of admissibility. The legitimization of the status is the result of a thorough and long assessment of the case, in which the applicant must adhere to strict stipulations of how to make themselves legible in terms of both the content and the language, which must remain infallible throughout (Bruce-Jones 2015; Razack 1995; Ticktin 2016). This is different from the legitimacy of immigration documentation, which is supposedly indexed by the material properties of the document or by calling in the bearer of the document to prove that they are indeed the person described in the document.

The decision to apply for refugee status is one that many people do not take lightly, especially in countries where the consequences of an application's rejection are more severe, like the United States. Also, it is a very expensive last resort, due to the high cost of lawyers, and has low chances of approval (Chu 2010). In Brazil, refugee status determination does not include a court hearing, and it is conducted entirely by the National Committee for Refugees. Rejected applicants can resort to public defenders to obtain information about the legal options available, or make the difficult decision to stay irregularly.

The wait time is so long that applicants start rebuilding their lives while the application is pending. The system is clogged, with a wait time of at least two years for a decision on an applicant's status. Brazil's understaffed National Committee for Refugees, responsible for assessing each individual case, saw a gradual increase in the number of applicants particularly with the dramatic influx in recent years of Haitians and Venezuelans. Between 2011 and 2017, Brazil received 126,102 refugee applications, and 84,162 were still pending by the end of 2017. While the refugee application is pending, spatial mobility within Brazil is absolute but international mobility is limited. Applicants can only reenter the country one time with prior authorization and the period abroad must not exceed ninety days. This is frustrating for many who want to be able to visit their loved ones and have additional reasons for wanting to access international mobility. It is particularly complicated for applicants and refugees to travel to their country of citizenship because that undermines their case of credible fear of persecution.

Meanwhile, Chinese applicants may start a family in Brazil, particularly if they have a child or marry someone who is a citizen or a visa holder, increasing their chances of regularizing their immigration status. Chinese migrants with whom I interacted viewed marriage and parenting as signs of social achievement and status complementing economic success as indicators of accomplishment in migration. While Yu's application was pending, he became the father of a baby born in Brazil to a Chinese migrant mother. Their baby is eligible to obtain birthright citizenship, which makes Yu and his wife eligible to regularize their immigration status and remain in Brazil regardless of the result of his asylum application. In Brazil, family reunification is a principle that supersedes unlawful entry and violations of immigration status, impeding the removal of parents of Brazilian citizens. However, the decision to acquire Brazilian citizenship is not an easy one, whether it is the case of the Brazilian-born child's birthright citizenship or the naturalization of an eligible Chinese migrant, because it implies abdicating Chinese citizenship.

NAVIGATING CITIZENSHIP STATUS

Johnny and Ming faced dilemmas when they learned that they were eligible to become naturalized Brazilians. Brazil has pathways to citizenship for eligible visa holders, including those who regularized their immigration situation in the regularization programs like Johnny and Ming. Migrants must meet a four-year residency requirement, which can be shortened if the applicant has a Brazilian spouse or child, or if the applicant has significant realty. However, one of the most difficult challenges that eligible Chinese visa holders face for naturalization, according to various interviewees, is the Portuguese language test. In the face of such challenges—lawful residency, financial resources, and language skills—many cannot apply for naturalization. Additionally, Chinese migrants who are permanent visa holders told me they see little incentive to become Brazilian citizens because visa holders enjoy nearly the same social rights as Brazilian citizens. However, the lack of citizenship status prevents one from exercising some political rights, notably voting, running for office, and holding civil service positions.

While the typical discourse about naturalization revolves around the trope that migrants want to benefit from welfare, for many Chinese migrants in Paraguay and Brazil, obtaining Paraguayan or Brazilian citizenship, if eligible, is a pragmatic decision about freedom of mobility as migrants. They want to increase their rights to presence in those countries and international mobility, showing that some undocumented migrants are demanding mobility before citizenship (Fernandez and Olson 2011). Johnny and Ming jokingly said that a "wedding anniversary celebration is only a real celebration if you are traveling to Paris free of visa." In a more sober tone, Johnny said that "for someone who had so many difficulties as an undocumented migrant, it feels reassuring to be able to travel internationally with less restrictions." Like them, others considered the higher level of international mobility when applying for naturalization in Paraguay and Brazil. Referring to the value of citizenship as indexed by the position of a passport in a ranking of freedom of international travel based on the number of countries a passport holder can travel free of visa, Yu made an allegory that is illustrative: "The ultimate test is to ask yourself which passport is easier to go to Disney with: the Brazilian or the Chinese? The answer tells you which is best. This is pure hierarchy between countries."

According to the data from the Federal Police of Brazil's National System of Enrollment and Records of Foreigners I obtained through freedom of information requests, 4,742 Chinese individuals were granted Brazilian citizenship between 1987 and 2015. This number is underestimated because it only includes those who had their alien identification number cancelled because of naturalization, excluding others who went through different paths. Yet, it is interesting to note that nearly 70% of these are concentrated in a few years: 2,239 and 404 in 1988 and 1989, respectively, and a total of 659 in 1998, 1999, and 2000 combined. One factor that might explain this is that around the 1988 and 1998 regularization policies for undocumented migrants, hometown associations and migrant advocacy groups championed immigration status awareness campaigns, makings migrants cognizant of their eligibility for naturalization, and provided legal counsel.

Yu said that "I love Brazil but do not feel Brazilian, I feel Chinese," an idea that I heard repeatedly from many other Chinese migrants I interviewed. For them, naturalization is not a sign of loyalty, allegiance, and cultural identification with the Paraguayan or Brazilian nation. In this, the overseas Chinese migrants in Paraguay and Brazil join a growing number of foreigners worldwide who seek to acquire citizenship for instrumental reasons rather than a national identity issue. Speaking about dual citizenship, sociologists Harpaz and Mateos define the concept of "strategic citizenship" as the "strategic-instrumental approach towards access to national citizenship" (2018, 843). This pragmatic approach to national citizenship informs new attitudes migrants and other transnationally oriented groups have developed such as novel acquisition strategies (for instance, based on ancestry), multiple practical uses of citizenship statuses (as premium passport or "insurance policy" if economic, political, or social conditions deteriorate in the country of first citizenship), and social understandings (as a status symbol or ethnic marker). The concept is useful to understand the case of overseas Chinese migrants in Ciudad del Este and São Paulo because it applies to the rise in instrumental attitudes towards nationality in the context in which the value of citizenship is increasingly shaped by global inequalities, including the unequal access to privileges and rights associated with international mobility.

Yet, the decision to naturalize poses dilemmas for eligible Chinese migrants because it decreases their mobility to and across China. China formally does not accept dual citizenship. In practice, it does not enforce the policy, and the Chinese elites increasingly hold dual citizenship (Spiro 2016). However, holding dual citizenship status remains controversial for Chinese migrants in Brazil. Many are not aware that the policy is largely not enforced, or do not want to take the risks associated with the violation. Zhou told me, "China is not like Brazil or the U.S. We can't hold two passports. I'd love to naturalize Brazilian but why would I want to lose my Chinese passport? Even without my passport, I'll remain culturally Chinese, no matter what. But should I just give it away?"

Paraguay and Brazil follow the rule of absolute birthright citizenship but, because China does not allow dual citizenship, many Chinese migrants are confronted with the difficult decision of choosing which nationality they want their children to have. On the one hand, undocumented migrants see their children's acquisition of Paraguayan or Brazilian citizenship at birth as a pragmatic choice to increase their own ability to regularize their immigration situation and to protect themselves against orders of departure or even removals. Paraguayan and Brazilian law dictates that parents of citizens at birth cannot be deported and that they are eligible to apply for family reunification visas. Migrants in São Paulo also said that they want their children to have Brazilian citizenship because they hope this will increase the children's opportunities to live in the United States, and dream of them eventually being able to also hold an American passport in the future. Taiwanese migrants in Ciudad del Este said that the Paraguayan passport is not as useful to them as the Taiwanese passport, but as both countries allow for dual citizenship, they do not hesitate to obtain Paraguayan citizenship, which is the most useful status for them in the country where they reside most of their life.

On the other hand, many migrants want their children to have Chinese citizenship either because of a cultural identification with the Chinese nationality or, more pragmatically, because of the rights associated with it, particularly if they send the children to be raised in China or plan on returning with the children in the future. Yet, migrants' cost-benefit analysis is not so straightforward in these cases either. For those who send their children to be raised in China, this is a crucial issue that raises questions about cultural adaptation and schooling. Children born in Brazil who are Chinese citizens have difficulties accessing public schools in China because they lack the local resident status known as *hùkǒu*. This significantly increases the cost of schooling and decreases their chances of attending school in the places where their grandparents live or accessing quality education (Chan and Buckingham 2008). Those who lack Chinese citizenship status have to observe applicable Chinese visa rules, including a validity period policy, which creates difficulties in following the school calendar and limits their right to stay, access to social rights, and their ability to travel internationally. Chinese migrants who are parents of children born in Brazil make complicated short- and long-term planning, where domestic class inequality and gaps in social rights intersect with inequality between nations and the various degrees of international mobility associated with the national citizenship status they elect for their children.

Chinese is in the top four nationalities of babies born to migrant women in Brazil in the last decade, with nearly seven thousand between 2013 and 2023, or 5.4% (Cavalcanti et al. 2023). A growing number of pregnant Chinese migrants use Brazil's public health system, which is free of charge and can be accessed by any individual irrespective of immigration status. In São Paulo, the health center in the district of the popular markets had the largest number of pregnant migrants of all public centers in the city in the 2010s. According to a Brazilian nurse I interviewed, there were roughly one hundred Chinese prenatal patients out of the approximately three hundred in total in 2015, and in 2016 nearly half of all prenatal patients were Chinese. Working-class migrants and vendors living in proximity to that health center constitute the majority of pregnant Chinese migrants who seek public services there. Additionally, many newly arrived migrants cannot afford private facilities. Social networks and an emergent services industry catering to pregnant Chinese migrants also facilitate their access to this unit. Chinese migrant and dentist Linda served as an interpreter between health providers and patients for over two decades. She also helped translate remotely for care providers and patients during home visits. In interviews I conducted, Linda and Brazilian health care providers reported that undocumented pregnant migrants expect to be able to remain lawfully in the country after the baby is born. Yet, the migrants I interviewed explained that the decision to have a child in Brazil is rather tough: it calls into question the family's migration plans and raises the issue of whether to return to China, stay in Brazil with the child, or send the child to the grandparents in China.

LEGIBILITY AGAINST ILLEGALIZATION

The immigration status of the overseas Chinese in Ciudad del Este and São Paulo is quite varied. Contrary to the typical depiction of those migrants, a great number are documented, though most experience a prolonged situation of living in a precarious immigration status. Some resort to tactics that include family arrangements and hired intermediaries to obtain legitimate papers or counterfeit documents needed for their international travels. Others are visa overstayers, who applied for a visa in China or Taiwan with the assistance of travel agencies or an affidavit of support letter from relatives in Brazil and Paraguay. Others yet are undocumented migrants who crossed borders illegally with the assistance of hired paper pushers, smugglers, and other intermediaries during their journey. A significant number of illegalized border crossers and overstayers regularized their immigration situation with regularization policies for undocumented migrants in the last four decades. The increase in visa holders and citizens, whether naturalized or acquired at birth, who may be eligible to sponsor visas for newcomers, contributed to an increase in regular migration.

Migrants' perspectives on the struggles to cross international borders and be in their place of choice show their mobility and emplacement contradict typical tropes of migration. Those perspectives are complex, filled with tensions and paradoxes in the migrants' abilities to use the state's official grammar of legality to achieve their migration plans as well as in their dilemmas and aspirations of obtaining a more stable immigration status and citizenship.

Migrants' dynamic relation between legibility and legality challenges the state-centric perspective of the legal/illegal binarism. That perspective naturalizes the "illegalization of migration," that is, how states alter legislation, policy, and jurisprudence to make it illegal and even criminal for noncitizens to cross international borders and remain in the country (de Genova 2004; Menjívar and Kanstroom 2013). Instead, the multiple meanings migrants make of a continuum between legal and illegal practices show the illegalization of migration cannot be dissociated from the uses of legality by the state and the migrants themselves. The migrants' uses of legality and strategic forms of legibility in the popular markets in São Paulo and Ciudad del Este are simultaneously a display of ingenuity in their struggles for mobility and emplacement and a limited attempt to regain control against the modes of extraction that depend on the illegalization of the migrant labor force. Economic crises, crackdowns on popular markets, and tougher border enforcement all pose additional challenges to the overseas Chinese migrants in the popular markets in Brazil and Paraguay. Yet, migrants show resilience to find resources and defiance to overcome an unjust system that restricts their mobility and emplacement.

CONCLUSION
SUBVERTING EXPLOITATION

IN 2022, A BILL WAS INTRODUCED in São Paulo City Council to establish the city's first Chinatown. The proposal focused on modernizing the shopping tourism infrastructure of an economically vibrant street in downtown. Its proponents promised "smart city" urban redevelopment with the creation of a technological hub and the use of clean energy to beautify the shopping facilities, enhance urban mobility, and create a "greener" shopping conglomerate. Chinatown, they insisted, would not only become São Paulo's largest shopping tourist destination, but South America's newest modern shopping experience featuring exquisite dining and authentic Chinese culture.

Behind the project is the president of the Brazil-China Social and Cultural Institute Thomas Law, a Brazilian born to Hong Kongese parents and a well-connected lawyer and business champion of the popular markets. Thomas Law introduced the bill in 2022 shortly after his father Law Kin Chong became the centerpiece of the City Council's investigation on the distribution of counterfeits imported from China and smuggled from Paraguay, nearly two decades after being convicted in a similar federal investigation. Expectedly, the Association of the Entrepreneurs of the Shopping

Circuit in São Paulo, linked to Thomas Law's institute, quickly showed support for the proposal, pointing out the need to revitalize the area. The project also received the support of many additional local groups, including Chinese associations, migrant-led chambers of commerce, and the Chinese-majority Community Safety Council. Even the Chinese Association of Brazil—a key supporter of Chinatown's main competitor, Shopping Circuit Consortium—also backed it, saying the Chinese community needs to unite for the shared goal of improving business in the popular markets. Hoping to implement his Chinatown project in time for the fiftieth anniversary of the diplomatic rapprochement between Brazil and China in 2024, Thomas Law received enthusiastic signs of cooperation from local politicians as well as from subnational Chinese governments during the visits of Brazilian presidents to China in 2021 and 2023 when he chaperoned South American business delegations.

Despite the growing presence of Chinese vendors in downtown São Paulo in the last three decades, Thomas Law's Chinatown will not be a historical district serving migrant communities like world-renowned Chinatowns in New York and San Francisco. Rather, it will be the epicenter of modern transnational commerce. For him, the model to follow is Dubai Chinatown. This Chinatown is a state-of-the-art shopping center with boutique stores and Chinese-themed atriums. It is a prime example of recent global Chinatowns built by public-private partnerships involving both local and Chinese governments as well as diasporic business groups to bolster trade and shopping tourism. Traditional Chinatowns have evolved from communities of working-class migrants who resisted gentrification largely because of family-owned real estate and community credit. The São Paulo Chinatown will, instead, be built not by ordinary vendors, but by wealthier merchants. The project is based on the idea that millionaires can create an upscale Chinese-themed shopping center and call it Chinatown on behalf of migrant vendors—who fear they will continue to be exploited.

In this book, I have analyzed how noncompliance, uneven enforcement, changes in legal parameters, and loopholes in the law affected the overseas Chinese communities in the informal economic circuit between Ciudad del Este and São Paulo. The situational application of legality (ranging from tax breaks and exclusive trade rights to the criminalization of vendors' activities and the privatization of public markets) boosted the popular markets while simultaneously restricting low-income vendors' ability to retain the revenue from their economic activities. By interrogating the effects of the flexible application of legality on markets at the fringes of the law, this book has shown the different ways in which overseas Chinese businesspeople and migrant vendors participated in a thriving economy that is at the brink of being shut down and, paradoxically, celebrated as a shopping tourism destination.

Overseas Chinese communities played a key role in the transformation of the informal economy between Paraguay and Brazil. The border market of Ciudad del Este emerged as a product of complex legislation that facilitated smuggling. As prominent importers, overseas Chinese elites held exclusive tariff-free trade concessions in Ciudad del Este supplying popular markets in São Paulo. With trade liberalization in Brazil and economic integration in South America—both of which represented a blow to Ciudad del Este's economy—the overseas Chinese importers successfully lobbied the Paraguayan government for tariff reductions and tax cuts.

A few overseas Chinese importers saw trade liberalization and economic integration as an opportunity for new businesses, rather than a threat. They moved back to São Paulo, where they replicated Ciudad del Este's successful business model, opening indoor markets and subleasing stalls to newly arrived Chinese migrants. By the 2010s, overseas Chinese individuals owned or managed the majority of indoor markets in São Paulo. As City Hall deployed a series of urban interventions promoting shopping tourism and popular entrepreneurialism, overseas Chinese importers and stall sublessors accepted leadership positions in the Shopping Circuit Consortium, an ambitious redevelopment project that privatized the Dawn Market. For Chinese vendors, however, the spread of indoor markets caused a mixed effect. On the one hand, these markets unlocked job opportunities for newcomers and protected them from the militarized policing of street vending, but, on the other hand, those markets also served as an outlet for capital expansion in the popular markets, increasing lease fees and siphoning off the revenue of Chinese vendors.

The overseas Chinese merchants' strong foothold in Ciudad del Este and São Paulo was a product of transnational business ties and diaspora policies connecting East Asia and South America. Migrants' associations in Ciudad del Este and São Paulo engaged with the local diaspora to implement trade promotion policies designed by governments in Taiwan and China. These associations also fostered migration to new destinations in Paraguay and Brazil, expanding the popular markets into far corners. The associations played an ambiguous role. On the one hand, they supported migrants' businesses, assisted with legal counseling, and represented vendors' interests in public and official affairs. On the other, they exercised tight control over vendors, keeping them in a precarious immigration status and a dire economic situation. For those vendors, street vending and selling from stalls were the only options available for an income, even if meager, and they were trapped in debts—a situation that did not match with the associations' misleading depiction of them as cosmopolitan entrepreneurs.

Despite the illegalization of irregular immigration status and the criminalization of the popular markets, overseas Chinese vendors deployed a range of tactics to redefine the terms of their own mobilities and enhance their ability to perform economic activities in Paraguay and Brazil. As global capitalism deepened an exploitative international division of labor at the same time that it mobilized the labor force of illegalized migrants, overseas Chinese vendors used transnational spatial mobility as an opportunity, albeit a risky one, to find new means to provide for themselves. They provisionally negotiated the display of a persona to convince gatekeepers of their legitimate migration purposes and made themselves legible in ways that were accepted by enforcers. Though limited both structurally (due to their immigration status and their economic activity in informal economies) and socially (due to their social membership in the migrant community and engagement with the diaspora associations), the overseas Chinese vendors skillfully made compromises in the attempt to maintain control over their mobility and subjecthood.

A key theoretical takeaway from the book is that cross-border spatial mobility is—despite all limitations—a practice of autonomy that migrants use to resist the systemic inequities pushing them towards unfreedom. Tougher border and immigration enforcement compound to current global capitalism's international division of labor and structural economic inequalities, facilitating the resurgence of unfree labor affecting migrants.

To counter that, migrants use the porous borders of legality to subvert exploitation and create opportunities to effect change. Chinese vendors rarely participated in political demonstrations in Ciudad del Este or São Paulo and only did so when local diaspora associations organized protests. However, on two occasions when Zhu Surong and Law Kin Chong were called to testify before City Council investigations in 2017 and 2023, Chinese vendors spontaneously rallied for better working conditions. Overcoming the fear of retaliation against their immigration status and economic reliance on distributors, vendors confronted powerful Chinese businesspeople and subverted exploitation.

While this broad takeaway speaks to a variety of lines of inquiry on topics such as labor, migration, borders, surveillance, and activism, this book makes pertinent contributions to a few fields of study in particular. It challenges the notion of informality prevalent in development and informality studies and goes against the tendency to separate the economy into two distinct spheres, the formal and the informal, in which the latter is seen simply as the survival economy of the poor and the disenfranchised. It advances a critical political economy approach that puts popular markets at the center of wealth circulation. It deploys the concept of "capture by illegality" to shed light on how the economic practices predominant in popular markets are shaped by power relations that reconfigure the boundaries between legal and illegal.

By centering the analysis on informal markets, the book advances the theory of postcolonial capitalism to explain accumulation in illegal economic circuits. It shows that restricting workers from accessing shared means of wealth generation does not simply serve the desire to eliminate their activities. Rather, the malleability of law seeks to differentiate labor and keep workers in a liminal position where they keep producing wealth, but only for capture. The extraction of wealth in informal economies in the Global South necessitates the discursive and practical redefinition of legality. In transnational markets at the fringes of legality, the flexible application of the law shapes accumulation through targeted surveillance and punishment of some, but not all, types of illegal economic behavior.

Another contribution the book makes to the field of border studies is to shed new light on the theoretical proposition that the border is a social relation—not simply a line demarcating geopolitical entities. Bringing together an analysis of the mobility of people and goods across the Global South, it argues that uneven development and the encounter between different economic models shaped the conditions of possibility for a foreign-oriented trade hub to emerge operated by migrants.

The book also makes major contributions to the field of migration studies. One such contribution is the focus on the role of local and transnational actors that implement diaspora engagement extraterritorially. Highlighting the diversity of South-South migration, the book shows how diaspora policies shape migrants' choice for a destination that offers income opportunities in the Global South rather than searching for a presumably more robust welfare system or economic opportunities in the Global North as it is often assumed. Another contribution of the book goes beyond the focus on the policies to stop and intercept migrant flows, acknowledging their impact but also moving away from a state-centric view concerning "suspicious" mobilities to focus instead on the migrants' multiple meanings and uses of legality.

The story told in this book offers a new perspective to the much-debated rise of China and opens a research agenda on its grassroots impact on globalization. While most accounts of China's economic and geopolitical ascension to the position of a unique global superpower might focus on macroeconomic trends or foreign affairs, my bottom-up approach shows that migrants and the diaspora are key transnational actors of China's global presence and strategic agents for its success. Local governments, diaspora agencies, and other unsuspected drivers of China's rise cooperate and compete to engage with the overseas Chinese populations. The growing presence of Chinese migrants, traders, and investors—in parallel to the unprecedented reach of China's soft and hard power—makes evident the need to render nuanced explanations of China's role in global affairs. This book unpacks the assumptions we make when we look at the state, the new forms of capital circulating transnationally, and the implication of the presence of China for global economies. It offers a fresh look at the way we conceptualize China in the world and the transformation of global power and geopolitical order. Future research must be done to investigate other grassroots actors and unexpected policy areas of China's rise, looking to understand their transnational role in shaping new directions of globalization.

Back to the circuit between Ciudad del Este and São Paulo, overseas

Chinese vendors are still recovering from the political and economic crises that affected the region. The coronavirus pandemic aggravated economic recession, slowing down the consumer market and exacerbating the unemployment crisis that drives workers to the informal economy. This posed challenges to overseas Chinese migrants, many of whom have economic disincentives to stay but do not have the means to return. Others, including newcomers in transit from Paraguay and Brazil to other South American countries, face stricter border enforcement and enter volatile consumer markets. For them, mobility is once again a promise of autonomy and a risk of entrapment. As they forge new paths, they are leading once again a quiet resistance to global systemic exploitation.

Translation Glossary

Except when the English translations below are official, they were translated by me. The original terms follow in Portuguese, Spanish, or Mandarin Chinese. When the original terms are bilingual, both versions are listed. Some bilingual terms diverge slightly between the Mandarin Chinese and Portuguese or Spanish versions; when that occurs, I privilege the Chinese version for my translation to English. Below, I maintain either the Traditional or the Simplified Mandarin Chinese characters as they appear in names, documents, and phrases. Throughout the book, I use the Hanyu Pinyin system for romanizing Mandarin Chinese.

Adaptation Regime | Régimen de Adecuación | Regime de Adequação

Association of Customs Brokers of Paraguay | Centro de Despachantes de Aduana del Paraguay

Association of the Cantonese of Brazil | Associação Geral dos Cantoneses do Brasil | 巴西廣東同鄉總會

Association of Fujianese in Brazil | Associação dos Chineses de Fujian do Brasil | 巴西福建同乡总会

Association of the Entrepreneurs of the Shopping Circuit in São Paulo | Associação Paulista dos Empreendedores do Circuito das Compras

Beijing Cultural Exchange Association of Brazil | Associação de Intercâmbio Cultural de Pequim do Brasil | 巴西北京文化交流协会

Brazilian Coffee Institute | Instituto Brasileiro do Café

Brazilian Council of Immigration | Conselho Nacional de Imigração

Brazilian Forum Against Piracy and Illegality | Fórum Nacional Contra a Pirataria e Ilegalidade

Brazilian Institute of Ethics in Competition | Instituto Brasileiro de Ética Concorrencial

Brazilian Project Structuring Company | Estruturadora Brasileira de Projetos

Brazilian Social Democracy Party | Partido da Social Democracia Brasileira

Brazilian Social Security Institute | Instituto Nacional do Seguro Social

Brazilian Health Regulatory Agency | Agência Nacional da Vigilância Sanitária

Brazil-China Social and Cultural Institute | Instituto Sociocultural Brazil-China

Chamber of Commerce of Information Technology Goods | Cámara de Comercio de Tecnología de la Información

China Travel Service | 中国旅行社, established in 1974 and merged with the Overseas China Travel Service (华侨旅行服务社)

Chinese Association of Brazil | Associação Chinesa do Brasil | 巴西华人协会

Chinese Association of Ciudad del Este-Paraguay | Asociación China de C.D.E. Paraguay | 巴拉圭東方市中華會館

Chinese Chamber of Commerce of Brazil | Câmara Chinesa de Comércio do Brasil | 巴西中国总商会

Chinese Dream | 中国梦

Chinese Social Center of Brazil in São Paulo | Centro Social Chinês de São Paulo | 巴西聖保羅中華會館

Colorado Party | Partido Colorado

Common External Tariff | Arancel Externo Común | Tarifa Externa Comum

Community Safety Council | Conselho Comunitário de Segurança

Consumer Protection Foundation of Rio de Janeiro | Fundação de Proteção e Defesa do Consumidor do Rio de Janeiro

Da Shan | 大山

Democratic Progressive Party | 民主進步黨

Democrats | Democratas

Downtown São Paulo Urban and Functional Revitalization Program (PROCENTRO) | Programa de Requalificação Urbana e Funcional do Centro de São Paulo

Employment Record Book | Carteira de Trabalho e Previdência Social

Encarnación Chapter of the Taiwanese Fellows' Solidarity and Aid Association | Asociación de Solidaridad y Ayuda de los Connacionales Taiwaneses de Encarnación | 巴拉圭恩卡納西翁僑界關懷救助協會

Federation of Chinese Businesspeople of Paraguay | Federación de Empresarios Chinos del Paraguay | 巴拉圭華商經貿聯誼會

Federation of Returned Overseas Chinese | 中华全国归国华侨联合会

General Association of the Chinese Businesspeople of Brazil | Associação Geral dos Empresários Chineses do Brasil | 巴西华人工商联合会

GSA Management of Fairs and Events LLC (GSA) | GSA Administração e Organização de Feiras e Eventos LTDA

Go Out Policy (also known as "Going Global Strategy") | 走出去战略

Hakka Social Center of Brazil | 巴西客家活動中心

Household Registration System | 户口

Independent Street Vendors Union | Sindicato dos Camelôs Independentes

Individual Micro-Entrepreneur | Microempreendedor Individual

Informal Economy Workers Union | Sindicato dos Trabalhadores da Economia Informal

Internal Revenue System of Brazil | Receita Federal do Brasil

In-Transit Customs Clearance Regime | Régimen de Despacho en Tránsito, also referred to as Régimen de Despacho Transitório

"Inviting in" (also known as "welcoming in" or "bringing in") | 请进来

Kuomintang (also known as Guomindang, Nationalist Party of China, or Chinese Nationalist Party) | 中國國民黨

"Large overseas Chinese affairs" | 大侨务

Licensed Retailer Importer Micro Company | Microempresa Importadora Varejista Habilitada

Licensed Street Vendors Union | Sindicato dos Permissionários em Ponto Fixo nas Vias e Logradouros Públicos do Município de São Paulo

Migrants' associations | 会馆

Min Nan Association of South America | Associação Min Nan da América do Sul | 南美洲闽南同乡联谊会

Ministry of Labor and Employment | Ministério do Trabalho e do Emprego

National Committee for Refugees | Comitê Nacional para os Refugiados

National System of Enrollment and Records of Foreigners | Sistema Nacional de Cadastro e Registro de Estrangeiros

Native-place associations | 同乡会

Natural Persons Register | Cadastro de Pessoa Física

Network of the Overseas Chinese in Brazil | Rede dos Chineses Ultramarinos do Brasil | 巴西华人网

Overseas Chinese | 华侨 (also referred to as 华侨华人)

Overseas Chinese affairs | 侨务

Overseas Chinese Affairs Office (OCAO) | 国务院侨务办公室

Overseas Chinese Association—Paraguay Chapter | Asociación de Chinos de Ultramar en Paraguay | 華僑協會總會巴拉圭分會

Overseas Chinese hometown associations | 侨乡会

Overseas Chinese hometowns | 侨乡

Overseas Chinese Service Center | 华助中心

Overseas Chinese Youth Federation of Brazil | Associação dos Jovens Chineses do Brasil | 巴西华人华侨青年联合会

Overseas Community Affairs Council, Republic of China (Taiwan) (OCAC) | 中華民國僑務委員會

Paraguay Chinese Club of Hometown Associations | Club Chino en Paraguay de Asociaciones de Ciudad de Origen | 巴拉圭台湾會館台湾同鄉會

People's Republic of China | 中华人民共和国

Popular Socialist Party | Partido Popular Socialista

Progressive Party | Partido Progressista

Qingtian Association of Brazil | Associação Geral de Qingtian do Brasil | 巴西青田县乡总会

Republic of China | 中華民國

"Reaching out" (also known as "going out") | 走出去

"Return and serve the country" | 回国服务

São Paulo Overseas Chinese Center | Centro de Apoio e Integração Social dos Migrantes Chineses | 圣保罗华助中心

Schedule of Capital Goods | Lista de Bienes de Capital | Lista de Bens de Capital

Schedule of Informatics and Telecommunication Goods | Lista de Bienes de Informática y Telecomunicaciones | Lista de Bens de Informática e Telecomunicações

Schedules of Exception to the MERCOSUR Common External Tariff | Listas de Excepción al Arancel Externo Común del MERCOSUR | Listas de Exceção à Tarifa Externa Comum do MERCOSUL

"Serve the country" | 为国服务

Simplified Importation Clearance | Despacho de Importador Simplificado

Social Democratic Party | Partido Social Democrático

South America Newspaper | *Diário Chinês Para a América do Sul* | 南美侨报

Southern Common Market (MERCOSUR) | Mercado Común del Sur | Mercado Comum do Sul

Special Tourism Regime | Régimen Especial de Turismo, officially Régimen Especial de Liquidación Impositiva

Street Vendors Permanent Council | Comissão Permanente de Ambulantes

Taipei Economic and Cultural Office | 臺北經濟文化辦事處

Taiwanese Association of Brazil | 巴西台灣同鄉會

Taiwanese Chamber of Commerce-Paraguay | Cámara de Comercio Taiwanés-Chino, Paraguay | 中華民國旅巴拉圭台灣商會

Transborder Trade Regime | Régimen Fronterizo de Comercialización

Unified Tax Regime | Regime de Tributação Unificado

Union of the Chinese Women of Brazil | União das Mulheres Chinesas do Brasil | 巴西中华妇女联合会

United Front Work Department | 中共中央统一战线工作部

Use of Public Space Permit | Termo de Permissão de Uso

Wenzhou Association of Brazil | Associação Wenzhou do Brasil | 巴西温州同乡联谊

Worker's Party | Partido dos Trabalhadores

World Federation of Taiwanese Associations | 世界台灣同鄉會聯合會

Notes

Introduction

1. Paramount leader of the People's Republic of China serving various positions from 1978 to 1989.
2. Foucault coined the neologism "illegalisms" (*illegalismes* in French) in the 1972–1973 lectures *The Punitive Society*. These lectures were published only in 2013 originally in French as *La Société Punitive* under Bernard Harcourt's edition. *The Punitive Society* (2015) is the first English translation of Foucault's work that accepts the term "illegalisms" instead of "illegalities," which had been used thus far in the translations of *Discipline and Punish* and other publications. Given its centrality in Foucault's work, it is surprising that the notion of illegalisms has remained largely ignored in Anglophone academia and has been understudied until very recently. While it is true that *La Société Punitive* was published late, *Dits et Écrits*, published in 1994, features various material in which Foucault presents the main arguments of the 1972–1973 lectures, including the course summary he wrote in 1973 (Foucault 1994). Additionally, *Dits et Écrits* includes texts in which the notion of "illegalisms" is ostensibly deployed: the conference "La Vérité et les Formes Juridiques" presented in May 1973 in Brazil and two interviews (Gros 2010). The term also appears in several publications of the mid-1970s, most notably *Discipline and Punish*, as well as in the work of the later Foucault, such as the 1982 essay "Le Sujet et le Pouvoir," republished in *Dits et Écrits*. The term appears more than 300 times in *The Punitive Society* and 120 times in *Discipline and Punish*.

Chapter 1

1. Colorado Party, 1954–1989.
2. Workers' Party, 2003–2010 and 2023–present.

Chapter 2

1. Head of the Kuomintang, he was the leader of the Republic of China in China from 1928 until 1949 and in Taiwan from 1949 until 1975.
2. Workers' Party, 1989–1992.
3. Progressive Party, 1993–1997.
4. Progressive Party, 1997–2000.
5. Workers' Party, 2001–2004.
6. Brazilian Social Democracy Party, 2005–2006.
7. Democrats, 2006–2008, and Social Democratic Party, 2009–2012. Kassab was deputy mayor and became mayor when José Serra stepped down to run for governor of São Paulo state in 2006. Kassab was later elected for the 2009–2012 term.
8. Workers' Party, 2012–2016.
9. Brazilian Social Democracy Party, 2017–2018 and 2018–2021. Covas was deputy mayor and became mayor when João Dória stepped down to run for governor of São Paulo state in 2018. Covas was later elected for the 2021–2024 term. He died while serving in April 2021, when then Deputy Mayor Ricardo Nunes was sworn in as mayor.

Chapter 3

1. Chinese Communist Party, 2013–present.
2. Popular Socialist Party, 2010–2012.
3. Progressive Party since 2016. Before, he was a member of the Brazilian Social Democracy Party, Popular Socialist Party, and Green Party.

Chapter 4

1. Brazilian Democratic Movement, 2016–2018.
2. In Brazil, the legal category "refugee" refers to someone who obtained refugee status, including those who applied in the country as well as those resettled. The category "asylee" refers to someone who receives protection from being extradited to their country of citizenship where the person was charged or sentenced for allegedly a political crime. Brazil and many other Latin American countries are different from countries that differentiate between the legal statuses of a refugee and asylee based on whether the applicant was in the territory of the country of application.

References

Aguiar, José Carlos. 2012. "Cities on Edge: Smuggling and Neoliberal Policies at the Iguazú Triangle." *Singapore Journal of Tropical Geography* 33 (2): 171–83.

Alba, Richard, Brenden Beck, and Duygu Basaran Sahin. 2018. "The U.S. Mainstream Expands—Again." *Journal of Ethnic and Migration Studies* 44 (1): 99–117.

Alba, Richard, Philip Kasinitz, and Mary C. Waters. 2011. "The Kids Are (Mostly) All Right: Second Generation Assimilation." *Social Forces* 8 (3): 763–74.

Alba, Richard, and Victor Nee. 2003. *Remaking the American Mainstream: Assimilation and Contemporary Immigration*. Cambridge, MA: Harvard University Press.

Alba Villalever, Ximena, and Felipe Rubio. 2018. "New Patterns of Chinese Migration to the Americas: Mexico City and Lima." In *New Migration Patterns of the Americas, Challenges for the 21st Century*, edited by A. Feldmann, X. Bada, and S. Schütze, 261–81. New York: Palgrave Macmillan.

Amar, Paul. 2013. *The Security Archipelago: Human-Security States, Sexuality Politics, and the End of Neoliberalism*. Durham, NC: Duke University Press.

Amicelle, Anthony. 2013. "Differential Management of Economic and Financial Illegalisms: Anti-Money Laundering and 'Tax Issues.'" *Champ Pénal/Penal Field* 10. Retrieved December 11, 2018 (http://journals.openedition.org/champpenal/8895).

Amicelle, Anthony, and Carla Nagels. 2018. "Les Arbitres de l'Illégalisme: Nouveau Regard sur les Manières de Faire du Contrôle Social" [Referees of illegalities: New perspectives on social control]. *Champ Pénal/Penal Field* 15. Retrieved December 11, 2018 (https://journals.openedition.org/champpenالسal/9774).

Antunes, Ricardo. 2007. "Dimensões da Precarização Estrutural do Trabalho" [Dimensions of the structural precarization of labor]. In *A Perda da Razão Social do Trabalho: Terceirização e Precarização,* 13–22. São Paulo: Boitempo.

Azaïs, Christian, Gabriel Kessler, and Vera da Silva Telles, eds. 2012. *Ilegalismos, Cidade e Política* [Illegalisms, city, and politics]. Belo Horizonte, Brazil: Editora Fino Traço.

Balibar, Étienne. 2002. "What Is a Border?" *Politics and the Other Scene,* edited by É. Balibar, 75–86. London: Verso.

Banerjea, Niharika. 2011. "Special Economic Zones and Middle-Class Connectivity in Urbanizing India." *Global Studies Journal* 3 (4): 127–39.

Barbosa, Alexandre Freitas. 2011. "O Conceito de Trabalho Informal, sua Evolução Histórica e o Potencial Analítico Atual: Para Não Jogar a Criança Fora Junto com a Água do Banho" [The concept of informal work, its historical evolution, and the current analytical potential: Not throwing the baby out with the bath water]. In *Marchas e Contramarchas da Informalidade do Trabalho: Das Origens às Novas Abordagens,* edited by R. V. de Oliveira, D. Gomes, and I. Targino, 105–59. João Pessoa, Brazil: Editora Universitária da UFPB.

Baxi Huaren Xun Wang Zi. 2019. "華僑協會巴拉圭分會歡慶108雙十國慶暨華僑節" [The Paraguay Chapter of Overseas Chinese Association celebrates the 108th Double Ten National Day and the Overseas Chinese Festival]. October 15, 2019. Retrieved January 6, 2021 (https://brazilhr.com/2019/10/461761).

Baxi Meizhou Huabao. 1998. 巴西華人耕耘錄 [Records of the diligent labor of Chinese Brazilians]. São Paulo: Baxi Meizhou Huabao.

Berman, Jacqueline. 2003. "(Un)Popular Strangers and Crisis (Un)Bounded: Discourses of Sex-Trafficking, the European Political Community and the Panicked State of the Modern State." *European Journal of International Relations* 9 (1): 37–86.

Bigo, Didier. 2002. "Security and Immigration: Toward a Critique of the Governmentality of Unease." *Alternatives* 27 (special issue 1): 63–92.

Bosniak, Linda. 2013. "Amnesty in Immigration: Forgetting, Forgiving, Freedom." *Critical Review of Social and Political Philosophy* 16 (3): 344–65.

Bourbeau, Philippe. 2001. "La Diaspora Chinoise Repensée" [The Chinese diaspora reimagined]. *Études Internationales* 32 (4): 745–67.

Braudel, Fernand. 2008 [1985]. *La Dynamique du Capitalisme* [The dynamics of capitalism]. Paris: Flammarion.

Brazilian Congress. 2004. "Notas Taquigráficas da Audiência Pública de 18 de Março de 2004 da Comissão Parlamentar de Inquérito com a Finalidade de Investigar Fatos Relacionados à Pirataria de Produtos Industrializados e à Sonegação Fiscal" [Transcription of the March 18, 2004 public hearing of the Brazilian Congress's Special Committee on Counterfeits and Tax Evasion].

Retrieved August 9, 2024 (https://www2.camara.leg.br/atividade-legislativa/comissoes/comissoes-temporarias/parlamentar-de-inquerito/52-legislatura/cpipirat/notas/nt180304.pdf).

Brito, José Maria de. 2005. *Descoberta de Foz do Iguaçu e a Fundação da Colônia Militar* [The discovery of Foz do Iguaçu and the founding of the military colony]. Curitiba, Brazil: Travessa dos Editores.

Bruce-Jones, Eddie. 2015. "Death Zones, Comfort Zones: Queering the Refugee Question." *International Journal on Minority and Group Rights* 22 (1): 101–27.

Büscher, Monika, and John Urry. 2009. "Mobile Methods and the Empirical." *European Journal of Social Theory* 12 (1): 99–116.

Cabrera, Luis. 2010. *The Practice of Global Citizenship*. Cambridge, MA: Cambridge University Press.

Cacciamali, Maria Cristina. 2000. "Globalização e Processo de Informalidade" [Globalization and the process of informalization]. *Revista Economia e Sociedade* 14: 153–74.

Cardin, Eric. 2010. "Expansão do Capital e as Dinâmicas da Fronteira" [Capital expansion and border dynamics]. Doctoral dissertation, Universidade Estadual de São Paulo, Brazil.

Cardin, Eric, and Cintia Fiorotti. 2018. "Dispositivos Estatales, Ilegalismos y Prácticas Sociales en la Frontera Brasil-Paraguay (1890–2015)" [State devices, illegalisms, and social practices on the Brazil-Paraguay border (1890–2015)]. *Estudios Fronterizos* 19 (e012): 1–17.

Cardoso, Fernando Henrique. 1971. "Comentário sobre os Conceitos de Superpopulação Relativa e Marginalidade" [Comments on the concepts of relative surplus population and marginality]. *Estudos CEBRAP* 1: 99–130.

Cardozo, José Eduardo. 2000. *A Máfia das Propinas: Investigando a Corrupção em São Paulo* [The bribery mafia: Investigating corruption in São Paulo]. São Paulo: Imprenta—Fundação Perseu Abramo.

Cavalcanti, Leonardo, Tadeu de Oliveira, and Sarah Lemos Silva. 2023. Relatório Anual OBMigra 2023—OBMigra 10 Anos: Pesquisa, Dados e Contribuições para Políticas [OBMigra 2023 annual report—OBMigra at 10 years: Research, data and policy contributions]. Observatório das Migrações Internacionais; Ministério da Justiça e Segurança Pública / Conselho Nacional de Imigração e Coordenação Geral de Imigração Laboral. Brasília, Brazil: OBMigra, 2023.

Ceccagno, Antonella. 2015. "The Mobile Emplacement: Chinese Migrants in Italian Industrial Districts." *Journal of Ethnic and Migration Studies* 41 (7): 1111–30.

Ceccagno, Antonella. 2017. *City Making and Global Labor Regimes: Chinese Immigrants and Italy's Fast Fashion Industry*. Cham, Switzerland: Palgrave Macmillan.

Cervo, Amado Luiz. 2001. *Relações Internacionais da América Latina: Velhos e*

Novos Paradigmas [Latin America's international relations: Old and new paradigms]. Brasília, Brazil: Instituto Brasileiro de Relações Internacionais.

Cesarino, Gabriela Krantz, and Valter Luiz Castana Junior. 2017. "Adaptação e Resiliência do Espaço Comercial de Rua: A 25 de Março" [Adaptation and resilience in a retail street: March 25th Street]. *Revista Rua* 23 (1): 117–39.

Chan, Carol. 2018. "Imagining and Linking Latin America: Chinese Regional Mobilities and Social Networks in Chile." *Journal of Latin American Geography* 17 (2): 23–45.

Chan, Carol. 2021. "Permanent Migrants and Temporary Citizens: Multinational Chinese Mobilities in the Americas." *Global Networks* 21 (1): 64–83.

Chan, Kan Wing, and Will Buckingham. 2008. "Is China Abolishing the *Hukou* System?" *China Quarterly* 195: 582–606.

Chan, Kwok-Bun. 2000. "Introduction: State, Economy and Culture: Reflections of the Chinese Business Networks." In *Chinese Business Networks: State, Economy and Culture*, edited by K. Chan, 1–13. Copenhagen: Prentice Hall.

Chan, Kwok-Bun. 2005. *Ethnic Relations and Chinese Business*. New York: Routledge.

Chan, Kwok-Bun, and Wai-Wan Chan. 2011. *Mobile Chinese Entrepreneurs*. New York: Springer.

Cheng, Joseph Y. S., and King-lun Ngok. 1999. "Government Policy in the Reform Era: Interactions Between Organs Responsible for Overseas Chinese and *Qiaoxiang* Communities." In *Qiaoxiang Ties: Interdisciplinary Approaches to "Cultural Capitalism" in South China*, edited by L. Douw, Cen Huang, and M. R. Godley, 113–42. London: Kegan Paul.

Chu, Julie. 2010. *Cosmologies of Credit: Transnational Mobility and the Politics of Destination in China*. Durham, NC: Duke University Press.

Circuito de Compras 2011: Projeto de Terminais Rodoviários e de Serviços de Transporte Dedicado. 18º Congresso Brasileiro de Transporte e Trânsito / VII INTRANS Exposição Internacional de Transporte e Trânsito 2015.

Ciudad del Este TI. 2011. "Dos Años Sabáticos de la C.C.T.I., el Retorno del Padre del RTU y la Formalización de CDE" [CCTI's two sabbatical years, the return of the father of RTU, and formalization in CDE]. *Ciudad del Este TI* 9 (80): 1. LatinMedia Publishing. Retrieved January 4, 2019 (https://issuu.com/latinmediapublishing/docs/cde80-marzo2011).

Cmasi. CC BY-SA 3.0 via Wikimedia Commons. Retrieved September 17, 2024, https://commons.wikimedia.org/wiki/File:Downtown_Ciudad_del_Este_view_134135.jpg.

Comaroff, Jean, and John Comaroff. 2016. *The Truth About Crime: Sovereignty, Knowledge, Social Order*. Chicago: University of Chicago Press.

Consumerism Leads to Economic Improvement. 2017. São Paulo, Brazil, October

31, 2017. Retrieved September 19, 2024, https://www.shutterstock.com/editorial/image-editorial/consumer-movement-shopping-center-s%C3%A30-paulo-household-9184869e.

Covas, Bruno. 2017. "São Paulo sem Ilegalidade" [São Paulo free of illegality]. *Folha de S. Paulo*, September 15, 2017. Retrieved September 27, 2023 (https://www1.folha.uol.com.br/opiniao/2017/09/1918600-sao-paulo-sem-ilegalidade.shtml).

DataMigra BI. n.d. OBMigra—International Migration Observatory. Retrieved May 20, 2024 (https://www.datamigra.unb.br/).

De Genova, Nicholas. 2004. "The Legal Production of Mexican/Migrant Illegality." *Latino Studies* 2: 160–85.

De Genova, Nicholas, Glenda Garelli, and Martina Tazzioli. 2018. "Autonomy of Asylum? The Autonomy of Migration Undoing the Refugee Crisis Script." *South Atlantic Quarterly* 117 (2): 239–65.

De Soto, Hernando. 1989. *The Other Path: The Invisible Revolution in the Third World*. New York: Harper and Row.

Délano, Alexandra, and Alan Gamlen. 2014. "Comparing and Theorizing State-Diaspora Relations." *Political Geography* 41: 43–53.

Deleuze, Gilles. 1985. *Foucault*. Paris: Editions de Minuit.

Denardi, Luciana. 2016. "Casetes, Redes y Banquetes: Prácticas Comerciales de Chinos, Taiwaneses y Argentinos en Buenos Aires" [Cassettes, networks, and banquets: Trade practices of the Chinese, Taiwanese, and Argentinians in Buenos Aires]. *Etnografías Contemporáneas* 2 (2): 134–60.

Dias, Guilherme Mansur, and Márcia Anita Sprandel. 2010. "A Temática do Tráfico de Pessoas no Contexto Brasileiro" [The theme of human trafficking in Brazilian context]. *Revista Interdisciplinar da Mobilidade Humana* 7 (35): 50–77.

Douw, Leo. 1999a. "Introduction." In *Qiaoxiang Ties: Interdisciplinary Approaches to 'Cultural Capitalism' in South China*, edited by L. Douw, Cen Huang, and M. R. Godley, 3–21. London: Kegan Paul.

Douw, Leo. 1999b. "The Chinese Sojourner Discourse." In *Qiaoxiang Ties: Interdisciplinary Approaches to 'Cultural Capitalism' in South China*, edited by L. Douw, Cen Huang, and M. R. Godley, 22–44. London: Kegan Paul.

Elyachar, Julia. 2005. *Markets of Dispossession: NGOs, Economic Development, and the State in Cairo*. Durham, NC: Duke University Press.

Escobar, Arturo. 1995. *Encountering Development. The Making and Unmaking of the Third World*. Princeton, NJ: Princeton University Press.

Fausto, Boris. 2009. *O Crime do Restaurante Chinês: Carnaval, Futebol e Justiça na São Paulo dos anos 30* [The Chinese restaurant crime: Carnival, soccer, and justice in 1930s São Paulo]. São Paulo: Companhia das Letras.

Ferguson, James. 2011. "Toward a Left Art of Government: From 'Foucauldian Critique' to Foucauldian Politics." *History of the Human Sciences* 24 (4): 61–68.

Ferguson, James. 2015. *Give a Man a Fish*. Durham, NC: Duke University Press.
Fernandez, Luis, and Joel Olson. 2011. "To Live, Love and Work Anywhere You Please: Critical Exchange on Arizona and the Struggle for Locomotion." *Contemporary Political Theory* 10 (3): 412–19.
Ferradas, Carmen. 1998. "How a Green Wilderness Became a Trade Wilderness." *Political and Legal Anthropology Review* 21 (2): 11–25.
Fiorotti, Cíntia. 2015. "História de Trabalhadores na Fronteira Brasil-Paraguai: 1960–2015" [The history of workers on the Brazil-Paraguay border: 1960–2015]. Doctoral dissertation, Universidade Federal de Uberlândia, Brazil.
Fischer, Nicholas, and Alexis Spire. 2009. "L'État Face aux Illegalisms" [State and illegal practices]. *Politix* 3 (87): 7–20.
Folha de S. Paulo. 2017. "Agentes da Receita Xingam Chineses em Ação contra Pirataria; Veja Vídeo" [Internal revenue agents curse the Chinese during operation against counterfeits: Watch the video]. October 11, 2017. Retrieved September 27, 2023 (https://www1.folha.uol.com.br/cotidiano/2017/10/1926134-agentes-da-receita-xingam-chineses-em-acao-contra-pirataria-veja-video.shtml).
Forment, Carlos. 2015. "Ordinary Ethics and the Emergence of Plebeian Democracy Across the Global South: Buenos Aires' La Salada Market." *Current Anthropology* 56 (S11): S116–S125.
Fórum Centro Vivo. 2001. *Contribuições para o Plano Reconstruir o Centro, da Prefeitura* [Contributions to city hall's plan "Rebuild Downtown"]. June 12, 2001. Retrieved January 4, 2018 (http://www.geocities.ws/forumcentrovivo).
Fórum dos Ambulantes. 2016. "Carta Aberta do Fórum dos Ambulantes ao Futuro Prefeito João Dória e à População de São Paulo" [Public letter to Mayor-Elect Dória and the population of São Paulo]. Retrieved March 9, 2020 (http://gaspargarcia.org.br/noticias/carta-aberta-do-forum-dos-ambulantes-ao-futuro-prefeito-joao-doria-e-a-populacao-de-sao-paulo/).
Foucault, Michel. 1994. *Dits et Écrits* [Sayings and writings]. Paris: Gallimard.
Foucault, Michel. 1995 [1975]. *Discipline and Punish: The Birth of the Prison*. New York: Vintage Books.
Foucault, Michel. 2008. *The Birth of Biopolitics: Lectures at the Collège de France 1978–1979*. New York: Palgrave Macmillan.
Foucault, Michel. 2009. *Security, Territory, Population: Lectures at the Collège de France 1977–1978*. New York: Palgrave Macmillan.
Foucault, Michel. 2015. *The Punitive Society: Lectures at the Collège de France 1972–1973*. New York: Palgrave Macmillan.
Freire da Silva, Carlos. 2008. "Trabalho Informal e Redes de Subcontratação: Dinâmicas Urbanas da Indústria de Confecções em São Paulo" [Informal work and subcontracting networks: Urban dynamics of the garment industry in São Paulo]. Master's thesis, University of São Paulo, Brazil.

Freire da Silva, Carlos. 2014a. "Das Calçadas às Galerias: Mercados Populares do Centro de São Paulo" [From the sidewalks to the galleries: Downtown São Paulo's popular markets]. Doctoral dissertation, University of São Paulo, Brazil.

Freire da Silva, Carlos. 2014b. "Ciudad del Este: Do Comércio de Fronteira ao Centro de São Paulo . . ." [Ciudad del Este: From border commerce to downtown São Paulo . . .]. *Travessia* 74: 75–92.

Freire da Silva, Carlos. 2018. "Conexões Brasil-China: A Migração Chinesa no Centro de São Paulo" [Brasil-China connections: Chinese migration in downtown São Paulo]. *Cadernos Metrópole* 20 (41): 223–43.

Freitas, Frederico. 2021. *Nationalizing Nature: Iguazu Falls and National Parks at the Brazil-Argentina Border*. Cambridge: Cambridge University Press.

Frúgoli, Heitor, Jr. 2000. *Centralidades em São Paulo: Trajetórias, Conflitos e Negócios na Metrópole* [Centralities in São Paulo: Trajectories, conflicts, and business in the metropolis]. São Paulo: Cortez/Edusp/Fapesp.

Frúgoli, Heitor, Jr. 2001. "A Questão da Centralidade em São Paulo: O Papel das Associações de Caráter Empresarial" [The issue of centrality in São Paulo: The role of corporate syndicates]. *Revista de Sociologia e Política* 16: 51–66.

Furtado, Celso. 1968. *Subdesenvolvimento e Estagnação na América Latina* [Underdevelopment and stagnation in Latin America]. Rio de Janeiro, Brazil: Editora Civilização Brasileira.

G1. 2008. "PRF Mapeia Rota Usada por Chineses Ilegais no País" [Highway police find the route illegal Chinese use in the country] October 27, 2008. Retrieved January 4, 2018 (http://g1.globo.com/Noticias/Brasil/0,,mul834105-5598,00-prf +mapeia+rota+usada+por+chineses+ilegais+no+pais.html).

Gago, Verónica. 2017. *Neoliberalism from Below: Popular Pragmatics and Baroque Economies*. Durham, NC: Duke University Press.

Gago, Veronica. 2018. "What Are Popular Economies?" *Radical Philosophy* 2 (2): 31–38.

Gago, Verónica, and Sandro Mezzadra. 2017. "A Critique of the Extractive Operations of Capital: Toward an Expanded Concept of Extractivism." *Rethinking Marxism* 29 (4): 574–91.

Gammeltoft-Hansen, Thomas, and Ninna Nyberg Sørensen. 2013. "Introduction." In *The Migration Industry and the Commercialization of International Migration*, edited by T. Gammeltoft-Hansen and N. N. Sørensen, 1–23. London: Routledge.

Gao, Weinong. 2012. 拉丁美洲华侨华人移民史、社团与文化活动远眺–上册 [Perspectives on the history, communities, and cultural activities of overseas Chinese migrants in Latin America, volume 1]. Guangzhou, China: Jinan University Press.

Gao, Weinong. 2017. "New Chinese Migrants in Latin America: Trends and Patterns of Adaptation." In *Contemporary Chinese Diasporas*, edited by M. Zhou, 333–48. Singapore: Palgrave.

Gao, Weinong. 2022. "巴西的中国大陆新移民：基于人口增长数据的探讨" [The new migrants from mainland China in Brazil: An exploration based on the data of population growth]. *Overseas Chinese Journal of Bagui* 4: 52–62.

Gao, Weinong, and Chang-Sheng Shu. 2023. "巴西华侨华人的前天、昨天与今天" [The day before yesterday, yesterday, and today of overseas Chinese in Brazil]. Guangzhou, China: Jinan University Press.

Garelli, Glenda, and Martina Tazzioli. 2017. *Tunisia as a Revolutionized Space of Migration*. New York and London: Palgrave Macmillan.

Glick-Schiller, Nina, and Noel Salazar. 2013. "Regimes of Mobility Across the Globe." *Journal of Ethnic and Migration Studies* 39 (2): 183–200.

Goffman, Erving. 1962. *The Presentation of Self in Everyday Life*. New York: Anchor Books.

Goldman, Márcio. 2006. "Alteridade e Experiência: Antropologia e Teoria Etnográfica" [Alterity and experience: Anthropology and ethnographic theory]. *Etnográfica* 10 (1): 161–73.

González, Freddy. 2017. *Paisanos Chinos: Transpacific Politics Among Chinese Immigrants in Mexico*. Oakland: University of California Press.

Gordon, Matthew, Gustavo Lins Ribeiro, and Carlos Alba, eds. 2012. *Globalization from Below: The World's Other Economy*. New York: Routledge.

Gros, Frédéric. 2010. "Foucault et 'La Société Punitive'" [Foucault and *The Punitive Society*]. *Pouvoirs* 135 (4): 5–14.

Hage, Ghassan. 1998. *White Nation: Fantasies of White Supremacy in a Multicultural Society*. Sydney, Australia: Pluto Press.

Hamlin, Rebecca. 2021. *Crossing: How We Label and React to People on the Move*. Stanford, CA: Stanford University Press.

Harcourt, Bernard. 2015. "Course Context." In Michel Foucault, *The Punitive Society: Lectures at the Collège de France 1972–1973*, 265–310. New York: Palgrave Macmillan.

Harpaz, Yossi, and Pablo Mateos. 2018. "Strategic Citizenship: Negotiating Membership in the Age of Dual Nationality." *Journal of Ethnic and Migration Studies* 45 (6): 843–57.

Hart, Keith. 1973. "Informal Income Opportunities and Urban Employment in Ghana." *Journal of Modern African Studies* 3 (11): 61–89.

Harvey, David. 2003. *The New Imperialism*. Oxford: Oxford University Press.

Hearn, Adrian. 2012. "Harnessing the Dragon: Overseas Chinese Entrepreneurs in Mexico and Cuba." *China Quarterly* 209: 111–33.

Hickey, Maureen, Elaine Lynn-Ee Ho, and Brenda Yeoh. 2015. "Introduction to the Special Section on Establishing State-Led 'Diaspora Strategies in Asia:

Migration-as-Development Reinvented.'" *Singapore Journal of Tropical Geography* 36 (2): 139–46.

Hirata, Daniel Veloso. 2012. "A Produção das Cidades Securitárias: Polícia e Política" [The making of securitarian cities: Police and politics]. *Le Monde Diplomatique*, April 2012. Retrieved December 11, 2018 (http://www.diplomatique.org.br/artigo.php?id=1123).

Hirata, Daniel Veloso. 2014a. "Street Commerce as a 'Problem' in the Cities of Rio de Janeiro and São Paulo." *Vibrant* 11 (1): 96–117.

Hirata, Daniel Veloso. 2014b. "Illegalismos" [Illegalisms]. In *Crime, Polícia e Justiça no Brasil*, edited by R. S. de Lima, J. L. Ratton, and R. G. de Azevedo. São Paulo: Contexto.

Ho, Elaine. 2016. "From *Guiqiao* to *Haidai*: Diaspora Engagement and the Evolving Politics of Return Migration in China." In *Handbook of Chinese Migration Identity and Wellbeing*, edited by R. Iredale and F. Guo, 199–214. Northampton, MA: Edward Elgar Publishing.

Ho, Elaine, and Mark Boyle. 2015. "Migration as Development Repackaged? The Globalizing Imperative of the Singaporean State's Diaspora Strategies." *Singapore Journal of Tropical Geography* 36 (2): 164–82.

Ho, Elaine, Maureen Hickey, and Brenda Yeoh. 2015. "New Research Directions and Critical Perspectives on Diaspora Strategies." *Geoforum* 59: 153–58.

Holston, James. 1991. "The Misrule of Law: Land and Usurpation in Brazil." *Comparative Studies in Society and History* 33 (4): 695–725.

Holston, James. 2008. *Insurgent Citizenship: Disjunctions of Democracy and Modernity in Brazil*. Princeton, NJ: Princeton University Press.

International Labor Organization. 1972. *Employment, Incomes and Equality: A Strategy for Increasing Productive Employment in Kenya*. Geneva: ILO. Retrieved February 17, 2020 (http://www.ilo.org/public/libdoc/ilo/1972/72B09_608_engl.pdf).

International Organization for Migration. 2010. "Perfil Migratório do Brasil 2009" [Brazil migration profile 2009]. Geneva: International Organization for Migration. Retrieved December 28, 2018 (https://repository.oim.org.co/handle/20.500.11788/1454).

Itikawa, Luciana Fukimoto. 2006. "Trabalho Informal nos Espaços Públicos no Centro de São Paulo: Pensando Parâmetros para Políticas Públicas" [Informal work in public spaces in downtown São Paulo: Parameters for public policies]. Doctoral dissertation, University of São Paulo, Brazil.

Kalir, Barak, Malini Sur, and Willem van Schendel. 2012. "Introduction: Mobile Practices and Regimes of Permissiveness." In *Transnational Flows and Permissive Polities: Ethnographies of Human Mobilities in Asia*, edited by B. Kalir and M. Sur, 11–26. Amsterdam: Amsterdam University Press.

Kara-José, Beatriz. 2010. "A Popularização do Centro de São Paulo: Um Estudo de

Transformações Ocorridas nos Últimos 20 Anos" [Popularization of downtown São Paulo: A study of transformations in the last 20 years]. Doctoral dissertation, University of São Paulo, Brazil.

Karam, John. 2006. "Margins of Memory on the Rua 25 de Março: Constructing the Syrian-Lebanese Past in São Paulo, Brazil." In *Arabs in the Americas: Interdisciplinary Essays on the Arab Diaspora*, edited by D. Zabel, 29–44. New York: Peter Lang Publishers.

Karam, John. 2010. "Atravesando las Américas: La Guerra contra el Terror, los Árabes y las Movilizaciones Transfronterizas en Foz de Iguazu y Ciudad del Este" [Crossing the Americas: The war on terror, the Arabs, and the cross-border mobilizations in Foz do Iguaçú and Ciudad del Este]. In *La Triple Frontera: Dinámicas Culturales y Procesos Transnacionales*, edited by V. Giménez Béliveau and S. Montenegro, 119–152. Buenos Aires: Espacio Editorial.

Karam, John. 2013. "The Lebanese Diaspora at the Tri-Border and the Redrawing of South American Geopolitics, 1950–1992." *Mashriq & Mahjar Journal of Middle East Migration Studies* 1 (1): 55–84.

Keshavarz, Mahmoud. 2018. *The Design Politics of the Passport: Materiality, Immobility, and Dissent*. London: Bloomsbury Academic.

Keshavarzian, Arang. 2010. "Geopolitics and the Genealogy of Free Trade Zones in the Persian Gulf." *Geopolitics* 15 (2): 263–89.

Khosravi, Shahram. 2010. *"Illegal" Traveller: An Auto-Ethnography of Borders*. Basingstoke and New York: Palgrave Macmillan.

Larner, Wendy. 2007. "Expatriate Experts and Globalising Governmentalities: The New Zealand Diaspora Strategy." *Transactions of the Institute of British Geographers* 32 (3): 331–45.

Lausent-Herrera, Isabelle. 2009. "Tusans (Tusheng) and the Changing Chinese Community in Peru." *Journal of Chinese Overseas* 7 (1): 115–52.

Lee, Ana Paulina. 2018. *Mandarin Brazil: Race, Representation, and Memory*. Stanford, CA: Stanford University Press.

Leite, José Roberto Teixeira. 1999. *A China No Brasil: Influências, Marcas, Ecos e Sobrevivências Chinesas na Sociedade e na Arte Brasileiras* [China in Brazil: Chinese influences, marks, echoes, and survival in Brazilian society and art]. Campinas, Brazil: Editora da Unicamp.

Lesser, Jeffrey. 1999. *Negotiating National Identity: Immigrants, Minorities, and the Struggle for Ethnicity in Brazil*. Durham, NC: Duke University Press.

Levien, Michael. 2011. "Special Economic Zones and Accumulation by Dispossession in India." *Journal of Agrarian Change* 11 (4): 454–83.

Levien, Michael. 2018. *Dispossession Without Development: Land Grabs in Neoliberal India*. New York: Oxford University Press.

Lindquist, Johan. 2013. "Beyond Anti-anti-Trafficking." *Dialectical Anthropology* 37: 319–23.

Liu, Hong. 1999. "Bridges Across the Sea: Chinese Social Organizations in Southeast Asia and the Links with *Qiaoxiang*." In *Qiaoxiang Ties: Interdisciplinary Approaches to "Cultural Capitalism" in South China*, edited by L. Douw, Cen Huang, and M. R. Godley, 87–112. London: Kegan Paul.

Liu, Hong. 2008. "Immigrant Transnational Entrepreneurship and Its Linkages with the State/Network: Sino-Singaporean Experience in a Comparative Perspective." In *Chinese Entrepreneurship in a Global Era*, edited by R. Wong, 117–49. London: Routledge.

Liu, Hong. 2016. "Opportunities and Anxieties for the Chinese Diaspora in Southeast Asia." *Current History* 115 (784): 312–18.

Liu, Hong, and Els van Dongen. 2016. "China's Diaspora Policies as a New Mode of Transnational Governance." *Journal of Contemporary China* 25 (102): 805–21.

Liu, Jiaqi M. 2022. "When Diaspora Politics Meet Global Ambitions: Diaspora Institutions Amid China's Geopolitical Transformations." *International Migration Review* 56 (4): 1255–79.

Ma Mung, Emmanuel. 2009. "La Nouvelle Géographie de la Diaspora Chinoise" [The new geography of the Chinese diaspora]. *Accueillir* 249/250: 33–35.

Macagno, Lorenzo. 2013. "From Mozambique to Brazil: The 'Good Portuguese' of the Chinese Athletic Club." In *Imperial Migrations: Migration, Diasporas and Citizenship*, edited by E. Morier-Genoud and M. Cahen, 239–62. London: Palgrave Macmillan.

Machado, Igor José de Renó. 2020. "Purity and Mixture in the Category of Refuge in Brazil." *Journal of Immigrant & Refugee Studies* 19 (53): 1–13.

Machado, Luiz Antônio. 2002. "Da Informalidade à Empregabilidade: Reorganizando a Dominação no Mundo do Trabalho" [From informality to employability: Reorganizing domination in the labor world]. *Caderno CRH* 15 (37): 81–109.

Marx, Karl. 1978. "Capital." In *The Marx-Engels Reader*, edited by R. Tucker, 294–442. New York: W. W. Norton & Company.

McNevin, Anne. 2011. *Contesting Citizenship: Irregular Migrants and the New Frontiers of the Political*. New York: Columbia University Press.

McNevin, Anne. 2014. "Global Migration and Mobility: Conceptual Approaches, Governing Rationalities and Social Transformations." In *Sage Handbook of Globalization*, edited by M. Steger, P. Battersby, and J. Siracusa, 644–61. London: Sage.

McNevin, Anne, Antje Missbach, and Deddy Mulyana. 2016. "The Rationalities of Migration Management: Control and Subversion in an Indonesia-Based Counter-Smuggling Campaign." *International Political Sociology* 10 (3): 223–40.

Meddeb, Hamza. 2015. "Rente Frontalière et Injustice Social en Tunisie" [Border rent and social injustice in Tunisia]. *L'État d'Injustice au Maghreb—Maroc et*

Tunisie, edited by I. Bono, B. Hibou, M. Hamza, and M. Tozy, 63–98. Paris: Editions Khartala.

Menezes, Alfredo da Mota. 1987. *A Herança de Stroessner: Brasil-Paraguai 1955–1980* [Stroessner's legacy: Brazil-Paraguay 1955–1980]. Campinas, Brazil: Papirus.

Menjívar, Cecília, and Daniel Kanstroom, eds. 2013. *Constructing Immigrant "Illegality": Critiques, Experiences, and Responses*. Cambridge: Cambridge University Press.

Mezzadra, Sandro. 2011. "How Many Histories of Labour? Towards a Theory of Postcolonial Capitalism." *Postcolonial Studies* 14 (2): 151–70.

Mezzadra, Sandro. 2016. "The Figure of the Migrant: Seeing Like a Migrant." An Und Für Sich. Retrieved December 20, 2018 (http://itself.blog/2016/06/24/book-event-the-figure-of-the-migrant-seeing-like-a-migrant-mezzadra/).

Mezzadra, Sandro, and Brett Neilson. 2013. *Borders as Methods, or the Multiplication of Labor*. Durham, NC: Duke University Press.

Mezzadra, Sandro, and Brett Neilson. 2019. *The Politics of Operations: Excavating Contemporary Capitalism*. Durham, NC: Duke University Press.

Milesi, Rosita. 2011. Regularização de Imigrantes no Brasil, pelo Sistema do Registro Provisório: Anistias de 1981, 1988, 1998 e 2009 [Immigrant regularization in Brazil through to the Temporary Registry: The amnesties of 1981, 1988, 1998, and 2009]. Retrieved December 4, 2011 (http://www.migrante.org.br).

Ministerio de la Hacienda de la República del Paraguay. 2000. *Régimen de Adecuación al MERCOSUR: Análisis de los Efectos Estimativos en la Política Fiscal* [MERCOSUR Adaptation Regime: An analysis of expected effects on fiscal policy]. Asunción, Paraguay.

Ministério Público Federal. 2009a. *Processo 2008.41.00.006612-1 IPL: 701/2008—Procuradoria da República no Estado de Rondônia* [Process 2008.41.00.006612-1 IPL: 701/2008—Public Prosecutor's Office in Rondônia]. July 23, 2009.

Ministério Público Federal. 2009b. "MPF-RO Denuncia 24 Envolvidos em Imigração Ilegal de Chineses" [Public Prosecutor's Office in Rondônia prosecutes 24 persons involved with illegal Chinese migration]. July 23, 2009. Retrieved March 4, 2020 (http://www.mpf.mp.br/ro/sala-de-imprensa/noticias-ro/mpf-ro-denuncia-24-envolvidos-em-imigracao-ilegal-de-chineses).

Miranda, Aníbal. 2000. *Dossier Paraguay: Los Dueños de Grandes Fortunas en Paraguay* [Dossier Paraguay: Large fortune owners in Paraguay]. Asunción: Miranda y Asociados.

Miranda, Fidel. 2009. *Historia del Centro de Despachantes de Aduana del Paraguay–Regional Alto Paraná: 20 Años De Vida Institucional* [History of the Custom Brokers Center of Paraguay–Alto Paraná Regional Branch: 20 years of institutional life]. Ciudad del Este, Paraguay: Sanchos Libros.

Moore, Henrietta. 1999. "Anthropological Theory at the Turn of the Century." *Anthropological Theory Today,* edited by H. Moore, 1–23. Cambridge: Polity Press.

Moraes, Ivy Mayumi de. 2018. *Locação Social em São Paulo entre 2001 e 2016: Definição da Agenda Governamental* [Social rental housing in São Paulo between 2001 and 2016: Setting the policy agenda]. Master's thesis, Fundação Getúlio Vargas, Brazil.

Moraga, Jorge. 2018. "Reparto Comunitario y Gasto Agonístico: Diferenciaciones y Hegemonías entre Antiguos y Nuevos Migrantes Chinos en Chile" [Community distribution and agonistic expenditure: Differentiations and hegemonies between old and new Chinese migrants in Chile]. *Rumbos* 8 (17): 133–52.

Morris, Julia. 2017. "Power, Capital and Immigration Detention Rights: Making Networked Markets in Global Detention Governance at UNHCR." *Global Networks* 17 (3): 400–422.

Muller, Juliane. 2019. "Andean-Pacific Commerce and Credit: Bolivian Traders, Asian Migrant Businesses, and International Manufacturers in the Regional Economy." *Journal for Latin American and Caribbean Anthropology* 23 (1): 18–36.

Muller, Juliane, and Rudi Colloredo-Mansfeld. 2019. "Entrepreneurship, Artisans, and Traders: The Remaking of China-Latin America Economies." *Journal for Latin American and Caribbean Anthropology* 23 (1): 9–17.

Mullings, Beverley. 2012. "Governmentality, Diaspora Assemblages and the Ongoing Challenge of 'Development.'" *Antipode* 44 (2): 406–27.

Nee, Victor, and Jimmy Sanders. 1987. "The Limits of Ethnic Solidarity in the Enclave Economy." *American Sociological Review* 52 (6): 745–73.

Neilson, Brett, and Ned Rossiter. 2008. "Precarity as a Political Concept, or, Fordism as Exception." *Theory, Culture & Society* 25 (7/8): 51–72.

Nickson, Andrew. 1997. "Corruption and the Transition." In *The Transition to Democracy in Paraguay* edited by P. Lambert and A. Nickson, 24–44. London: Palgrave Macmillan.

Nun, José. 1969. "Superpoblación Relativa, Ejército Industrial de Reserva y Masa Marginal" [Relative surplus population, industrial reserve army, and marginal mass]. *Revista Latinoamericana de Sociología,* 5 (2): 178–236.

Núñez de Báez, Guillermina. 2003. *Reseña Historica del Alto Paraná* [Historical review of Alto Paraná]. Ciudad del Este, Paraguay: Papyru's Impresiones.

O Estado de S. Paulo. 2009. "PF Prende Quadrilha Acusada de Trazer Chineses Ilegais ao Brasil" [Federal police arrest group accused of bringing illegal Chinese to Brazil]. May 22, 2009. Retrieved January 4, 2019 (https://www.estadao.com.br/noticias/geral,pf-prende-quadrilha-acusada-de-trazer-chineses-ilegais-ao-brasil,375346).

O Estado de S. Paulo. 2012. "Brasil é a Bola da Vez para Chinês Imigrante" [For Chinese migrants, Brazil is the new destination of choice]. August 11, 2012. Retrieved January 4, 2018 (https://sao-paulo.estadao.com.br/noticias/geral, brasil-e-a-bola-da-vez-para-chines-imigrante-imp-,915194).

Oliveira, Francisco. 1972. "A Economia Brasileira: Crítica à Razão Dualista" [The Brazilian economy: Critique of the dualist reason]. *Novos Estudos* 2: 3–82.

Oliveira, Francisco. 2003. *Crítica à Razão Dualista / O Ornitorrinco* [Critique of the dualist reason / The platypus]. São Paulo: Boitempo.

Oliveira, Lineu Francisco. 2010. *Mascates e Sacoleiros: Empreendedores que Construíram uma Região* [Peddlers and *Sacoleiros*: Entrepreneurs who built a neighborhood]. São Paulo: Scortecci.

Ong, Aihwa. 1999. *Flexible Citizenship: The Cultural Logic of Transnationality*. Durham, NC: Duke University Press.

Penner, Reinaldo. 1998. "Movimiento Comercial y Financiero de Ciudad del Este: Perspectivas dentro del Proceso de Integración" [Ciudad del Este's commercial and financial flows: Perspectives from the integration process]. Banco Central del Paraguay. Gerencia de Estudios Económicos. Departamento de Economía Internacional. Asunción, Paraguay.

Penner, Reinaldo. 2005. "Informe sobre el Comercio de Productos Informáticos en Ciudad del Este: La Gran Oportunidad de Industrialización" [Report on computer goods in Ciudad del Este: The great opportunity for industrialization]. United States Agency for International Development and Cámara de Comercio de Tecnología de la Información. July 2005.

Penner, Reinaldo. 2006. "Segundo Informe sobre el Comercio de Productos Informáticos en Ciudad del Este: La Gran Oportunidad de Industrialización" [Second report on computer goods in Ciudad del Este: The great opportunity for industrialization]. United States Agency for International Development. December 2006.

Peraldi, Michel. 2007. "Aventuriers du Nouveau Capitalisme Marchand: Essai d'Anthropologie de l'Éthique Mercantile" [Adventurers of the new commercial capitalism: Essay on the anthropology of mercantile ethics]. In *Voyage du Développement: Emigration, Commerce, Exil*, edited by F. Adelkhah and J. Bayart, 73–114. Paris: Karthala.

Pieke, Frank. 2007. "Les Migrations Chinoises Contemporaines: Nouveaux Régimes et Nouvelles Activités en Europe" [Contemporary Chinese migrations: New regimes and new activities in Europe]. In *Nouvelles Migrations Chinoises et Travail en Europe*, edited by L. Roulleau-Berger, 19–43. Toulouse, France: Presses Universitaires du Mirail.

Pieke, Frank, Pál Nyíri, Mette Thunø, and Antonella Ceccagno. 2004. *Transnational Chinese: Fujianese Migrants in Europe*. Stanford, CA: Stanford University Press.

Pinheiro-Machado, Rosana. 2010. "Uma ou Duas Chinas?" [One or two Chinas?]. *Civitas* 10 (3): 468–89.

Pinheiro-Machado, Rosana. 2017. *Counterfeit Itineraries in the Global South*. London and New York: Routledge.

Pinheiro-Machado, Rosana. 2018a. "Rethinking the Informal and Criminal Economy from a Global Commodity Chain Perspective: China-Paraguay-Brazil." *Global Networks* 18 (3): 479–99.

Pinheiro-Machado, Rosana. 2018b. "The Power of Chineseness: Flexible Taiwanese Identities During Times of Change in Asia and South America." *Journal of Latin American and Caribbean Anthropology* 23 (1): 56–73.

Piza, Douglas de Toledo. 2012. *Comerciantes Chineses: Um Pouco da Mundialização Contada a Partir da Região da rua 25 de Março* [Chinese sellers: A tale of globalization in 25 de Março Street]. Master's thesis, University of São Paulo, Brazil.

Piza, Douglas de Toledo. 2015. "Circuitos do Comércio Chinês em São Paulo" [Circuits of Chinese commerce in São Paulo]. In *Ilegalismos na Globalização: Trabalho, Migrações, Mercados*, edited by V. Telles and A. Peralva, 304–19. Rio de Janeiro: Editora da UFRJ.

Pliez, Olivier. 2010. "Toutes les Routes de la Soie Mènent à Yiwu (Chine): Entrepreneurs et Migrants Musulmans dans un Comptoir Économique Chinois" [All silk roads lead to Yiwu (China): Muslim entrepreneurs and migrants at a Chinese trading post]. *L'Espace Géographique* 39 (2): 132–45.

Portal da Prefeitura. 2013. "Prefeitura Irá Priorizar Segurança e Diálogo na Feira da Madrugada." May 28, 2013. Retrieved March 26, 2019, https://www.prefeitura.sp.gov.br/cidade/secretarias/subprefeituras/noticias/?p=148969.

Portes, Alejandro. 1994. "The Informal Economy and Its Paradoxes." In *The Handbook of Economic Sociology*, edited by N. Smelser and R. Swedberg, 426–52. Princeton, NJ: Princeton University Press.

Portes, Alejandro. 2010. *Economic Sociology: A Systematic Inquiry*. Princeton, NJ: Princeton University Press.

Qu, Xiaolei. 2016. "Utilitarian Cultural Affinity: Transnational Ties Between China and Singapore's Voluntary Associations." *Sungkyun Journal of East Asian Studies* 16 (1): 91–112.

Quintino, Felipe, and Tania Tonhati. 2017. "Uma Análise das Autorizações de Trabalho Concedidas a Estrangeiros pela Coordenação Geral de Imigração (CGIg), 2011–2016" [Analysis of work authorizations granted to foreigners by the general coordination of immigration, 2011–2016]. In *A Inserção dos Imigrantes no Mercado de Trabalho Brasileiro: Relatório Anual 2017*, edited by L. Cavalcanti, T. Oliveira, D. Araujo, and T. Tonhati, 16–33. Brasília: OBMigra.

Rabossi, Fernando. 2004. "Nas Ruas de Ciudad del Este: Vidas e Vendas num Mercado de Fronteira" [In the streets of Ciudad del Este: Lives and sales in a

border market]. Doctoral dissertation, Universidade Federal do Rio de Janeiro, Brazil.
Rabossi, Fernando. 2007. "Árabes e Muçulmanos em Foz do Iguaçu e Ciudad del Este: Notas para uma Re-interpretação" [Arabs and Muslims in Foz do Iguaçu and Ciudad del Este: Notes for re-interpretation]. In *Mundos em Movimento: Ensaios sobre Migrações*, edited by G. Seyferth, H. Póvoa, M. C. Zanini, and M. Santos, 287–312. Santa Maria, Brazil: Editora da Universidade Federal de Santa Maria.
Rabossi, Fernando. 2010. "Made in Paraguai. Notas Sobre la Producción de Ciudad del Este" [Made in Paraguay: Notes on production in Ciudad del Este]. *Papeles de Trabajo* 6: 1–21. Retrieved January 30, 2019 (http://www.idaes.edu.ar/papelesdetrabajo/paginas/Documentos/7%20Rabossi.pdf).
Rabossi, Fernando. 2013. "Dinámicas económicas en la Triple Frontera (Brasil, Paraguay y Argentina)" [Economic dynamics in the tri-border area (Brazil, Paraguay, and Argentina)]. In *Seguridad, Planificación y Desarrollo en las Regiones Transfronterizas*, edited by F. Carrión, 167–93. Quito, Ecuador: FLACSO and Centro Internacional de Investigaciones para el Desarrollo (IDRC-CRDI).
Rabossi, Fernando. 2014. "Terrorism Frontier Cell or Cosmopolitan Commercial Hub? The Arab and Muslim Presence at the Border of Paraguay, Brazil, and Argentina." In *The Middle East and Brazil: Perspectives on the New Global South*, edited by P. Amar, 95–115. Bloomington: Indiana University Press.
Ragazzi, Francesco. 2009. "Governing Diasporas." *International Political Sociology* 3 (4): 378–97.
Razack, Sherene. 1995. "Domestic Violence as Gender Persecution: Policing the Borders of Nation, Race and Gender." *Canadian Journal of Women and the Law/Revue Femmes et Droit* 8 (1): 45–88.
Ribeiro, Gustavo Lins. 2006. "Economic Globalization from Below." *Etnográfica* 10 (2): 233–49.
Roitman, Janet. 2004. *Fiscal Disobedience: An Anthropology of Economic Regulation in Central Africa*. Princeton, NJ: Princeton University Press.
Rojas Villagra, Luis. 2014. *La Metamorfosis del Paraguay: Del Esplendor Inicial a su Traumática Descomposición* [Paraguay's metamorphosis: From an initial splendor to its traumatic decay]. Asunción, Base-IS.
Rosales, Rocío. 2020. *Fruteros: Street Vending, Illegality, and Ethnic Community in Los Angeles*. Oakland, CA: University of California Press.
Rostow, Walt Whitman. 1960. *The Stages of Economic Growth: A Non-Communist Manifesto*. Cambridge: Cambridge University Press.
Roulleau-Berger, Laurence, ed. 2007. *Nouvelles Migrations Chinoises et Travail en Europe* [New Chinese migrations and work in Europe]. Toulouse: Presses Universitaires du Mirail.

Roy, Ananya. 2005. "Urban Informality: Toward an Epistemology of Planning." *Journal of the American Planning Association* 71 (2): 147–58.
Ruiz Díaz, Francisco. 2006. "Regímenes Especiales de Importación en el Paraguay" [Special importation regimes in Paraguay]. Asunción, Paraguay: Secretaría del MERCOSUR.
Ruiz Díaz, Francisco, and Álvaro Ons. 2013. "La Política Comercial Externa del Paraguay en el MERCOSUR" [Paraguay's external trade policy in MERCOSUR]. In *Paraguay en el MERCOSUR: Asimetrías Internas y Política Comercial Externa*, edited by F. Masi, 128–200. Asunción: Centro de Análisis y Difusión de la Economía Paraguaya.
Samson, Melanie. 2015. "Accumulation by Dispossession and the Informal Economy: Struggles over Knowledge, Being and Waste at a Soweto Garbage Dump." *Environment and Planning D: Society and Space* 33 (5): 813–30.
Santos, Artur Henrique da Silva, ed. 2016. *Desenvolvimento, Trabalho e Inovação: A Experiência da Cidade de São Paulo* [Development, labor, and innovation: The experience of the city of São Paulo]. São Paulo: Fundação Perseu Abramo.
Sanyal, Kalyan. 2007. *Rethinking Capitalist Development: Primitive Accumulation, Governmentality, and Post-Colonial Capitalism*. London: Routledge.
São Paulo City Council. 2017. "Relatório da Comissão Parlamentar de Inquérito da Feira da Madrugada" [Report of the São Paulo City Council Special Committee on the Dawn Market]. Retrieved August 9, 2024 (http://www.saopaulo.sp.leg.br/wp-content/uploads/2017/06/relat%c3%b3rio-final-cpi-feira-da-madrugada.pdf).
São Paulo City Council. 2023. "Relatório da Comissão Parlamentar de Inquérito sobre Pirataria e Evasão Fiscal" [Report of the São Paulo City Council Special Committee on Counterfeits and Tax Evasion]. Retrieved August 9, 2024 (https://www.saopaulo.sp.leg.br/wp-content/uploads/2023/03/relatorio-cpi-pirataria-relator-ver-isac-felix-1.pdf).
São Paulo Department of Labor, Development, and Entrepreneurship. 2015. "Projeto Circuito das Compras: Concessão Pública para o Desenvolvimento Socioeconômico e Requalificação da Região Central de São Paulo, através da Interligação dos 4 Maiores Centros Comerciais da Região e do Fomento ao Comércio e ao Empreendedorismo" [Shopping circuit project: Public concession for the socioeconomic development and requalification of downtown São Paulo, interlinking the four largest commercial centers and fomenting commerce and entrepreneurship]. July 2015.
Sassen, Saskia. 1994. "The Informal Economy: Between New Developments and Old Regulations." *Yale Law Journal* 103 (8): 2289–304.
Sassen, Saskia. 2014. *Expulsions: Brutality and Complexity in the Global Economy*. Cambridge, MA: Harvard University Press.

Sbardelotto, Denise. 2010. "Resenha: *Descoberta de Foz do Iguaçu e a Fundação da Colônia Militar*" [Review: *The Discovery of Foz do Iguaçu and the Founding of the Military Colony*]. *Educere et Educare* 5 (9): 293–97.

Scheel, Stephan. 2019. *Autonomy of Migration? Appropriating Mobility Within Biometric Border Regimes*. London and New York: Routledge.

Schuster, Caroline. 2015. *Social Collateral: Women and Microfinance in Paraguay's Smuggling Economy*. Oakland: University of California Press.

Scott, James C. 1998. *Seeing Like a State: How Certain Schemes to Improve the Human Condition Have Failed*. New Haven, CT: Yale University Press.

Secretaria de Estado de Comunicação Social, 2008. "Ipardes Apresenta Estudo sobre o Oeste do Paraná." August 27, 2008. Retrieved August 15, 2024, https://arquivo2003.aen.pr.gov.br/Noticia/Ipardes-apresenta-estudo-sobre-o-Oeste-do-Parana.

Secretaria Nacional de Justiça. 2018. "Refúgio em Números" [Asylum in numbers]. Retrieved December 28, 2018 (https://www.acnur.org/portugues/wp-content/uploads/2018/04/refugio-em-numeros_1104.pdf).

Shachar, Ayelet. 2009. *The Birthright Lottery: Citizenship and Global Inequality*. Cambridge, MA: Harvard University Press.

Sheller, Mimi. 2018. "Theorising Mobility Justice." *Tempo Social* 30 (2): 17–34.

Sheller, Mimi, and John Urry. 2006. "The New Mobilities Paradigm." *Environment and Planning A* 38 (2): 207–26.

Shu, Chang-Sheng. 2009. "Imigrantes e Imigração Chinesa no Rio de Janeiro (1910–1990)" [Immigrants and Chinese migration in Rio de Janeiro (1910–1990)]. *Leituras da História* 17 (2): 44–53.

Shu, Chang-Sheng. 2023. *Chinese Migration to Brazil: History, Mobility and Identities*. Newcastle-upon-Tyne, UK: Cambridge Scholars Publishing.

Silva, Marcos de Araújo. 2008. "Guanxi nos Trópicos: Um Estudo sobre a Diáspora Chinesa em Pernambuco" [Guanxi in the tropics: A study of the Chinese diaspora in Pernambuco]. Master's thesis, Federal University of Pernambuco, Brazil.

Silva, Micael Alvino da. 2010. "Notas sobre a Administração Pública de Foz do Iguaçu (1889–1937)" [Notes on the public administration of Foz do Iguaçu (1889–1937)]. *História na Fronteira* 3 (3): 115–37.

Silva, Sidney. 2006. "Bolivianos em São Paulo: Entre o Sonho e a Realidade" [Bolivians in São Paulo: Between dream and reality]. *Estudos Avançados* 20 (57): 157–70.

Spiro, Peter. 2016. *At Home in Two Countries*. New York: New York University Press.

Sprandel, Marcia Anita, Rosita Milesi, William Cesar de Andrade, Ana Paula da Cunha, Daniela Drummond, and Helen Leal Melo Lima. 2013. "Migración

Extracontinental en Brasil: El Caso de los Ciudadanos Africanos y Asiáticos" [Extracontinental migration in Brazil: The case of African and Asian citizens]. In *Cuadernos Migratorios N°5—Migraciones Extracontinentales en América del Sur: Estudios de Caso*, 115–67. Geneva, Switzerland: International Organization for Migration. Retrieved December 28, 2018 (https://repository.oim.org.co/handle/20.500.11788/1392).

Standing, Guy. 2011. *The Precariat: The New Dangerous Class*. New York: Bloomsbury.

Stenberg, Josh. 2012. "The Chinese of São Paulo: A Case Study." *Journal of Chinese Overseas* 8 (1): 105–22.

Stenberg, Josh. 2016. "An Overseas Orthodoxy? Shifting Toward Pro-PRC Media in Chinese-Speaking Brazil." In *Media and Communication in the Chinese Diaspora: Rethinking Transnationalism*, edited by W. Sun and J. Sinclair, 115–67. Abingdon, UK: Routledge.

Stoler, Ann Laura. 2022. *Interior Frontiers: Essays on the Entrails of Inequality*. New York: Oxford University Press.

Strathern, Marilyn. 2004. *Partial Connections*. Oxford: Altamira Press.

Taiwanese Chamber of Commerce-Paraguay and Chinese Association of Ciudad del Este-Paraguay. 2015. 歡迎僑務委員會陳委員長士魁專刊 [Special issue to welcome the Overseas Community Affairs Council Chairman Chen]. Ciudad del Este, Paraguay.

Tang, Shi-Yeoung. 2013. "巴西招徠臺灣人移民—1960年代我國政府的態度與人民的反應" [Brazil recruits Taiwanese immigrants: The attitude of the Chinese government and the reaction of the people in the 1960s]. 人口學刊 46: 87–119.

Tarrius, Alain. 2002. *La Mondialisation par le Bas* [Globalization from below]. Paris: Balland.

Tassi, Nico, Alfonso Hinojosa Gordonava, and Richard Canaviri Paco. 2015. *La Economía Popular en Bolivia: Tres Miradas* [Popular economy in Bolivia: Three views]. La Paz: Centro de Investigaciones Sociales.

Tazzioli, Martina. 2016. "Foucault and the Irreducible to the Population: The Mob, the Plebs, and Troubling Subjectivities in Excess." In *Foucault and the Making of Subjects*, edited by L. Cremonesi, O. Irrera, D. Lorenzini, and M. Tazzioli, 175–210. London: Rowman & Littlefield.

Tazzioli, Martina. 2017. "The Government of Migrant Mobs: Temporary Divisible Multiplicities in Border Zones." *European Journal of Social Theory* 20 (4): 473–90.

Telles, Vera da Silva. 2009. "Ilegalismos Urbanos e a Cidade" [Urban illegalisms and the city]. *Novos Estudos* 84: 142–73.

Telles, Vera da Silva. 2010. "Nas Dobras do Legal e Ilegal: Ilegalismos e Jogos de Poder nas Tramas da Cidade" [Between the legal and the illegal: Illegalisms and power play in the city]. *Dilemas: Revista de Estudos de Conflito e Controle Social* 2 (5/6): 97–126.

Telles, Vera da Silva. 2012. "Jogos de Poder nas Dobras do Legal e Ilegal: Anotações de um Percurso de Pesquisa" [Power play between the legal and the illegal: Notes of a research journey]. In *Ilegalismos, Cidade e Política*, edited by C. Azaïs, G. Kessler, and V. Telles, 27–56. Belo Horizonte, Brazil: Fino Traço.

Thunø, Mette. 2001. "Reaching Out and Incorporating Chinese Overseas: The Trans-Territorial Scope of the PRC by the End of the 20th Century." *China Quarterly* 168: 910–29.

Thunø, Mette, ed. 2007. *Beyond Chinatown: New Chinese Migration and the Global Expansion of China*. Copenhagen: NIAS Press.

TNS Research International. 2009. "25 de Março—Laboratório de Consumo" [25 de Março Street—A laboratory for consumption]. Retrieved May 28, 2012 (http://www.tnsglobal.com.br/site2006/mkt/varejo/25.pdf).

Ticktin, Miriam. 2016. "Thinking Beyond Humanitarian Borders." *Social Research: An International Quarterly* 83 (2): 255–71.

Tilly, Charles. 1990. *Coercion, Capital, and European States, A.D. 990–1990*. Oxford: Blackwell.

To, James Jiann Hua. 2014. *Qiaowu: Extra-Territorial Policies for the Overseas Chinese*. Leiden and Boston: Brill Academic Publishers.

Tracy, Noel, and Constance Lever-Tracy. 2002. "A New Alliance for Profit: China's Local Industries and the Chinese Diaspora." In *Chinese Entrepreneurship and Asian Business Networks*, edited by T. Menkhoff and S. Gerke, 65–83. London and New York: Routledge.

Truzzi, Oswaldo Mário Serra. 1993. *Patrícios: Sírios e Libaneses em São Paulo* [*Patrícios*: Syrians and Lebanese in São Paulo]. Doctoral dissertation, Universidade Estadual de Campinas, Brazil.

Truzzi, Oswaldo Mário Serra. 2008. Sociabilidades e Valores: Um Olhar sobre a Família Muçulmana em São Paulo" [Sociability and values: A view on the Muslim family in São Paulo]. *Dados* 51 (1): 37–74.

Tucker, Jennifer. 2017a. "City-Stories: Narrative as Diagnostic and Strategic Resource in Ciudad del Este, Paraguay." *Planning Theory* 16 (1): 74–98.

Tucker, Jennifer. 2017b. "Affect and the Dialectics of Uncertainty: Governing a Paraguayan Frontier Town." *Environment and Planning D: Society and Space* 35 (4): 733–51.

Tucker, Jennifer. 2020. "Outlaw Capital: Accumulation by Transgression on the Paraguay-Brazil Border." *Antipode* 52 (5): 1455–74.

Tucker, Jennifer. 2023. *Outlaw Capital: Everyday Illegalities and the Making of Uneven Development*. Atlanta: University of Georgia Press.

Valverde, Mariana. 2016. "Review of *The Punitive Society: Lectures at The Collège De France 1972–73*." *British Journal of Criminology* 57 (1): 238–46.

Van Schendel, Willem, and Itty Abraham. 2005. "Introduction: The Making of Illicitness." In *Illicit Flows and Criminal Things: States, Borders, and the Other Side of Globalization*, edited by W. van Schendel and I. Abraham, 1–37. Bloomington: Indiana University Press.

Veras, Daniel. 2009. "A Imigração Chinesa em São Paulo: Importante Ponto de Contato entre Brasil e China" [Chinese immigration in São Paulo: A link between Brazil and China]. In *Nós e a China*, edited by L. Paulino and M. Pires, 183–99. São Paulo: LCTE Editora.

Wallerstein, Immanuel. 1992. "The Concept of National Development, 1917–1989: Elegy and Requiem." *American Behavioral Scientist* 35 (4): 517–29.

Waters, Mary C., Van Tran, Philip Kasinitz, and John Mollenkopf. 2010. "Segmented Assimilation Revisited: Types of Acculturation and Socioeconomic Mobility in Young Adulthood." *Ethnic and Racial Studies* 33 (4): 1168–93.

Xavier, Iara Rolnik. 2010. "Projeto Migratório e Espaço: Os Migrantes Bolivianos na Região Metropolitana de São Paulo" [Migratory project and space: Bolivian migrants in the São Paulo metropolitan area]. Master's thesis, Universidade Estadual de Campinas, Brasil.

Xiang, Biao. 2007. "A New Mobility Regime in the Making: What Does a Mobile China Mean to the World?" *Idées Pour le Débat* 10: 1–19.

Zhang, Sheldon, Gabriella Sanchez, and Luigi Achilli. 2018. "Crimes of Solidarity in Mobility: Alternative Views on Migrant Smuggling." *Annals of the American Academy of Political and Social Science* 676 (1): 6–15.

Zhou, Min, and Rennie Lee. 2013. "Transnationalism and Community Building: Chinese Immigrant Organizations in the United States." *Annals of the American Academy of Political and Social Science* 647 (1): 22–49.

Zhou, Min, and Hong Liu. 2016. "Homeland Engagement and Host Society Integration: A Comparative Study of New Chinese Immigrants in the United States and Singapore." *International Journal of Comparative Sociology* 57 (1/2): 30–52.

Index

Note: Some entries below are English translations as they appear in the book and do not include the corresponding terms in Mandarin Chinese, Spanish, or Portuguese. For a list of the terms in the original language, consult the Translation Glossary above.

Accounting Court (São Paulo), 88
accumulation, 21, 24, 25, 160; capitalist, xi, 78, 84; by dispossession, xii, 22, 23; by exploitation, xii; primitive, xii, 22, 42; by transgression, 23; of wealth, 3, 26, 42
Adaptation Regime, 55–56, 63. *See also* Southern Common Market (MERCOSUR)
Administration Commission of Puerto Presidente Stroessner, 39, 40
Africa, 18, 21
Agreement of Mutual Protection and Promotion of Investments (Paraguay-Taiwan, 1992), 53
Amazon, Brazilian, 139, 140
amnesty (immigration regularization), 120, 129, 143–146
Amorim, Celso, 58
Angolans, 70

anti-Chinese, 119
anti-communism, 102
Anti-Mafia Police (Paraguay), 55
Argentina, xvii, 37, 44, 58, 125; MERCOSUR, 53; Tierra del Fuego, 54; tourists' view of, 59; in tri-border area with Brazil and Paraguay, 7f; in *triple frontera*, x
Argentinians, 41
Armenian migrants, 67
Asia, 43, 102, 109, 113; diaspora agencies, 32; East, 67, 159; exports, 64, 69, 70; informal economy in, 21; migration from to South America, 24, 33; overseas Chinese affairs agencies in, 98; Southeast, 16, 99, 103; West, 67
Asian Tigers, 41
Association of Customs Brokers of Paraguay, 41
Association of Fujianese in Brazil, 104

Association of the Cantonese of Brazil, 104
Association of the Entrepreneurs of the Shopping Circuit in São Paulo, 104, 156–157
associations (Ciudad del Este), 101–103
associations (São Paulo), 103–106
associations, Chinese, 49, 120, 121, 157; Chinese Association of Brazil, 72, 96, 103, 104, 107–108, 111, 113–116, 119; Chinese Association of Ciudad del Este-Paraguay, 50, 57, 96, 101–102, 110, 115–116, 147, 148; Overseas Chinese Association-Paraguay Chapter, 102, 113
associations, diaspora, 98, 101, 122, 159, 160
associations, hometown (*qiáoxiānghuì*), 11, 14, 99, 100, 102, 108, 151
associations, native-place (*tóngxiānghuì*), 99, 101, 103–105, 114–118, 122
associations, surname/kin, 99
associations, trade/business, 59, 99, 105, 106, 122
Asunción, Paraguay, 29, 38, 40, 52, 101; Treaty of Asunción, 53
associations, vendors', 75, 78, 93
asylum, 33, 129, 147, 148, 150, 170n4.2. *See also* refuge/refugees
atheism, 14
Australia, 11, 134

Beijing, China, 10, 104, 134; Beijing Cultural Exchange Association (Brazil), 105; government, 99, 100
Beijing Cultural Exchange Association of Brazil, 105
belonging, 12, 99, 107
Bigo, Didier, 128
Bolivia, 139
Bolivians, 68, 70, 92, 117
Border Clearance Regime (Paraguay), 44

border studies, 128, 160
borderlands, 62, 63, 101, 131, 139, 141; Paraguay's, 44; trade in, 36–43
Bosniak, Linda, 145
Brás (São Paulo neighborhood), 67, 69, 73
Brasília, Brazil, 40, 56
Braudel, Fernand, 42
Brazil-China Business Council, 106
Brazil-China Chamber, 106
Brazil-China Economic Development Chamber, 106
Brazil-China Social and Cultural Institute, 106, 156
Brazilian Coffee Institute, 44
Brazilian Council of Immigration, 133
Brazilian Forum against Piracy and Illegality, 118
Brazilian Health Regulatory Agency, 142
Brazilian Institute of Ethics in Competition, 81, 118
Brazilian Project Structuring Company, 86
Brazilian resellers, 35, 58, 61, 62
Brazilian Social Security Institute, 142
Brazilian vendors, 70, 71, 75, 78, 85
Brazil-Paraguay-Brazil smuggling scheme, 44, 56
bribery, 1, 62, 73, 75, 79, 119, 120, 136. *See also* corruption
brokering, 26, 50, 95, 98, 123; Association of Customs Brokers of Paraguay, 41; for Chinese governments, 111–113; in global economy, 98, 123–124; import, 105; migration, 14; political, 117
Buddhism, 14, 119
Bureau of Diaspora Affairs (Republic of China), 99
Business Company SRL, 41–42, 43

Camilo, Álvaro, 87
Canada, 11, 134

INDEX   195

Cantonese (language), 14
Cantonese distributors, 69
Cantonese migrants, 16, 47, 68, 103; Association of the Cantonese of Brazil, 104
capitalism, 24; contemporary, ix–xii; global, 19, 89, 159; neoliberal, 23, 24; postcolonial theory of, xii, 24, 160; spread of, 22; transition to, 18–19
capture by illegality, xii, 21–28, 94, 124
Caruaru, Brazil, 115
Catholicism, 14, 15
Central Bank (Brazil), 45
Central Bank (Paraguay), 6, 51–52, 53
Chamber of Commerce and Services of Ciudad del Este, 59, 60
Chamber of Commerce of Information Technology Goods (Ciudad del Este), 60
Chiang, Kai-shek, 69, 102
China-Brazil Chamber of Commerce, 106
China Overseas Exchange Association (China), 101
Chinatowns, 120, 156, 157
China Travel Service (China), 101
Chinese Association of Brazil, 72, 96, 114, 115, 157; assists São Paulo Chinese community, 103; converges with OCAO's agenda, 104; Heida Li as president of, 119; holds workshops for importers/vendors, 111; partners with Department of Migrant Support, 108; partners with São Paulo Chinese consulate, 107; promotes Network of the Overseas Chinese in Brazil, 116; Yiwu China Commodities City Group's ties with, 113
Chinese Association of Ciudad del Este-Paraguay, 48, 50, 57, 96, 101–102, 110, 115–116
Chinese businesspeople, 66, 85, 107, 158, 160; accumulate wealth circulating illegally, 28; bend law, 2–3; Federation of Chinese Businesspeople of Paraguay, 49, 57, 101–102; General Association of the Chinese Businesspeople of Brazil, 105, 109, 112; interdependent with migrant vendors, 32; lead migrants' associations, 92; open indoor markets, 86; use legality to reframe informality, 21; Young Chinese Businesspeople Association, 118
Chinese Chamber of Commerce of Brazil, 106
Chinese Communist Party (China), 14, 15, 47, 100, 103, 114
Chinese communities, x, 16, 112; business groups controlled by, 115; Chinese Association of Brazil, 103, 157; in Ciudad del Este/São Paulo, 10, 14, 30, 70–74, 97; diaspora agencies connect with, 114; migrants' associations represent, 119–122; in Paraguay/Brazil, 12; role in informal economy, 158; Zhu Surong leads, 66
Chinese consulate (São Paulo), 106
Chinese Cultural Association of Brazil, 103
Chinese diaspora, xi, 4, 12, 85, 95, 98, 157
Chinese distributors, 2, 3, 6, 14, 83, 160; accused of smuggling migrants, 142; control undocumented Chinese migrants, 138; Law Kin Chong, 71; own indoor markets, 73; siphon wealth off vendors, 32
Chinese Dream (Zhōngguó mèng), 114
Chinese identity, 12, 107. See also Chineseness
Chinese importers, 55, 62–64, 113; in Ciudad del Este/São Paulo, 31, 35–36, 42; deal in electronics, 58; distribute smuggled goods, 69; in informal economy, 3; in Shopping Circuit Consortium, 158; vendors' relations with, x

Chinese investors, 42, 67, 94, 161
Chinese mafia, 2
Chinese migration, x, 11, 16, 72, 105, 132, 133; to Brazil, 14, 15; to Paraguay/Brazil, 126; to South America, ix
Chinese Nationalist Party (Guomindang/Kuomintang; Republic of China), 13, 100
Chineseness, 12–13, 107
Chinese Question, 15
Chinese Social Center of Brazil in São Paulo, 103
Chinese sojourners, 12
Chinese stallholders, xviii, xix, 35, 118; in Dawn Market, 8, 67, 94; in General Association of the Chinese Businesspeople of Brazil, 109; in illegalized markets, 3; indoor market shutdowns affect, 117; Law Kin Chong subleases to, 71; management companies aid, 27; precarious position of, 72; relocate to indoor markets, 86; Shopping Circuit Consortium against, 65, 66, 92, 95; socioeconomic stratification of, 14; street vending policies affect, 32; in Taiwanese shops, 50
Chinese takeover, 96
Chinese traders, 41, 42, 69
Chinese vendors, xii, 125, 127, 162; access opportunities for, 105; change São Paulo markets, 71; in Ciudad del Este/São Paulo, xix, 72f, 80, 98, 141, 157–160; Civil Police profile, 82; General Association of the Chinese Businesspeople of Brazil to aid, 109; importers' relations with, 2–3; indoor markets' effect on, 27; in informal economy, 18; interaction with state institutions, 121; navigate illegality, 33; not represented in informal workers' unions, 76; Paraguay/Brazil, 135; protest indoor market shutdowns, 117; shape popular markets, 28; street vending regulations affect, 31; undocumented, 139

Chu, Julie, 129
citizenship, 126–129, 144, 150–151; acquisition, 129, 152; birthright, 150, 152; Brazilian, 150–151, 153; British 16; Chinese 12, 150, 153; dual, 152–153; national, 127, 146, 152, 153; Paraguayan, 153; participatory, 117, 121; Portuguese 16; rights, 88; social 23; status, 144, 150–155; strategic, 152; Taiwanese 12; theory, 127; transmission of, 133
City Council (São Paulo), 74, 79, 91, 119, 120, 157; Committee on the Bribery Mafia, 75; Committee on the Dawn Market, 65; investigates Law Kin Chong, 156, 160
City Free of Counterfeits and Illegal Commerce (program), 81
City Free of Piracy (program), 82, 83, 94–95, 115, 116
Ciudad del Este, Paraguay, 5f, 7f; Lai-Lai Center, 48f; skyline, 51f
Civil Police (Brazil), 77, 79, 81, 120; Department of Crime Investigation, 82
class, 17, 26, 77, 89; capitalist-entrepreneurial, 21, 63; conflict, 26; inequalities, 4, 153; lower, 7, 25, 68, 90, 114; middle, xvii, 8, 16, 46, 59, 70, 76; relations, 22; social; struggle, 22; upper, 8, 25, 67, 68; working x, xix, 4, 16, 46, 60, 67, 68, 88, 94, 154, 157
Clean City (slogan), 93
colonialism, x, 14, 16, 18–19, 24
Colorado Party (Paraguay), 38, 40
commodity circuits, x, 3, 4, 17; China-Taiwan-Paraguay, 35; Ciudad del Este-São Paulo, 30; transnational, 21, 66
Common External Tariff, 53; Schedules of Exception to, 55–58, 63

INDEX   197

Community Safety Council (Brazil), 109, 120, 121, 157
concessioners, 26, 35, 36, 63, 83, 91
confiscation, 62, 77, 79, 82, 117, 118
Congress (Brazil), 1, 144
Congress (Paraguay), 41
conspiracy, 1, 80, 82, 83
Consumer Protection Foundation of Rio de Janeiro, 142
Conventions of Tourism and Investment (Paraguay-Taiwan), 102
corruption, 39, 73, 119. *See also* bribery; money laundering
counterfeiting, 29, 83, 95, 118, 120, 140–142, 156; anti-counterfeits operations, 4; Chinese migrants distribute, 105; City Free of Counterfeits and Illegal Commerce, 81; City Hall attacks, 77; crackdown on, 45, 55, 82, 93, 117, 119, 147; documents, 154; as international crime, 58; Law Kin Chong accused of, 1, 2, 119, 156, 160; policies on, 74; regulation of, 27, 32, 66, 67, 73, 78, 94; Special Committee on Counterfeits and Tax Evasion, 1
Covas, Bruno, 92–93, 118, 170n2.9
crime, 83, 120, 121; Civil Police investigate, 79, 82; conspiracy, 80; human trafficking, 140; political, 170n4.2; prevention, 109; property, 25; transnational, 58, 141
criminality, 3, 4, 80, 82, 120, 137, 155; Civil Police investigate, 79; criminal organizations, 2, 55, 126, 139; criminal records, 144; forgery, 147; against migrants, 142; smuggling, 44
criminalization, 26, 88, 140, 157–159; of economic activities, xii, 3, 126; of vendors, 67, 95
Cultural Revolution (China), 16, 100, 103

Culture Center of Taipei Economic and Cultural Office, 103
Customs Statute (Paraguay), 54

Dawn Market, 8, 65–67, 84–88, 85f, 89–92, 92f, 94–95; Chinese migrants run stalls in, 73; City Hall polices on, 78; developers and realtors build stalls in, 83; Military Police officers in, 81; privatization of, 97, 123, 158; Zhu Surong subleases stalls in, 71
Day of the Chinese Migrant (Brazil), 120
degradation, 68, 70
Democratic Progressive Party (Taiwan), 13, 100
Deng, Xiaoping, x, 16, 100, 112, 114
Department of Labor, Development, and Entrepreneurship (São Paulo), 8, 77, 90
Department of Migrant Support, 108. *See also* Qingtian Association of Brazil
development, 18, 36, 124; economic, 11, 36–39, 52, 64, 67; international organizations 19; national 18, 19, 39; models 36–39, 52, 62, 64; policy 18, 20; social, 42, 67; real estate, 17; studies, 160; uneven, x, 6, 33, 161; urban ix, 3, 23, 26, 27, 39, 83, 95, 156, 158
developmentalism, 19–20, 89
de-Sinicization, 13, 100
deterrence, 81–83, 132
diaspora engagement, 97–98, 109, 122–124, 159, 161
dictatorship, 38; civil-military (Brazil, 1964-1985), 51, 74, 81; Paraguay, x, 102; Taiwan, 102
Discipline and Punish (Foucault), 26, 169n2
documentation, 50, 139, 144, 151–153; employment record book, 146–147;

documentation (*cont.*)
forged, 125, 129, 135–138, 147, 154; of immigration, 129, 149, 154; Natural Persons Register, 147. *See also* paper selves; undocumented migrants/migration
Dog Meat Festival, 142
Dominguez, Humberto Dibb, 38–39
Dória, João, 92–93, 170n2.9
Double Ten, 8, 10, 11. *See also* National Day of the Republic of China
Downtown São Paulo Urban and Functional Revitalization Program (PROCENTRO), 75–77
Duty Free Shop Puerto Iguazu, 59

Ecuador, 139, 140
Ecuadorian investor visas, 139
emplacement, 126–128, 132, 134, 141, 146, 155. *See also* mobility
employment record book, 146–147
Encarnación, Paraguay, 58, 101, 116
Encarnación Chapter of the Taiwanese Fellows' Solidarity and Aid Association, 116
enforcement, border, 33, 126, 127, 130, 139–143, 145, 155, 162
entrepreneurialism, 104, 124; popular, xii, 8, 21, 88–94, 95, 158
Erundina, Luiza, 74
ethnography, 28–30
Europe, 10, 16, 17, 59, 67, 68, 69, 133
extortion, 1, 27, 73, 75, 79, 83

family reunification visas, 129, 133, 143, 150, 153
Federal Highway Police (Brazil), 141
Federal Police (Brazil), 46, 55, 71, 126, 139–142, 144; National System of Enrollment and Records of Foreigners, 151
Federation of Chinese Businesspeople of Paraguay, 49, 57, 101–102

Federation of Returned Overseas Chinese (China), 101, 114
Ferguson, James, 89
fiscal evasion, 81, 82
Fordism, 19
Foreign Markets Trading Corporation, 40, 41
forgery, 33, 129, 135, 136–139, 141, 147
formalization, 94; of triangle commerce, 60–62
Foucault, Michel, xii, 24–26; governmentality, 98; illegalisms, 169n2
Foz do Iguaçu, Brazil, xv, xvii, 10, 101; border with Ciudad del Este, 58, 60, 139; Chinese migration to, 8, 50, 134; Federal Police of Brazil in, 46; trading houses in, 43; in tri-border area, 7f
free-trade zones, x, 26, 35–36, 40–45, 48, 52–56, 63, 158
freedom, 10, 20, 28, 47, 129, 137, 151; amnesty and, 143–146; unfreedom, 159
Friendship Treaty (Paraguay-Taiwan, 1968), 102
Fujianese migrants, 16, 72, 135, 139, 140, 142; Association of Fujianese (Brazil), 104
Fujian province, China, 101, 104, 114, 134, 139, 141, 143
Futian Market, 112

Galeria Pagé, 71
GDP (gross domestic product), 6
Gehl Architects, 90
General Agreement on Tariffs and Trade, 49
General Association of Chinese Businesspeople of Brazil, 105, 109, 112, 118
Germans/Germany, 148
Global North, xi, 21, 33, 161
Global South, xi, 6, 33, 160–161; informal economy in, 3, 18, 21, 22, 24

Goffman, Erving, 130
Go Out Policy/Going Global Strategy (*zǒuchūqù zhànlüè*), 111
government (Brazil), xi, 37, 58, 60, 148; Brazilian Coffee Institute lobbies, 44; against counterfeiting, 147; demands end of cigarette smuggling under Adaptation Regime, 56; federal, 84, 86, 88; on labor-contract migration, 15; negotiates Transborder Trade Regime, 61
government (China), xi, 16, 47, 98, 101; brokering for, 111–113, 123; Chinese Dream, 114; diaspora policy of, 97; establishes Overseas Chinese Affairs Commission, 100; imperial, 12, 99; on labor-contract migration, 15; on overseas Chinese affairs, 99; subnational, 157; on Taiwan's political sovereignty, 69; trade policies of, 105, 159
government (Paraguay), 6, 35, 40, 41, 46, 53, 55; Chinese importers lobby, 64, 158; Ciudad del Este interest groups lobby, 59; import legislation of, 6; Taiwanese community leaders pressure, 49, 50; Taiwanese government lobbies, 134; Taiwanese importers lobby, 31; vision of large social transformations, 37
government (Taiwan), xi, 13, 55, 98, 100; agenda regarding Paraguay, 122; diaspora policy of, 97; establishes Parque Industrial Oriente, 53; helps establish diaspora associations, 101–102; lobbies Paraguayan government, 134; migrants' associations and, 110; on overseas Chinese affairs, 99; recognition of, 50, 103, 113; trade policies of, 157
governmentality, xii, 129; neoliberal, 98, 107, 123
GSA Management of Fairs and Events LLC, 84, 86

Guangdong, China, 15, 101, 114, 116
Guangxu Emperor, 15
Guayaquil, Ecuador, 139
Guomindang/Kuomintang (Nationalist Party of China; Republic of China), 13, 100

Haddad, Fernando, xii, 88, 89, 90, 91
Haitians, 70, 149
Hakka (language), 14
Hakka community, 103
Hakka Social Center of Brazil, 103
Harpaz, Yossi, 152
Hart, Keith, xi, 18
Harvey, David, xii, 22
Hokkien (language), 14
hometown associations (*qiáoxiānghuì*), 11, 14, 32, 99, 100, 102, 108, 151
Hong Kong, 1, 11, 12, 41, 55, 70, 100
Hong Kongese, xviii, 43, 103, 119, 156; in Ciudad del Este, 14; importers/distributors, 6, 55, 69; migrants, 16, 43, 119; as São Paulo vendors, 8
Hotel Acaray, 38
Hualien, Taiwan, 16
huáqiáo (overseas Chinese), 12
huárén, 12
hùkou (local resident status), 153
Human Rights Committee of the São Paulo Bar Association, 118
human smuggling, 126, 139, 140, 141, 142, 143, 155
human trafficking, 29, 105, 126, 139–143. *See also* slavery

Iguazu Falls, Brazil-Argentina, xvii, 46, 59, 131
Iguazú River, Brazil-Argentina, 7f
illegalisms, xii, 25–26, 169n2. *See also* Foucault, Michel
illegality. *See* capture by illegality
illegalization, 3, 126, 128, 143, 159; legibility against, 154–156

imperialism, 18, 20, 24, 106
importation, 43–45, 69, 102, 104; from Asia to São Paulo, 70; border trade in Ciudad del Este, 36; of Brazilian cigarettes, 56; in capture by illegality, 26; catering to foreigner buyers, 40; Chinese share of grows, 35; in Ciudad del Este, 31, 54; in Paraguay, 51; to São Paulo, 123; Simplified Importation Clearance, 60; unrecorded, 6
Import Substituting Industrialization, 39
Independent Street Vendors Union, 83
indeterminacy, 43
Individual Micro-Entrepreneur, 61
Indonesia, 16
Indonesians, 14, 103
indoor markets, 17, 73, 83, 86, 95, 97, 119; in 25 de Março Street district, 71; Chinese-owned, 75, 93; closed, 117–118; effect on Chinese vendors, 27; illegal commerce in, 121; Law Kin Chong opens, 2; in Operation Delegated, 81; São Paulo, 72f, 123, 158. *See also* Dawn Market
Informal Economy Workers Union, 61, 74
informal sector, xi, 18–20
informality, xi, 19–25, 43, 81, 127; dispossession by, 23; from to entrepreneurship, 32; studies, 160
intellectual property rights, 21, 45, 77, 81, 82
Inter-American Development Bank, 75, 76
Internal Revenue System of Brazil, 60, 118
International Cooperation and Development Fund (Taiwan), 55
International Federation of Taiwanese Associations, 103
International Fraternity Bridge, 59
International Friendship Bridge, xv, xix, 7f, 8, 38, 125
International Labor Organization (ILO), 18–19, 20
international trade, 7, 19, 39, 41, 106; promoting, 97, 98, 104, 123, 124
In-Transit Customs Clearance Regime, 44, 45, 47, 63
inviting in/welcoming in (*qǒngjìnlái*), 114
irregular commerce, 93, 116–119
Itaipú Dam, Brazil-Paraguay, 47
Italian migrants, 67

Japanese-Brazilian community, 120
Jewish migrants, 67, 68
Johnson, Lyndon, 18

Kang, Youwei, 15
Kassab, Gilberto, 78–81, 83, 86–88, 91, 170n2.7
Kennedy, John F., 18
Kuomintang/Guomindang (Nationalist Party of China; Republic of China), 13, 100

Lai-Lai (shopping center), 47, 48f
large overseas Chinese affairs (*dàqiáowù*), 114
Latin America, ix, x, xi, 8, 17, 19, 20, 21; real estate syndicate, 83
Law, Kin Chong, 71–72, 156, 160; arrest and imprisonment, 1–2, 119; business of, 11, 27, 36, 63; in São Paulo, 64
Law, Thomas, 119, 156, 157
law enforcement, xii, 31, 44, 93, 126; revitalization and, 74–76
Lebanese, 41, 47, 55, 58, 67, 68
LED Manufacturers Association of Shenzhen, 112

Legality Movement, 118
legibility, 128, 132, 136, 143; against illegalization, 154–156
Li, Heida, 119
Licensed Retailer Importer Micro Company, 60
Licensed Street Vendors Union, 74
licensing, 51, 61, 86, 93; driver's licenses, 135–136; of indoor markets, 117; Licensed Retailer Importer Micro Company, 60; Licensed Street Vendors Union, 74; of stallholders, 109; of street vending, 76, 77, 78, 79, 84, 119
Lula da Silva, Luiz Inácio, 60, 88, 89

Macanese migrants, 14, 16
Macau, 12
mafia, 2, 79; Anti-Mafia Police (Paraguay), 55; Committee on the Bribery Mafia, 75
Maluf, Paulo, 74–75, 77
Manaus, Brazil, 54, 55
Mandarin Chinese (language), 14, 29, 106, 118
march to the east, 38
march to the west, 38
Marx, Karl, xii, 22–24
Marxism, xii, xxiii, 20, 22–25
Mateos, Pablo, 152
Mediterranean, 21
Memorandum of Adjustment of Conduct, 119
Metropolitan Civil Guard (São Paulo), 79
Mezzadra, Sandro, 24
Miami, Florida, 50, 69
migrant integration, 47, 104, 109, 127
migrants' associations (*huìguǎn*), xii, 99–106, 110; bridge diaspora policies with migrants, 32, 123; Chinese businesspeople in, 86, 92; in Ciudad del Este/São Paulo, x, 97, 124, 159; in ethnography, 29; in overseas Chinese communities' interests, 119; in Taiwanese migrants' socioeconomic integration, 47; in trade promotion, 98; undocumented vendors blame, 138

migration channels, 43, 129–134, 143
migration studies, ix, 28, 127, 161
Military Police (São Paulo), 77, 79–82, 85, 89, 93; Álvaro Camilo, 87
minister of foreign affairs, 40, 58
Ministry of Foreign Affairs (Paraguay), 52
Ministry of Labor (Brazil), 133
Ministry of Labor and Employment (Brazil), 142
Min Nan Association of South America, 104, 118
mobility, 28, 31, 64, 132, 137, 141; across Global South, 161; of Brazilian stallholders, 86; brokers, 123–124; of Chinese vendors, 117, 159; demobilization, 83; ethnography of, xiii, 28–30; of market subjects, 28; of migrants, 28, 123, 128–129, 132, 134, 155, 159, 161; social, xvii, 16, 90; within South America, 162; traders, 123–124; trans/international, 33, 35, 127, 138, 143, 146, 149–153, 159; urban, 156; of vendors, 126. *See also* emplacement
mobilities turn, 28
money laundering, 1, 55, 56, 58, 77. *See also* corruption
Movement in Defense of the Brazilian Legal Market, 118
Mozambique, 16
Mutual Defense Treaty (US-Taiwan), 47

National Committee for Refugees (Brazil), 149

National Day of the Republic of China, 113. *See also* Double Ten
Nationalist Party of China (Guomindang/Kuomintang), 13, 100
National System of Enrollment and Records of Foreigners (Brazil), 151
native-place associations, 99, 101, 103–105, 114–118, 122
Natural Persons Register, 147
neoliberalism, 18, 20–24, 33, 58. *See also* governmentality
Network of the Overseas Chinese in Brazil, 116
New China, 15
New York, 40, 157
North America, 17, 133. *See also* United States (U.S.)

Oceania, 133
Office of the United States Trade Representative, 58, 81
officialness, 40–43, 137
Oliveira, Francisco de, 20
Open-Door Policy, 100
Operation Clean, 77
Operation Da Shan, 139–143
Operation Delegated, 79–83, 89, 93, 94, 115, 116
Operation Revitalization, 77
Operation Sentinel, 142
Operation September, 118
Operation Yulin, 142
Orient Industrial Park (Parque Industrial Oriente), 53, 54, 55, 122
overseas Chinese affairs (*qiáowù*), 99, 101, 113
overseas Chinese affairs, large (*dàqiáowù*), 114
overseas Chinese affairs agencies, 98, 111
Overseas Chinese Affairs Commission (OCAC), 99–101, 110, 111, 113, 115, 122; establishes Culture Center of Taipei Economic and Cultural Office, 103; founds Taiwanese Chamber of Commerce-Paraguay, 102; Office of the State Council, 100
Overseas Chinese Affairs Office of the State Council (OCAO), 100, 103, 104, 108, 109, 113; local OCAOs, 101, 111, 112, 114–116
Overseas Chinese Association-Paraguay Chapter, 102, 113
overseas Chinese associations, 120, 121
overseas Chinese communities/populations, 97, 100, 103, 112, 114–115, 157–158, 161; associations representing, 119–122; Chineseness of, 12; in commodity circuit, 30, 70, 73; role of migrants' associations for, 123, 124; socioeconomic stratification of, 14; ties with hometowns, 99
Overseas Chinese Festival, 113
Overseas Chinese Service Center, 109
Overseas Chinese Youth Federation of Brazil, 105, 106, 108, 118, 123, 124
Overseas Community Affairs Council, Republic of China (Taiwan), 100. *See also* Overseas Chinese Affairs Commission (OCAC)
Overseas Compatriot Affairs Commission, 100. *See also* Overseas Chinese Affairs Commission (OCAC)

Palermo Protocol, 140
paper selves, 129–130, 132, 134, 137, 138, 148. *See also* documentation
Paraguayan vendor exporter, 61
Paraguay Chinese Club of Hometown Associations, 102
Paranaguá Port, Brazil, 37, 38, 43, 69
Paraná River, Brazil-Paraguay-Argentina, xv, 7f
passports, 151–153

Pedro Juan Caballero, Paraguay, 58, 101, 116
peoplehood, 107
People's Republic of China (PRC), x, 12, 16, 100, 103. *See also* government (China)
Pericás Neto, Bernardo, 52
personhood, 33, 135
Peru, 139
Peruvians, 70, 117
piracy. *See* Brazilian Forum against Piracy and Illegality; City Free of Piracy (program)
Pitta, Celso, 74–75, 77
policies, popular markets, 74–78
policies, diaspora, 32, 97, 107, 109, 114, 124, 161; agencies, 99–106; connecting East Asia and South America, 158–159; *huárén*, 12; shape migrants' destination choice, 161; of Taiwanese/Chinese governments, 123
policies, regularization, 94; immigration, 129, 144, 146, 151, 155; revitalization plan and, 76–78; social movements and, 74
policies, trade, 36, 49, 52, 57, 70, 105
popular entrepreneurialism, xii, 8, 21, 88–94, 158
popular illegalisms, 26
popular markets and shopping tourism, 3–8
Portugal, 15, 16
Portuguese (language), 11, 29, 50, 60, 131, 141; on goods in popular markets, 112; in Mozambique, 16; skill in for naturalization, 150
Portuguese Empire, 15
primitive accumulation, xii, 22, 42
PROCENTRO (Downtown São Paulo Urban and Functional Revitalization Program), 75–77
protectionism, xviii, 35, 39, 46, 70

Protestantism, 14
Protocol of Ouro Preto, 53. *See also* Southern Common Market (MERCOSUR)
Protocol to Prevent, Suppress and Punish Trafficking in Persons, Especially Women and Children, 140
Public Prosecutor's Office (Brazil), 86, 140
Puerto Iguazú, Argentina, 7f, 59
Puerto Presidente Stroessner, Paraguay, 38, 39

Qing dynasty, 12, 15, 99
Qingtian, China, 16, 71, 116, 130, 131
Qingtian Association of Brazil, 104, 107, 108, 111, 113, 115

reaching out/going out (*zǒuchūqù*), 111, 113, 114
real estate, 39, 71, 83, 157; developers, 36, 68, 72; investors, 74; market, 32; owners, 17, 27, 73, 95
Rebuild Downtown (city hall plan), 76. *See also* Downtown São Paulo Urban and Functional Revitalization Program (PROCENTRO)
Recife, Brazil, 115
refuge/refugees, 84, 146–150, 170n4.2; National Committee for Refugees, 149. *See also* asylum
regional integration, 52, 53, 58, 64
Regularization Bill of 2009 (Brazil), 120
relations of production, 20, 22–23
Republic of China (Taiwan), 8, 12, 13, 99, 103, 113; Overseas Community Affairs Council, Republic of China (Taiwan), 100. *See also* government (Taiwan)
resistance, 33, 128–129, 162; vendor's, 82, 83

return and serve the country (*huíguó fúwù*), 111
revitalization, 70, 74–76, 76–78, 83, 94, 157; Downtown São Paulo Urban and Functional Revitalization Program (PROCENTRO), 75; Operation Revitalization, 77
Rio de Janeiro, Brazil, 15, 103; Consumer Protection Foundation of Rio de Janeiro, 142
Rostow, Walt Whitman, 18

sacoleiros (shoppers), 6
Salto del Guairá, Paraguay, 58, 116. *See also* Southern Common Market (MERCOSUR)
Samson, Melanie, 23
Santos, Artur Henrique da Silva, 90, 91
Santos Port, Brazil, 43
Sanyal, Kalyan, 24
São Paulo, Brazil, 5f
São Paulo Bar Association, 118
São Paulo City Council Committee on the Dawn Market, 65
São Paulo downtown, 87f
São Paulo Overseas Chinese Center, 108
Schedule of Capital Goods, 57. *See also* Southern Common Market (MERCOSUR)
Schedule of Exceptions, 57, 59
Schedule of Informatics and Telecommunication Goods, 57
Schedules of Exception to the MERCOSUR Common External Tariff, 55, 56, 57, 58, 63
Scott, James, xiii, 128
securitization, 58, 81, 128
seeing like a migrant, xiii, 128, 129
selfhood, 107, 132
Senegalese, 70
Serra, José, 76–78, 84, 170n2.7

serve the country (*wèi guó fúwù*), 111
Shachar, Ayelet, 127
Shanghai, China, 15, 139
Shopping Circuit Consortium, 65, 66, 91, 92, 93, 95, 157, 158; Zhu Surong heads, 72
Shopping Circuit Project, 65–66, 83, 84–88, 87f, 90, 91, 94, 95
Shopping Circuit—The New Dawn Market, 91, 92f
shopping tourism, 21, 32, 66, 84, 91, 95, 156–158; popular markets and, 3–8
Simplified Importation Clearance, 60
Singapore, 16, 41, 100
Singaporeans, 14, 41, 63, 103
slavery, 15, 24, 126, 140, 141, 142. *See also* human trafficking
smuggling, 29, 31, 36, 40, 43, 45–46, 83, 120; anti-smuggling operations, 4; Border Clearance Regime contributes to, 44; to Brazil, 51, 55, 58; Brazil-Paraguay-Brazil smuggling scheme, 44, 56; Chinese importers in, 69; Chinese migrants in, 105; crackdown on, 117, 118; Law Kin Chong involved in, 1–2, 71, 119; legislation facilitates, 158; from Paraguay, 2, 51–52, 55, 69, 156; raids tackling, 144; sold in popular markets, 74; under Stroessner regime, 63; under Unified Tax Regime, 60, 62; whiskey, 41. *See also* human smuggling
social control, 22, 25, 26, 80, 82, 97, 104, 124, 129, 138, 159. *See also* surveillance
social movements, 74–78
solidarity economy, 76, 90
South America, 3, 21, 125, 156, 159; Chinese born in, 14; Chinese diaspora to, 111, 114; Chinese mafia in, 2; Chinese migration to, ix, 32, 50, 162;

economic integration in, 158; geopolitical shifts in, 102; informal economies in, 14, 95; migrants' associations in, 32; migration from Asia to, 24, 33; Min Nan Association of, 104, 118; popular markets in, 4, 98, 112; smuggling to, 56; Southern Common Market (MERCOSUR), 52; travel outside, 46
South America Newspaper, 108
South Americans, 157
Southern Common Market (MERCOSUR), 52–57, 59, 63, 64, 116
South Koreans, 68
South-South migration, 24, 161
sovereignty, 129; state, 127–128, 136, 138, 146; Taiwan's political, 69
Spanish (language), 10, 11, 29, 50, 112
Special Committee on Counterfeits and Tax Evasion, 1
special economic zones, x, 42
Special Tourism Regime/Special Tax Regime, 49, 50, 51, 52, 56, 61, 63
state repression, 26, 62
state-diaspora relations, 97–98. *See also* diaspora engagement
street vending, 9f, 70, 75–79, 80, 159; in 25 de Março Street, 9f; deterring, 95; enforcement, 73, 81, 83, 84, 94; grows, 69; licensing, 74, 84, 119; Military Police control, 93; permits, 90; policies, 32, 66, 74; policing, 158; regulations, 4, 23, 27, 29, 31, 67, 73, 121; Street Vending Council, 90; Street Vending Plan, 90
street vendors, xi, xiii, xviii, 47, 91, 93–94; Bolivian, 92; Chinese, xix, 3, 32, 66, 74, 77, 78, 83; in Dawn Market, 84–85; Department of Labor supports, 77; goods of, 8; governing by force, 78–83; income opportunities for, 70; in informal economy, 18; law enforcement's perceptions of, 75; migrants become, 114; operate illegally, 26; Paraguayan, 35; perspectives of, 138; precarious condition of, 17, 67, 111; procure imported goods, 69; sell Chinese imports, 104–105; socioeconomic stratification of, 14; Street Vendors Permanent Councils, 76; upward social mobility of, 90; work early hours, 72
Street Vendors Forum, 78
Street Vendors Permanent Councils, 74, 76, 78
Stroessner, Alfredo, x, 29, 38–40, 42, 48–49, 52, 63, 102
subjecthood, 159
subjectivity, 107, 129, 132
Sulanca, Brazil, 115
Suplicy, Marta, 76
surveillance, 26, 128, 160
Syrian-Lebanese migrants, 67
Syrians, 38, 70

Taichung, Taiwan, 10, 14, 16, 47, 116
Taipei, Taiwan, 10, 99, 100, 101, 122; government recognition of, 16, 50, 102, 103, 113; to promote trade through diaspora, 110
Taipei Economic and Cultural Office, 103
Taiwanese Association of Brazil, 103
Taiwanese Chamber of Commerce-Paraguay, 49, 57, 96, 101, 102, 110, 115, 122
Taiwanese communities, 10–11, 16, 34, 49, 50; of Ciudad del Este, Paraguay, 55, 96, 122
Taiwanese distributors, 8, 10, 97, 110
Taiwanese Fellows' Solidarity and Aid Association, Encarnación Chapter, 116
Taiwanese identity, 13

Taiwanese importers, 31, 34, 49, 57; in Ciudad del Este, 46, 50, 53, 54, 56; in São Paulo, 47
Taiwanese migrants, in Ciudad del Este, 47
Taiwan Industrial Park (Ciudad del Este), 55
Temer, Michel, 144
Tierra del Fuego, Argentina, 54, 55
trade liberalization, xviii, 7, 35, 49, 52, 58, 63–64, 70, 116, 158
Trade and Economic Cooperation Treaty, 102
trade liberalization, xviii, 7, 35, 49, 52, 58, 62, 64, 70, 116, 158. *See also* World Trade Organization
Transborder Trade Regime, 61, 63
Treaty of Asunción, 53. *See also* Southern Common Market (MERCOSUR)
triangle commerce (*comercio de triangulación*), 36, 43, 45, 47–48, 63–64, 97, 113; formalizing, 60–62; paradoxes of, 49–52; under regional integration, 53–60; saving, 52
tri-border area (Brazil, Paraguay, Argentina), 7f, 58
triple frontera, x
Tucker, Jennifer, 23
turismo comprista/turismo de compra, 6, 7. *See also* shopping tourism
25 de Março Street (market), 67–69, 71, 73, 79, 81, 85, 90, 139; street vending, 9f

underdevelopment, 3, 19. *See also* development
undocumented migrants/migration, 121, 125–126, 130, 136, 140, 144, 147, 153; amnesty for, 120; Chinese distributors control, 138; Chinese migrants as, 132, 143; Chinese vendors, 135, 139; income opportunities for, 73; injustices against, 146; under Operation Clean, 77; under Operation Delegated, 80; pregnant, 154; regularization of, 145, 151, 155
Unified Tax Regime, 60–62
Union of the Chinese Women of Brazil, 105
unions, customs, 53, 54, 64
unions, labor, 76, 78; Artur Henrique da Silva Santos, 90; Independent Street Vendors Union, 83; Informal Economy Workers Union, 61, 74; Licensed Street Vendors Union, 74; Union of the Chinese Women of Brazil, 105
United Front Work Department, 101, 114
United Nations, 16, 102
United Nations Convention against Transnational Organized Crime, 140
United States (U.S.), 11, 13, 18, 47, 134, 149, 152, 153; Office of the United States Trade Representative, 58, 81
Uruguay, 53
Use of Public Space Permit, 74

Vargas, Getúlio, 38
Venezuelans, 149

wage labor, xi, 89, 4, 19, 20–23, 25
war on terror, 55, 58
WeChat, 65, 108, 117
Wen Zhou, China, 11, 16, 72, 143
Wenzhou Association of Brazil, 11, 104
Wenzhounese migrants, 11, 80, 82
Western countries, 15, 18, 77, 133
Woo, William Boss, 120
Workers' Party (Brazil), xii, 58, 60, 89
World Trade Organization, 57, 77

Xi, Jinping, 114

Yiwu, China, 112, 115
Yiwu China Commodities City Group, 112
Ynsfrán, Edgar, 39, 40
Yuen Control (Taiwan), 55

Zhejiangese migrants, 15, 16, 72
Zhejiang province, China, 71, 72, 112, 114, 134, 136, 143
Zhu, Surong, 65, 66, 71, 72, 85, 91, 160

**GLOBALIZATION
IN EVERYDAY LIFE**

*The Stigma Matrix: Gender, Globalization, and
the Agency of Pakistan's Frontline Women*
    Fauzia Husain   2024

*Aid and the Help: International Development and the
Transnational Extraction of Care*
    Dinah Hannaford   2023

Forbidden Intimacies: Polygamies at the Limits of Western Tolerance
    Melanie Heath   2023

Unruly Speech: Displacement and the Politics of Transgression
    Saskia Witteborn   2023

Seeking Western Men: Email-Order Brides under China's Global Rise
    Monica Liu   2023

Children of the Revolution: Violence, Inequality, and Hope in Nicaraguan Migration
    Laura Enríquez   2022

At Risk: Indian Sexual Politics and the Global AIDS Crisis
    Gowri Vijayakumar   2021

*Here, There, and Elsewhere: The Making of Immigrant
Identities in a Globalized World*
    Tahseen Shams   2020

Beauty Diplomacy: Embodying an Emerging Nation
    Oluwakemi M. Balogun   2020

The authorized representative in the EU for product safety and compliance is:
Mare Nostrum Group
B.V Doelen 72
4831 GR Breda
The Netherlands

www.ingramcontent.com/pod-product-compliance
Lightning Source LLC
Chambersburg PA
CBHW031812220426
43662CB00007B/608